Frankenstein and Philosophy

Popular Culture and Philosophy® Series Editor: George A. Reisch

VOLUME 1 *Seinfeld and Philosophy: A Book about Everything and Nothing* (2000)

VOLUME 2 *The Simpsons and Philosophy: The D'oh! of Homer* (2001)

VOLUME 3 *The Matrix and Philosophy: Welcome to the Desert of the Real* (2002)

VOLUME 4 *Buffy the Vampire Slayer and Philosophy: Fear and Trembling in Sunnydale* (2003)

VOLUME 5 *The Lord of the Rings and Philosophy: One Book to Rule Them All* (2003)

VOLUME 9 *Harry Potter and Philosophy: If Aristotle Ran Hogwarts* (2004)

VOLUME 12 *Star Wars and Philosophy: More Powerful than You Can Possibly Imagine* (2005)

VOLUME 13 *Superheroes and Philosophy: Truth, Justice, and the Socratic Way* (2005)

VOLUME 19 *Monty Python and Philosophy: Nudge Nudge, Think Think!* (2006)

VOLUME 25 *The Beatles and Philosophy: Nothing You Can Think that Can't Be Thunk* (2006)

VOLUME 26 *South Park and Philosophy: Bigger, Longer, and More Penetrating* (2007)

VOLUME 30 *Pink Floyd and Philosophy: Careful with that Axiom, Eugene!* (2007)

VOLUME 33 *Battlestar Galactica and Philosophy: Mission Accomplished or Mission Frakked Up?* (2008)

VOLUME 35 *Star Trek and Philosophy: The Wrath of Kant* (2008)

VOLUME 36 *The Legend of Zelda and Philosophy: I Link Therefore I Am* (2008)

VOLUME 37 *The Wizard of Oz and Philosophy: Wicked Wisdom of the West* (2008)

VOLUME 38 *Radiohead and Philosophy: Fitter Happier More Deductive* (2009)

VOLUME 39 *Jimmy Buffett and Philosophy: The Porpoise Driven Life* (2009) Edited by Erin McKenna and Scott L. Pratt

VOLUME 41 *Stephen Colbert and Philosophy: I Am Philosophy (And So Can You!)* (2009) Edited by Aaron Allen Schiller

OLUME 42 *Supervillains and Philosophy: Sometimes, Evil Is Its Own Reward* (2009) Edited by Ben Dyer

VOLUME 43 *The Golden Compass and Philosophy: God Bites the Dust* (2009) Edited by Richard Greene and Rachel Robison

VOLUME 44 *Led Zeppelin and Philosophy: All Will Be Revealed* (2009) Edited by Scott Calef

VOLUME 45 *World of Warcraft and Philosophy: Wrath of the Philosopher King* (2009) Edited by Luke Cuddy and John Nordlinger

Volume 46 *Mr. Monk and Philosophy: The Curious Case of the Defective Detective* (2010) Edited by D.E. Wittkower

Volume 47 *Anime and Philosophy: Wide Eyed Wonder* (2010) Edited by Josef Steiff and Tristan D. Tamplin

VOLUME 48 *The Red Sox and Philosophy: Green Monster Meditations* (2010) Edited by Michael Macomber

VOLUME 49 *Zombies, Vampires, and Philosophy: New Life for the Undead* (2010) Edited by Richard Greene and K. Silem Mohammad

VOLUME 50 *Facebook and Philosophy: What's on Your Mind?* (2010) Edited by D.E. Wittkower

VOLUME 51 *Soccer and Philosophy: Beautiful Thoughts on the Beautiful Game* (2010) Edited by Ted Richards

VOLUME 52 *Manga and Philosophy: Fullmetal Metaphysician* (2010) Edited by Josef Steiff and Adam Barkman

VOLUME 53 *Martial Arts and Philosophy: Beating and Nothingness* (2010) Edited by Graham Priest and Damon Young

VOLUME 54 *The Onion and Philosophy: Fake News Story True, Alleges Indignant Area Professor* (2010) Edited by Sharon M. Kaye

VOLUME 55 *Doctor Who and Philosophy: Bigger on the Inside* (2010) Edited by Courtland Lewis and Paula Smithka

VOLUME 56 *Dune and Philosophy: Weirding Way of the Mentat* (2011) Edited by Jeffery Nicholas

VOLUME 57 *Rush and Philosophy: Heart and Mind United* (2011) Edited by Jim Berti and Durrell Bowman

VOLUME 58 *Dexter and Philosophy: Mind over Spatter* (2011) Edited by Richard Greene, George A. Reisch, and Rachel Robison-Greene

VOLUME 59 *Halo and Philosophy: Intellect Evolved* (2011) Edited by Luke Cuddy

VOLUME 60 *SpongeBob SquarePants and Philosophy: Soaking Up Secrets Under the Sea!* (2011) Edited by Joseph J. Foy

VOLUME 61 *Sherlock Holmes and Philosophy: The Footprints of a Gigantic Mind* (2011) Edited by Josef Steiff

VOLUME 62 *Inception and Philosophy: Ideas to Die For* (2011) Edited by Thorsten Botz-Bornstein

VOLUME 63 *Philip K. Dick and Philosophy: Do Androids Have Kindred Spirits?* (2011) Edited by D.E. Wittkower

VOLUME 64 *The Rolling Stones and Philosophy: It's Just a Thought Away* (2012) Edited by Luke Dick and George A. Reisch

VOLUME 65 *Chuck Klosterman and Philosophy: The Real and the Cereal* (2012) Edited by Seth Vannatta

VOLUME 66 *Neil Gaiman and Philosophy: Gods Gone Wild!* (2012) Edited by Tracy L. Bealer, Rachel Luria, and Wayne Yuen

VOLUME 67 *Breaking Bad and Philosophy: Badder Living through Chemistry* (2012) Edited by David R. Koepsell and Robert Arp

VOLUME 68 *The Walking Dead and Philosophy: Zombie Apocalypse Now* (2012) Edited by Wayne Yuen

VOLUME 69 *Curb Your Enthusiasm and Philosophy: Awaken the Social Assassin Within* (2012) Edited by Mark Ralkowski

VOLUME 70 *Dungeons and Dragons and Philosophy: Raiding the Temple of Wisdom* (2012) Edited by Jon Cogburn and Mark Silcox

VOLUME 71 *The Catcher in the Rye and Philosophy: A Book for Bastards, Morons, and Madmen* (2012) Edited by Keith Dromm and Heather Salter

VOLUME 72 *Jeopardy! and Philosophy: What Is Knowledge in the Form of a Question?* (2012) Edited by Shaun P. Young

VOLUME 73 *The Wire and Philosophy: This America, Man* (2013) Edited by David Bzdak, Joanna Crosby, and Seth Vannatta

VOLUME 74 *Planet of the Apes and Philosophy: Great Apes Think Alike* (2013) Edited by John Huss

VOLUME 75 *Psych and Philosophy: Some Dark Juju-Magumbo* (2013) Edited by Robert Arp

VOLUME 76 *The Good Wife and Philosophy: Temptations of Saint Alicia* (2013) Edited by Kimberly Baltzer-Jaray and Robert Arp

VOLUME 77 *Boardwalk Empire and Philosophy: Bootleg This Book* (2013) Edited by Richard Greene and Rachel Robison-Greene

VOLUME 78 *Futurama and Philosophy* (2013) Edited by Courtland Lewis and Shaun P. Young

VOLUME 79 *Frankenstein and Philosophy: The Shocking Truth* (2013) Edited by Nicolas Michaud

VOLUME 80 *Ender's Game and Philosophy: Genocide Is Child's Play* (2013) Edited by D.E. Wittkower and Lucinda Rush

IN PREPARATION:

How I Met Your Mother and Philosophy (2014) Edited by Lorenzo von Matterhorn

Jurassic Park and Philosophy (2014) Edited by Nicolas Michaud

The Devil and Philosophy (2014) Edited by Robert Arp

Justified and Philosophy (2014) Edited by Rod Carveth

Leonard Cohen and Philosophy (2014) Edited by Jason Holt

Homeland and Philosophy (2014) Edited by Robert Arp

For full details of all Popular Culture and Philosophy® books, visit www.opencourtbooks.com.

Popular Culture and Philosophy®

Frankenstein and Philosophy

The Shocking Truth

Edited by

NICOLAS MICHAUD

OPEN COURT
Chicago

Volume 79 in the series, Popular Culture and Philosophy®, edited by George A. Reisch

To order books from Open Court, call toll-free 1-800-815-2280, or visit our website at www.opencourtbooks.com.

Open Court Publishing Company is a division of Carus Publishing Company, dba ePals Media.

First printing 2013

Printed and bound in the United States of America.

ISBN: 0-8126-9836-7

Library of Congress Control Number 201393090

Contents

Acknowledgments

I have many people I would like to thank for helping me stitch this project together. First and foremost, I owe a great deal of thanks to David Ramsay Steele for making this project happen—without his help and guidance there would be no book . . . Thank you, David.

I also owe George Reisch my deep thanks for helping me get this project off the ground and giving me the chance to take it on. Thank you, also, to my authors in this volume . . . you are awesome!

I owe unending thanks to the many people who put up with me while I tromp around grumpily trying to make my deadlines (in alpha order to avoid any angry mobs): Thomas Arden, Jake and Jessica May, Powell Kreis, and Joan and Ken Michaud. And a very special thank-you to my grandmother, Nelkis Cobas, whose own writing continues to inspire me. You are the best family a mad scientist could create. I love you all!

And thank you to our readers and fans of *Frankenstein* for keeping alive a story far bigger than any one short (or not so short) human lifespan.

That Vital Spark of Life

Igor, Show them in. . . .

"It's Alive! . . . It's Aliiiive!!!!"

With those immortal words, Mary Shelley, the author of *Frankenstein*, . . . well, did nothing. Shelley never wrote those words. Where did we hear them? We heard them at the movies. We heard them on TV. We heard our maniacal biology professor shout them from the top of the science building! (What some people will do for a research grant.)

Shelley's creation keeps coming back. The creature has lived many lives and stalks the Earth in many creepy forms, in hundreds of movies, dozens of TV shows, in comic books, and even in many new novels which seek to re-engineer Shelley's creature. So this book can dissect not just one body of work, but a vast proliferating corpus (or should I say corpse?) of popular entertainment, a monstrous mythology slouching through the mass mind.

This book stitches together assorted corporeal parts scavenged from many a fetid graveyard. We're here to investigate and pay homage to a pop culture icon, and to have a bit of fun with it—and by fun, I do mean something a bit disgusting.

When you enter into the massive world that is Frankenstein, you find a whole bunch of philosophical—and, let's be honest, shocking—toys to play with . . . Mel Brooks's *Young Frankenstein*, the lovable Herman Munster, Dean Koontz's Dr. Helios, the terrifying monster brought to life by Boris Karloff, and the newly re-animated Adam Frankenstein, to name but a few.

Not that we don't pay plenty of attention to Shelley's towering masterwork, but you just may find that some of our chapters mention Mary Shelly and *Frankenweenie* in the same sentence . . . and what's *Frankenstein* about if it's not about breaking rules? So, if there's a good place to tread where only God should, while wearing a pair of heavy black boots with studs in them, it's here.

And you'll find that once we start trampling upon those boundaries, our investigative probe unveils some blood-chilling questions: We will ask you if a re-animated corpse-man has a soul. We will consider the chilling question, "If it is wrong to make monsters, is it wrong to make babies?" And perhaps most pressingly, we'll reflect on whether Frankenstein's maligned creation would be wrong in seeking to end all of us . . .

So, dim the lights, sit back by the flickering glow of a candle, and let's look deeply into the dull, yellow eyes of the dark doctor's foul creation.

On second thoughts, leave the lights on—and while you're at it, bar the door.

I

Dr. Frankenstein's Easy Guide to Eternal Life

1
Wanna Live Forever? Don't Pull a Frankenstein!

MICHAEL HAUSKELLER

"It's aliiiiiive, it's aliiiiiiiiiive!!!" Who could forget that moment in James Whale's 1931 film *Frankenstein*? The scene is one of the reasons why the monster's creator, played by Colin Clive, comes across as being more than just slightly disturbed. Although he keeps denying it ("Crazy, am I?"), the mad gleam in his eyes clearly marks him as an outright fruitcake. No wonder he has become the model for one of our most-cherished stereotypes, the "mad scientist."

In Mary Shelley's novel, however, there's no hint of fruitcakeyness. Shelley's Victor Frankenstein might be slightly obsessed, but otherwise he seems to be quite sane. He is ambitious, as good scientists tend to be, and basically just wants to make the world a better place by ridding it of death, "that most irreparable evil," and of disease. If that's a sign of lunacy, then lately we seem to be surrounded by lunatics.

For thousands of years we've been dreaming about immortality, but only now, for the first time in history, radical life extension seems to be a real possibility. Scientists are close to figuring out what makes us age, and many are hopeful that very soon we'll be able to halt and possibly even reverse the ageing process, which would make us virtually immortal. At least we would no longer *have* to die. And could anything be more desirable than that? Dedicated anti-ageists such as Aubrey de Grey, moral philosophers such as John Harris, and transhumanists such as Max More and Nick Bostrom assure us that death is the greatest of all evils and that nothing could be more important than getting rid of it. If that's true, then it seems that Frankenstein's ambition was actually quite sensible.

So why exactly did everything go so terribly wrong? Why did Victor Frankenstein, instead of becoming mankind's greatest benefactor as he had planned to, end up creating something that he himself chooses to see, or perhaps cannot help but see, as a monster?

Playing God

In Shelley's novel, Frankenstein himself blames the whole mess on his ill-considered attempt to "learn the hidden laws of nature," to "penetrate" the "physical secrets of the world," to "unveil the face of Nature" and to pursue her "to her hiding-places." Frankenstein talks about nature as if she were a woman that he wants to bed and that he is determined to have whatever it takes. And if she doesn't readily give herself to him, well, then she must be taken by force. The whole thing comes very close to a rape fantasy.

But after the rape comes remorse, and punishment. Or perhaps punishment first, and then remorse. After his creature has gone rampant, Frankenstein expresses disgust at his own actions. He speaks of his "unhallowed arts," which led him, despite his good intentions, to commit "deeds of mischief beyond description horrible." He doesn't talk about God directly, but his choice of words ("unhallowed") suggests that he feels he committed a sacrilege, an act that somehow defied God's will and the natural and at the same time divine order of things, and that he has been justly punished for this.

The movie version is far more explicit. In Whale's *Frankenstein* he shouts, after his creation has actually begun to move and shown that it is indeed alive: "In the name of God, now I know what it feels to *be* God!" And in the prologue that was added to the film to warn viewers of the shocking nature of the events that they were going to see, the presenter summarizes the whole story by saying that "Frankenstein sought to create a man after his own image, without reckoning upon God."

In *Bride of Frankenstein*, James Whale's 1935 sequel to *Frankenstein*, Mary Shelley herself, played by Elsa Lanchaster who later remorphs so splendidly as the Bride, conveniently explains what her story is all about. Her purpose was, she says, to "write a moral lesson about a mortal man who dared to emulate God." All this strongly suggests that the violation, the crime that Frankenstein committed, was that he assumed a power that only God should have. The ancient Greeks called this *hubris*. Frankenstein made himself *like* God and was punished for it *by* God.

Traditionally, the power to give life was seen to be God's prerogative. It was the ultimate power that only God possessed. But what exactly does that mean? Does it mean that it's *impossible* for us ever to gain the power to give life? Or does it simply mean that whoever acquired it would be like God himself, equal to him in power and knowledge?

This thought, or hope, inspired not only the efforts of Dr. Frankenstein, but also those of countless alchemists, those harbingers of modern science, when they were trying to figure out how to transform things into other things: lead into gold, dead matter into something living. In their search for the *philosopher's stone* and the *elixir of life*, often seen as the same substance, which was supposed to give those who got hold of it wealth, wisdom, and power over life and death, they followed the path that was already suggested by the Genesis chapter in the Bible. We are used to thinking that Adam and Eve were expelled from the Garden of Eden for having eaten from the tree of the knowledge of good and evil, but that's not entirely true. If you read closely you'll find that in fact God wants them out because he's afraid that now that they have smartened up they might also eat from the second unusual tree in the Garden, namely the tree of life:

> Behold, the man has become like one of Us, knowing good and evil; and now, he might stretch out his hand, and take also from the tree of life, and eat, and live forever. (Genesis 3:22)

If they *did* eat from it, they would be, in all relevant respects, just like him, and he can't have that. Adam and Eve's expulsion from the Garden of Eden is not so much a punishment as a preventative measure: God protects his privilege.

It's not really clear, though, why we shouldn't aspire to become immortal, why this is being withheld from us. God's jealousy seems to be all that stands between us and eternal life. There's no consideration of what is good for *us*. Of course we don't necessarily need a better reason or any reason at all. Perhaps all we need to know is that if we try to pull a Frankenstein we *will* be punished. It could be just a fact of life that certain things need to be left alone, because if they are not, then we'll have to deal with some very unpleasant consequences.

So what we are being warned against is simply that if we cross certain lines and enter areas that have never been explored before, then the consequences are unforeseeable and likely to be bad. We are not made for crossing those lines. Better safe than sorry. Beware of the unknown. So the message is perhaps not that it is in some way morally *wrong* to cross those boundaries and "emulate God," but simply that it is highly *dangerous*.

Frankenstein's story brings to mind that of the sorcerer's apprentice. While his master's away, the apprentice can't resist the temptation to play master himself. He tries out the magic spells he has heard his master use, and it's working just fine. He gets the broom to fetch water to prepare a bath for him. That was easy. Unfortunately, when the bath is full the broom keeps fetching water. The house floods, and the apprentice has no idea how to stop it. Not quite so easy anymore. Luckily, before everything goes to hell, the sorcerer returns and brings things back to normal.

In Frankenstein's case, the master stays absent. Things really *do* go to hell. Yet the message is the same: there are things that are too big for us and that can easily get out of control. We can only ever *play* at being God, like children who dress up as adults. We deceive ourselves into believing that we have godlike power and wisdom, while in fact we don't. And that is why sooner or later we will screw up.

But is so much caution really necessary? Whale's Frankenstein, in the 1931 movie, clearly thinks that things only get interesting when they get dangerous. After all, "where would we be if nobody tried to find out what lies beyond" and to discover "what eternity is for example?" If we take our caution too far, there can be no science, and without science no progress. And isn't it even our *right* to know things, and to live?

We've been condemned to ignorance and death by an unjust God or perhaps an indifferent nature. So why not fight? Why meekly accept the death penalty? Why not *change* the order of things? It seems we've got nothing to lose, even though that doesn't seem to be what Mary Shelley believed. Although . . .

Gods Have Duties, Too!

Both in Shelley's novel and in most of the many movie versions of *Frankenstein* (including *I, Frankenstein*) there are plenty of hints that prompt us to read the story as being about a man who commits a sacrilege by violating the natural order of things and who, as a direct consequence, unleashes a terrible evil that comes to haunt him. And that's how people tend to remember the story. In the public imagination, Frankenstein is the guy who, driven by curiosity and ambition, creates a monster which then wreaks havoc wherever it goes.

However, what does not quite accord with this common reading is the fact that the creature actually appears to be rather nice at first. In the novel, his only fault is his ugliness, which is inexplicable since he was actually designed to be beautiful. But although the parts still are beautiful, together they form a whole that clearly is not. It is repulsive, and this repulsive *appearance* is all that Frankenstein ever sees when he refers to his creation as a "demoniacal corpse," a "vile insect," or an "abhorred devil." Yet in truth the creature is anything but an insect or a devil. His natural impulses are good and he's far from stupid.

After being rejected by his creator, he wanders about until he finds a safe place to hide. From his hiding place he's able to observe a family of three, and by listening to their conversations he quickly learns the human language. After a couple of years he is able to read, and not just any stuff, but things like Plutarch's *Lives*. And he can talk about philosophy and the natural sciences as if he had studied them at the university in Ingolstadt just like his creator. A monster that reads the classics and that speaks like a romantic poet does not seem to be much of a monster at all.

Boris Karloff does a much better job at being a monster, with his constant grunting, outstretched arms, stiff walk and limited mental ability, but his monster too can be rather sweet, delighting in sunshine, flowers, and even cigars. Although he's a bit short-tempered and can be quite deadly when provoked, he is actually quite a gentle creature, more like a frightened child or animal than a born "fiend." Whatever the "abnormal brain" that Frankenstein's assistant mistakenly pinched did to him, it clearly hasn't made him evil. The reason why the creature starts killing people is that he is being treated very badly by almost everyone he meets. He defends himself.

In the novel, things are a bit more complicated because he is much more human, or much more adult, than in most of the movies. The reason for his violence is a very human one: he wants to take revenge, and he executes his revenge with a coolness and determination that only a human could muster. And why? Because wherever he went, all he has ever met with is hate and abhorrence. Experience has embittered him, and he has every right to be mad. "I was benevolent and good; misery made me a fiend." His "accursed," "unfeeling," "heartless" creator has abandoned him for no good reason. And he had no right to do that because a creator has a *moral obligation* to look after his creation.

We should not give life to a being that can think and feel and suffer, and then just leave it to fend for itself. Instead, we have a duty to make sure that it gets what it needs, not only to survive, but also to live well. And that includes, perhaps more than anything else, love. Frankenstein should have loved his creation. Instead he hated him right from the start. And *that* is when things began to go wrong. If he had loved him, as a father loves his child, there would have been no monster. But he didn't. So who is the monster now, Frankenstein or his creation?

But if Frankenstein is to his creature what a father is to his child and also what God is to man, then we can read the whole story as a comment on our relation to God, and God's failure to provide for us as he should have. If we understand ourselves as God's (or Nature's) children, then by denying us eternal life and instead condemning us to die and to rot in our graves, whoever has made us has failed in his duty. "You purpose to kill me," the creature chides his creator, "How dare you sport thus with life? Do your duty towards me, and I will do mine to you." This is man complaining to God about the injustice of mortality. "I ought to be thy Adam, but I am rather the fallen angel, whom thou drivest from joy from no misdeed." And that is also what happened to Adam eventually, and what will happen to each one of us. "You accuse me of murder, and yet you would, with a satisfied conscience, destroy your own creature." Just as Frankenstein demands that his creature be good while at the same time doing his best to destroy it, or to wish that it had never come into existence, God asks us to be just and good, while at the same time condemning us to death and eternal darkness through no fault of our own.

We feel we haven't deserved this. And that is why some of us rebel against the natural order of things, like Dr. Frankenstein. Because it's unjust. So we are the badly mistreated creature, but we are also Dr. Frankenstein trying to fight back. We are both, and that means that Dr. Frankenstein is also the monster that he created. They are mirror images of each other. Victor Frankenstein is the "modern Prometheus," who steals fire from the Gods to protect us and who is severely punished for it and made miserable. He is also Lucifer, the "archangel who aspired to omnipotence." But Lucifer is also the "light-bringer," planning to "pour a torrent of light into our dark world." Yet Frankenstein's creation compares himself to Lucifer when he explains his actions to his creator: the "fallen angel becomes a malignant devil."

Monsters are made, not born. But the greatest monsters are those who make monsters. "Am I to be thought the only criminal?" the creature asks defiantly. The greatest monster is not the creature. It is not Dr. Frankenstein either. The greatest monster, it appears, is God himself.

Are Things Really That Bad?

This is *one* way of looking at the world. It's the way that Frankenstein looks at it before he succeeds in his endeavor. Before the catastrophe that turns his thinking around. It *may* be the way, or one of the ways, that Mary Shelley, perhaps without being fully aware of it, looked at the world.

It's also the way today's transhumanists look at it. As the arch-transhumanist Max More puts it:

> No more gods, no more faith, no more timid holding back. Let us blast out of our old forms, our ignorance, our weakness, and our mortality.

The world is bad, so let's create another. But is that really so? *Is* death the greatest evil? *Have* we been treated unjustly?

Do we really have a good reason to rebel against the natural order?

Of course, growing old is no fun. It's not easy getting used to it. And that we will all, each and every one of us, one day, and much sooner than we would like, cease to exist is a thought that is almost incomprehensible. How can *I* die? Will not the world end with me? (And in a sense it does.) And whenever we try to get our heads around this, we are struck by the horror of non-existence, "the void that presents itself to the soul," as Shelley's Frankenstein tells us.

Yet the Greek philosopher Epicurus pointed out a long time ago that once we're dead, we couldn't care less. Death is no harm because we won't be aware of it. As long as we are, death is not, and as soon as death is, we are no longer there to suffer from it. We are not scared of dying because death is an evil. Rather, death is only an evil to the extent that we are scared of it. Get rid of the fear and everything is fine.

Besides, if we look at the bigger picture, we may find that the death of the individual is actually quite useful. If people didn't die, we would probably not even exist because nobody would have bothered to create us. In a world in which nobody dies, or at least nobody has to die, there would be little need for children. They would only increase the problem of overpopulation, and since we would have no reason to make room for the young, our children would find it very difficult to create a place for themselves in society. So a world in which people didn't die would very likely be a world without children.

There would be no fresh eyes with which to look at the world. No sense of wonder, no surprises. There would be little change, and no progress, or at least no moral progress. When we get older we tend to become quite inflexible in our views. We know how the world works. We have settled down, not only in the world, but also in our own minds. Death allows the world to move on, to explore new avenues of being. We live only because others have died.

If Frankenstein were real and if he had succeeded in discovering the "secret of eternal life," then we would all be pre-Victorians now with an early nineteenth-century frame of mind. Or rather, we wouldn't exist at all. Because *they* would. So all things considered, the fact that people die and don't live forever is actually quite a good thing.

But what about knowledge, and power? Should we not try to gain more control over things, and over our own lives, so that we are more able to protect ourselves and others from a world that at times can be very cruel and hostile indeed? Yes, perhaps, but how far are we willing to go with this? How far is it *good* for us to go? How likely is it that our aspirations will contribute to making this world a better place? And is making the world a better place really what people want when they strive for more knowledge and power?

There is such a thing as "senseless curiosity." It is what Shelley's Frankenstein later in the book believes he was driven by when he set out to uncover the secret of eternal life. At first he flattered himself with the thought that he'd become mankind's greatest benefactor, their very own Prometheus. But perhaps it was all a sham. Perhaps it was just plain old curiosity, of the kind that kills the cat, without a clear purpose, just the desire to find out whether it can be done, whether *we* can do it, whether *he* can do it.

Should there really be a limit? *Must* we accept that we are finite creatures? Let's go and find out. Let's acquire knowledge, for knowledge is power, and we like power, not so much because we can do certain things with it, things that we are interested in doing, not because there is really a *need* to have more of it, but for its own sake.

In fact, power is felt to be so desirable that we're willing to do almost anything to get it.

> One man's life or death were but a small price to pay for the acquirement of the knowledge which I sought, for the domination I should acquire and transmit over the elemental foes of our race.

In other words, eternal life is, paradoxically, something worth dying for, and perhaps also worth killing for, because eternal life is the acme of power. Frankenstein is well aware of the contradiction: "Who shall conceive the horrors of my secret toil as I dabbled among the unhallowed damps of the grave or tortured the living animal to animate the lifeless clay?" Life is destroyed to be created anew. But at least Dr. Frankenstein regrets his actions, although he never fully realizes to what extent he may have been motivated not by benevolence, but by sheer power hunger. His self-awareness is constrained by his need to think of himself as a fundamentally good man, one that has erred and sinned, yes, but still one who always wanted to do good.

Professor Pretorius in *Bride of Frankenstein*, who is yet another of Frankenstein's alter egos, has no such scruples. He is said to be even crazier than Frankenstein, but only because he has no illusions about what he wants and why he wants it. Moral concerns hold no sway over him. He is crazy because he is so damn rational, a perfect illustration of G.K. Chesterton's witty remark about the madman being not the one who has lost his reason, but rather the one who has lost everything *but* his reason. He kills without remorse to get what he wants, and what he wants is to bring about "a new world of gods and monsters" by creating a whole race of new humans that would serve him as their God. A race of naturally born slaves, play things for their all-powerful ruler.

And that's the trouble with both knowledge and the power that springs from it. The more knowledge and power we have, as a species, the more easily can it be used against us, as individuals. The atom bomb is a powerful tool, but if you are one of those on whom it is used, you won't feel very powerful at all. Each new power also makes us more vulnerable. The power over life and death might appeal to you as long as you imagine that power to be in your own hands. But chances are that it is not you at all, but rather someone else who possesses it, and who wields it to make you do his will.

Mark Twain once said that to a man with a hammer everything looks like a nail. The question is, will you be the man with the hammer, or will you be the nail? Perhaps a world in which people do not have *too* much power is far better for most of us in the long run, for our weaknesses do also protect us from each other.

How to Be Happy

"Learn from me, if not by my precepts, at least by my example, how dangerous is the acquirement of knowledge and how much happier that man is who believes his native town to be the world, than he who aspires to become greater than his nature will allow." This is Frankenstein's final resumé, the lesson that he has learned from his experience and that he urges us to take to heart. Trying to become greater than our current nature will allow, so that in order to succeed we will have to change that very nature, is dangerous. But it is dangerous not so much because it might invite trouble by provoking the wrath of the gods or anything like that, but rather because we can't be really happy when we're constantly chasing a dream that may well turn out to be a nightmare—and that might not even be possible to realize.

We always need to ask ourselves, and reflect very carefully about, what we want and why we want it. Knowledge appears to be a good thing, but too much knowledge, or perhaps pursuing that knowledge with too much determination, may very well make our lives pretty miserable. One reason for this is that pursuing knowledge beyond certain limits might be nothing but a fool's errant. We are somehow assuming that we can know everything, that our minds are powerful enough. But why should we assume that? We are ourselves a work of nature, and if nature is powerful enough to create something that is capable of understanding all its workings, then it must also be powerful enough to conceal things from us. There is no guarantee, and in fact it's very unlikely, that we are actually capable of understanding more than a tiny fraction of the universe.

However, the most important thing to remember is that we shouldn't get too obsessive about anything, be that knowledge, life itself, or some other thing. As the ancient Greek philosopher Aristotle knew, the route to a good life and to happiness lies in finding the right balance between the extremes.

The pursuit of knowledge is fine as long as it is just one of many activities that make up our lives. And so with everything else. It is fine as long as it does not become an obsession to weaken our affections and destroy our taste for what life has to offer us. Then, and only then, will it become "unlawful, that is to say, not befitting the human mind." That is what happens to Frankenstein. He postpones his own life to pursue a specter, in his case the specter of an eternal life.

Victor Frankenstein's life is a failure not so much because his creature does not turn out the way he conceived it, but rather because he fails to see that eternity can be found only in the present, in the here and now. The secret of happiness is the discovery that our native town *is* the world, and that whatever we may find when we venture beyond its boundaries, it is not likely to make our lives any better.

2
Victor Frankenstein in the Twenty-First Century

Danilo Chaib

Today a real Frankenstein walks among us. I realized this in May 2010 when I was taking the subway in London and read in the newspaper *Metro*:

> Maverick Frankenstein Scientist Creates Artificial Life.[1]

I thought: "Whaaaaat?" Could it be just the sensationalist press trying to get attention? But then, in another newspaper the next day I read: "Frankenstein's Lab creates Life in a Test Tube."[2] "OMG," I thought, "Is this for real? Who is this Frankenstein anyway? Is he a philosophical clone of Victor Frankenstein? Is he going to fashion a creature and let it loose in the world, only worrying about the consequences when it's too late?"

Conspiracy Theory!

"It's Alive! It's Alive!" cried Craig Venter, along with his team of biologists of the J. Craig Venter Institute[3] in May 2010. The speech was published by the famous TED series.[4] "Perhaps it's

---

1 <http://metro.co.uk/2010/05/20/maverick-frankenstein-scientist-dr-craig-venter-creates-artificial-life-321593>.

2 <www.express.co.uk/news/uk/176331/Frankenstein-lab-creates-life-in-a-test-tube>.

3 <www.jcvi.org>.

4 <www.ted.com/talks/craig_venter_unveils_synthetic_life.html>.

a giant philosophical change in how we view life," said Craig Venter about his creation of a living bacterium with synthetic DNA. Craig went on to explain that the practical implications of this new life form could help society in ecological matters: "Also, at Synthetic Genomics, we've been working on major environmental issues. I think this latest oil spill in the Gulf is a reminder."

But how, we wonder, can these little bacteria help us with the oil spill in the Gulf of Mexico? Now, let's fast forward to November 2010, when British celebrity Stephen Fry appeared in a video posted by the BBC on a page dedicated to the oil spill entitled "Has the Oil Really Gone?" Stephen Fry and Mark Cawardine asked Mike Utsler, COO Gulf Coast Restoration, BP, whether it was really accurate to state that the vast majority of the oil spilled by the Deepwater Horizon had been successfully dispersed. The answer Mr. Utsler provided was really the seed of countless blogs to say that Frankenstein's monster was actually on the loose: "The oil plume is actually disappearing, the plume is biodegrading, there is a new form of microbiology that is attacking this plume and using it as a food source." Whaaaaat?

To add more scariness to this scenario, just after Utsler uttered those words, some "staff men" showed up and said that he could no longer stay for the remainder of the interview. But, hey, what's so polemical about all this? What drives so many curious nerds to endlessly discuss on blogs the consequences of a new life form on the loose? Apparently, this new life form was created to help society, isn't that right?

What's the problem with creating new life to help us? That was exactly, you might remember, what Mary Shelley's *Frankenstein* was about, what the "Modern Prometheus" was doing. For Shelley, we can pave Hell with good intentions, but not Heaven . . . or Earth. The same thought is brought to light by philosopher Jürgen Habermas. Habermas believes that inequalities and injustices can actually go away in our society, but not when science is dictating the dominant ideology. Rather, the improvement should be in the human heart, on a moral level. For Habermas, we already have the tools to reach an egalitarian society, where morality is always a dynamic value, being constructed every day by social relations.

The Habermas Corpus

The huge monster in Shelley's novel doesn't have a name. In our case, the little artificial bacterium created by Venter does. Many biologists started to call the first being having an entirely synthetic genome by the nickname "Synthia." Habermas argues against creations like Synthia, especially in his 2003 book *The Future of Human Nature*, which voices a criticism against human cloning and other practices promoted by the idea of *liberal eugenics*.

Liberal eugenics advocates the use of reproductive and genetic technologies where the choice of enhancing human characteristics and capacities is left to the individual preferences of parents acting as consumers, rather than the public health policies of the state. From this idea, a bio-social movement had sprung, defending practices that would improve the genetic composition of a population, usually a human population, but without the intervention of public opinion or the state. Habermas criticizes the philosophical and moral intentions of scientists who claim that they're doing research in order to improve humanity for the better. Do you remember Victor Frankenstein in Mary Shelley's book? He was obsessed with helping society, but without really interacting with society itself.

Craig Venter claims to be helping society too. We can actually see those claims two years before Synthia had been born, in a video published by TED in March 2008.[5] In this video, at time 14:42, we can see Craig Venter showing a slide to the public, explaining that the future uses of synthetic and engineered species are to: 1. increase basic understanding of life; 2. replace the petrol-chemical industry; 3. become a major source of energy; 4. enhance Bioremediation; and 5. drive antibiotic and vaccine discovery and production.

All of Venter's predictions worry Habermas. He thinks liberal eugenics is a threat to the foundations of the human moral community. He also argues that liberal eugenics will fundamentally alter relationships in the moral community, since with it reproduction will change from a natural process of

[5] <www.ted.com/talks/craig_venter_is_on_the_verge_of_creating_synthetic_life.html>.

creation to an artificial process of manufacture. That manufacture will undermine moral equality, and thereby human rights. And, as a result, liberal eugenics will undermine individual freedom and autonomy. For Habermas, what seems good for society (as Victor Frankenstein thought when creating his monster) is actually, as Mary Shelley explained in her book, an irresponsible act, leading innocents like Justine to suffer the injustice of a horrible death as a consequence of the uncontrollable behavior of Frankenstein's monster.

Good Synthetic Intentions

Craig Venter, still on TED's presentation, gives us more clues of why he is producing synthetic life: "Why do this?" asks Craig Venter at minute 10:45 of the video. He continues:

> I think this is pretty obvious in terms of some of the needs. We're about to go from six and a half to nine billion people over the next forty years. To put it into context for myself: I was born in 1946. There are now three people on the planet for every one of us that existed in 1946; within forty years, there'll be four. We have trouble feeding, providing fresh, clean water, medicines, fuel for the six and a half billion. It's going to be a stretch to do it for nine. We use over five billion tons of coal, 30 billion-plus barrels of oil—that's a hundred million barrels a day. When we try to think of biological processes or any process to replace that, it's going to be a huge challenge. Then of course, there's all that CO_2 from this material that ends up in the atmosphere.

Habermas's retort is that, everything Craig Venter says above is sustained by a group of ideas that justify society as it is. But this paradigm works for society *as it is*, and doesn't look for any structural social transformation. But what if countries decide to change their policies, and have a huge worldwide agrarian reform? It's known that much of the land owned by the cattle industry in Brazil, for example, could be used to create little villages, each one sustained by their own agricultural production. This ultimately would decrease the immigration from small cities to big cities, like São Paulo (with more than twenty million people). People unemployed in big cities would eventually find employment in small cities and miserable areas in big cities, like the "*favelas*" (slums) could disappear.

This solution, to share land to solve the problem of poverty was actually proposed in a book by Thomas More (1478–1535). The book is about a little island where equality was finally achieved by its inhabitants. The island's name gave the book its title, *Utopia*. Although criticized for being unrealistic, many arguments in this book are actually prevalent even today, and many philosophers have tried to bring that distant island within our horizon. More's book seems to be the opposite of the dystopian vision gifted to us by Mary Shelley, but perhaps there is a reason for some hope.

What's true for many philosophers, including Habermas, is that the growth of world population is not something "natural" and "unstoppable." It is instead a symptom of the inequalities that persist in a society centered on the individual, the same society that drove Victor Frankenstein away from his loved ones in pursuit of his own selfish and egotistical aims. Music teacher and philosopher Jean-Jacques Rousseau, in his *Discourse upon the Origin and the Foundation of the Inequality Among Mankind*, agreed with More, saying that lands and cattle are the primary private property and the seed for all inequality. Rousseau imagined that the first person, who, after enclosing a piece of land, took it in to his head to say, "This is mine," and found people ignorant enough to believe it, was the true founder of the society for which Craig Venter is justifying his acts. Rousseau wonders: "How many crimes, how many wars, how many murders, how many misfortunes and horrors, would that person who said 'This is mine' have saved the human species, who pulling up the stakes or filling up the ditches should have cried to his fellows: Be sure not to listen to this imposter; you are lost, if you forget that the fruits of the Earth belong equally to us all, and the Earth itself to nobody!"

So basically, for More, Rousseau, and Habermas, the way to eradicate hunger is not "more food!" Among the practices in the food industry to keep up the price of the product is to control the quantity. There are several cases of food being wasted while confined in storehouses in order stop the decrease in price for the products. Robert H. Frank, a professor of management and economics at Cornell University, affirmed in 2009 that paying farmers not to grow crops was a substitute for agricultural "price support programs." The "price support program meant" that farmers had to incur the expense of plowing their fields, fertilizing, irrigating, spraying, and harvesting them, and then selling their crops to the government, which stored them in silos until they either rotted or were consumed by rodents. According to Robert Frank, it was much cheaper just to pay farmers not to grow the crops in the first place.[6]

If those practices from both government and farmers are real, then the problem of hunger in the world is not scarcity of food. Shelley's Frankenstein actually developed the same argument and excuse to create "synthetic life" as Craig Venter. Victor Frankenstein wanted to free mankind from disease and natural death: "what glory would attend the discovery if I could banish disease from the human frame and render man invulnerable to any but a violent death!"

This hope justified his production of a new life form; but when he finally achieved his goal, instead of giving love to the creature, he abandoned it. Victor's abandonment of his creation reveals that he never really cared about society. He wanted personal gain, and he then realized too late that his creature wouldn't fulfill his ambitions. Mary Shelley was the daughter of a philosopher, founder of the feminist movement worldwide, Mary Wollstonecraft (1759–1797). Shelley's mother wrote books such as *A Vindication of the Rights of Woman*, where she writes that women should participate more actively in history. Shelley knew then, that a character isolated from society, like Victor Frankenstein, and at the same time obsessed with helping the very society he ignored, would never have the courage to face such a *different* creature! Victor was not used to dealing with different people; he had no education in understanding other cultures. And so he had to abandon the creature and save himself, because he could not accept anything so different from himself.

Despite all the melancholic drama perpetrated by Victor Frankenstein and his whining throughout Shelley's book, he is seen as a villain by many, as depicted in the comic books series published by DC Comics, *Frankenstein, Agent of S.H.A.D.E.* There, the "creature" actually leads a group of super-humans fight against many villains, of which the most powerful villain is, guess who? Victor Frankenstein, of course! He is there, as a

---

6 <www.pbs.org/newshour/businessdesk/2009/08/why-does-the-govt-pay-farmers.html>.

bloody villain threatening the world with biotechnology. There are people who interpret Shelley's Victor Frankenstein as a villain for imposing his egoistic wishes upon nature. Most people make the moral judgment that, when we interfere in another person's life and make this life worse, this is wrong. This morality is well depicted in a hilarious Tim Burton's version of Frankenstein, *Frankenweenie.*

Be Your Own Frankenstein

Let's give *you* the opportunity to create your own synthetic life form. What would you like to create? A bacterium? A protozoa? A fish? A dinosaur? Or maybe, would you like to reincarnate someone? Like your beloved doggy? Tim Burton did this twice, actually. In 1984, he filmed *Frankenweenie*, as the ad for the film said, "A Comic Twist on a Classic Tail." More than twenty-five years later, in 2012, Burton re-animated *Frankenweenie* and got nominated for the Academy Award for Best Animated Feature.

Frankenweenie, in a really smart way, evidences Habermas's point of view, even using Victor Frankenstein as the hero. This time Victor is a boy who loves his doggy Sparky and does everything to be with him (even bringing the doggy back from the dead). However, many school colleagues of Victor's learn his techniques, and in order to win a science competition, they start to bring other dead pets back to life. Things don't go well, as every animal they try to reincarnate turns out to be evil. The logic of the movie is clear: If you don't have love, your creations will turn against you and against others, as well.

It's not just that you have to care about your creation and then your creation will care about you. It's more than that. You have to care about the interactions your creation will have with others. It's no wonder that, at the end of *Frankenweenie* (Spoiler alert!!) Sparky, Victor's *creature*, saves everyone from the evil pets! There is a morality in Sparky that motivates him to care about others. Hannah Arendt (1906–1975) pointed out that the life of a human being proceeds only on the condition that there is interaction with other human beings: For human beings, "to live" means—according to the expression in Latin, "to be among men" (*inter homines esse*), and to die, "to cease to be among men." In other words, the verb "to live" can't be seen as singular: *to live* is always plural.

It's Alive! It's Aliiive . . . and Controlled—(Really?)

Craig Venter in an interview in *Time* magazine in July 2012, praised Shelley's *Frankenstein*. Apparently he is writing a book on synthetic life and going through all the history of "Vitalism", a theory which posits that living things are materially different from nonliving things, and tries to explain the background to that kind of thinking. Venter said that this was first clearly articulated by Mary Shelley in *Frankenstein*.[7]

The reporter was surprised by Venter's raising the topic of Shelley's book, and took the opportunity to ask Venter what we have discussed throughout this chapter: about the laws of unintended consequences! Venter answered that when his team cried "It's Aliiive!" in May 2012 and made their announcement of having created synthetic life in the laboratory, President Obama himself asked his new commission to look at this issue. This commission's report stressed that Venter and his colleagues are building components to be able to terminate or limit the spread of any new life form.

As an example, Venter mentioned the tens of millions of experiments that he has been doing since the 1970s, like putting genes of every organism into *E. coli* in laboratories, and declared that there's never been a problem. The reason for this is that the laboratory *E. coli* has a chemical dependency. It can't survive outside the special lab medium. So, Synthia is under control! Conspiracy theorists would respond: Really? Have you never heard of chaos theory, Craig Venter? Or better yet, have you never seen any horror movies? It always starts with someone saying "Everything's under control" and then suddenly, Frankenstein's monster is pulling the heart out of the body of some innocent little girl!

If You Want Immortality, Do Something Meaningful During Your Life—(Really?)

Victor Frankenstein went in search of immortality, and accordingly to Venter, he found it. Venter categorically says that if you

---

[7] Well, not really. The first to articulate Vitalism was actually a contemporary of Plato's, Hippocrates of Cos (460 B.C.–c. 370 B.C.).

want immortality, you should do something meaningful during your lifetime. Victor Frankenstein did something meaningful in his lifetime: a 'scientific act' that set a monster loose and killed his entire family and friends. Well, this type of immortality, apart from making a good gothic novel, doesn't seem so great. What is meaningful, really? Is the love of Tim Burton's Victor for his dog meaningful? The attitude towards life and society should be considered by everybody in their actions.

As Habermas sees it, the problem is not genetic engineering itself, but the mode and scope of its use. In a world with wars, hunger, and social inequality, science should focus on changing the structure of society rather than the individual. The program of liberal eugenics blinds itself to this task because it ignores how biotechnology can be used collectively, serving society as a whole, rather than doing what Victor Frankenstein did, isolating himself from society, and trying to "cure" a society that he never interacted with and maybe never even really loved.

3
Embracing the Corpse-People

GREG LITTMANN

Mary Shelley's *Frankenstein* is one of the greatest horror novels ever written, as well as one of the greatest works of science fiction. Like all great horror writers, Shelley drew on her own fears to inspire her work. *Frankenstein* is her nightmarish fantasy about scientific exploration taken too far. But how far is too far?

For Shelley, the perfect example of going too far is creating artificial life. Yet creating artificial life is a goal of modern scientific research, both for geneticists editing DNA to produce new forms of biological life and for computer programmers working in artificial intelligence to produce thinking machines. So asking, "How wise is Shelley's attitude in *Frankenstein*?" is not just an excuse to wallow in a wonderful book. If we're going to be consistent, what we say about the *Frankenstein* case will have implications for what we should say about the development and use of technologies in the real world.

What's Wrong with Monsters?

Why not create artificial life? Mary Shelley saw it as overstepping human prerogatives. Creating life is only for God. In her Author's Introduction to the 1831 edition of *Frankenstein*, she writes: "Frightful must it be, for supremely frightful would be the effect of any human endeavor to mock the stupendous mechanism of the Creator of the world. His success would terrify the artist; he would rush away from his odious handy work, horror-stricken."[1] Dr. Victor Frankenstein likewise views his act as trespassing on God's turf. He complains: "How much happier that man is who believes his native town to be the world, than he who aspires to become greater than his nature will allow?" (p. 31). The full title of the novel, *Frankenstein or the Modern Prometheus*, is a reference to Victor's usurping of God's prerogative, Prometheus being the Titan in Greek mythology who stole fire from the gods and gave it to humanity.

As it turns out, though, we weren't created by a god but arose through billions of years of evolution. In the absence of God, no divine law holds us back. Of course, just because we aren't forbidden to do something doesn't make it a good idea. The arctic explorer Robert Walton, whose letters frame the novel, asks, "What can stop the determined heart and resolved will of man?" (p. 7) as he proudly sails his ship north into the icy waters on a doomed voyage of discovery. His excessive human pride is not challenging God here, at least not directly, but it is leading him to go beyond the limits of what human beings should do.

One good reason to be wary of creating new life is that it could be dangerous. Victor refuses to build a mate for his creation for fear that they will populate the world with their kind and perhaps wipe out humanity. He need not have worried. Modern genetics reveals that there is no way that two people made out of corpses sewn together could produce babies made out of baby corpses sewn together, or anything similar. Sewing human parts together doesn't rewrite their DNA, so any monster children will be built on normal human DNA. Stephen King also notes that "Shelley apparently never considered the idea that for a man capable of creating life from moldering spare parts, it would be child's play to create a woman without the capacity for conceiving a child"[2] It might be added that if what the monster really needs is a friend, as he keeps insisting, Victor should be able to haggle him into accepting a male companion.

Still, Victor certainly has a point that creating new life could potentially have disastrous consequences. If artificially created creatures happen to kill off or outcompete some established

---

[1] Mary Shelley, *Frankenstein* (Dover, 1983), pp. viii–ix.

[2] *Danse Macabre* (Berkley, 1983), p. 39.

species, they could collapse an entire ecosystem. Likewise, the development of biological weapons intended to spread contagion among human populations is madness. Given the potential consequences for humanity, the human propensity for making mistakes, and the ability of humans to be shockingly evil, developing these technologies just isn't worth the risk.

However, this is not the sort of case we find in *Frankenstein*, even if we allow that in the universe of the novel, the children of corpse-monsters will be corpse-monsters too. Let's imagine that Victor had built his creature a mate, and together the two monsters became the Adam and Eve of a new race that spread over the Earth. One day a family of cadaver folk might move in next door to you, the Smith-Jones-Black-Shelley-Wilkinson-And-A-Bit-Of-Phelps family; two gigantic but wizened adults and three gaunt, necrotic children. What, exactly, is so bad about that?

Certainly, they are ugly. But so what? So am I and I bet you are too. Yet you would think it rude if your neighbor complained about your face. More to the point, some of the best people I know are ugly. They have the hearts of angels and faces like the devil's backside.

When Victor sees the monster for the first time since the night of his creation, he immediately concludes that it was the monster who murdered his brother William. He accuses: "Nothing in human shape could have destroyed that fair child. *He* was the murderer. I could not doubt it!" (p. 50). But Victor's judgment is unfair. Very ordinary humans kill children, while nothing in the monster's makeup requires him to be a killer. Victor calls him wretch, fiend, daemon, monster, and devil, but never so much as gives his creation a name, let alone offers him help and guidance. If anyone had ever befriended the poor "devil" and taught him that humanity is not his enemy, he would not have reached for William's neck, but for his hand. Victor is right of course—the monster *did* murder his brother. But nothing Victor had learned up to that point justifies his conclusion. Little does he realize it, but his own prejudices against his creation are the greatest part of the problem.

As the monster frequently points out, and as he demonstrates by trying to make friends with the cottager family, all he really wants is to be loved. If Victor had treated the monster as his family treated the needy child Elizabeth Lavenza, and taken him under his protection, the monster too would have grown up to be "the living spirit of love." Even after the monster turns to murder, he'd be perfectly happy to reform if shown a little basic decency. He complains: "I was benevolent and good; misery made me a fiend. Make me happy, and I shall again be virtuous" (p. 69). In fact, he would reform if just one person would show him kindness: "If any being felt emotions of benevolence towards me, I should return them an hundred and an hundredfold; for that one creatures sake, I would make peace with the whole kind" (p. 105).

It's true that the corpse-people are, on average, a lot stronger, healthier, more agile, and more intelligent than humans. If a sufficiently large population of them decided to wipe us out, there's not much that we could do to stop them. But that's not grounds to prevent them from existing. If it were, I would be justified in preventing the birth of a human child in case it ever decided to buy a gun and shoot me.

Direct killing isn't the only way to bring disaster to a species. What if they used their superior intelligence to outcompete us, as we *Homo sapiens* used our superior intelligence to outcompete our cousins the Neanderthals? Again, though, such a standard is obviously unfair when we apply it to other humans. We wouldn't want to prevent the births of particularly intelligent or healthy babies on the grounds that we don't want our children having to compete for resources with *their* children. Besides, why would a race as intelligent as the monsters want to allow us to become extinct? Imagine what our own scholars would give to reverse the extinction of the Neanderthal. How much more would a race of geniuses give to preserve the only other species whose intelligence resembles theirs, and the one that gave them existence in the first place?

Learning to Love Monsters

Stripped of the religious preconceptions that make the artificial creation of life seem like the violation of divine law, the value system underlying *Frankenstein* is more supportive of creating artificial life than the author seems to realize. The primary virtue celebrated in *Frankenstein* is not reverence for divine law but kindness. Victor is a man of "benevolence and sweetness" with "manners . . . conciliating and gentle." His entire family is likewise characterized by gentleness and benevolence. His parents were "possessed of the very spirit of kindness and indulgence" and his upbringing was such that "during every hour of my infant life I received a lesson of patience, of charity, and of self-control" (p. 16).

Nor do they limit their compassion to family and friends alone. Victor's father and mother were frequently in the habit of visiting the poor to relieve their distress and go so far as to taking the penniless orphan Elizabeth into their family. Elizabeth herself, as noted above, is "the living spirit of love," "unfolding . . . the real loveliness of beneficence" for others. Victor's best friend Henry Clerval, everything that a man should be, is "perfectly humane . . . thoughtful in his generosity . . . full of kindness and tenderness." Even the explorer Walton is a man capable of loving a friend of brief acquaintance "like a brother."

Shelley rightly rejects material gain as the basis for a fulfilling human life. Clerval refuses to follow his father's wish that he devote himself solely to business, becoming "chained to the miserable details of commerce." His life must have travel, poetry, and adventure, and he must be allowed to cultivate his mind with education. She also rightly rejects the quest for fame, and especially placing such a goal over loving relationships. She invites us to see foolishness in Walton, the mirror of Victor, when he writes to his beloved sister, "My life might have been passed in ease and luxury; but I preferred glory to every enticement that wealth placed in my path. . . . If I succeed, many, many months, perhaps years, will pass before you and I may meet. If I fail, you will see me again soon, or never" (p. 3).

Even so, Shelley's concern with the importance of family and friendship makes her too narrow-minded about how people should spend their time. To her mind, dedication to socializing with family and friends must be so complete that, as a repentant Victor puts it shortly before his death, "If the study to which you apply yourself has a tendency to weaken your affections, and to destroy your taste for those simple pleasures in which no alloy can possibly mix, then that study is certainly unlawful, that is to say, not befitting the human mind." It would be better if "no man allowed any pursuit whatsoever to interfere with the tranquility of his domestic affections" (p. 34).

It's interesting that Shelley places such limitations on the study of the natural world when her love of nature so permeates her novel. Victor and the monster alike are both uplifted by scenes of natural beauty even in their deepest despair. Clerval and Elizabeth, representatives of the healthy-minded man and healthy-minded woman, are both regularly enchanted by nature, to the point that Clerval goes into aesthetic rapture at least twice a day, when the sun rises and sets. Forgetting to admire nature is a sign of Victor's moral decline: "My eyes were insensible to the charms of nature. And the same feelings which made me neglect the scenes around me caused me also to forget those friends . . ." (p. 33). Yet Shelley's love of nature does not extend to love of understanding nature. For her, nature is to be appreciated as it strikes the senses, but the causes of natural phenomena are no part of their beauty.

When Victor condemns scientific obsession, it's not scientific activity per se that Shelley is objecting to, but what she sees as the unnatural devotion of some scientists. The monster attacks not Victor, but his friends and family, like a personification of the scientific curiosity that alienates him from his loved ones. But simple pleasures, nice as they are, are not the only pleasures that entice us, and we should not feel bound to forgo sophisticated pleasures for simple ones.

As to letting nothing interfere with the tranquility of our domestic affections, in practice that would mean getting next to no work done at all. We could *always* be spending quality time with friends or family instead of working, a very serious dilemma, but not one that should prevent us from pursuing projects that give our lives meaning. More importantly, we must not let the desire for the happiness of our loved ones prevent us from promoting the happiness of others in general. Kindness that applies only to those we know is not kindness enough. Researchers like Victor Frankenstein, who devote long hours to their work away from home, save other people's family and friends through their discoveries.

A Future of Cosmic Horror and Other Benefits of Being Kind

A good guiding principle to direct our kindness is the one adopted by the monster himself when making sense of human history. "I read of men concerned in public affairs, governing or massacring their species. I felt the greatest ardour for virtue rise within me, and abhorrence for vice, as far as I understood the signification of those terms, relative as they were, as I applied them, to pleasure and pain alone" (p. 92). The monster has invented the moral theory known as "utilitarianism," the view that the rightness or wrongness of acts depends solely on how much pleasure or suffering they cause. Mary Shelley's father, the political philosopher William Godwin (1756–1836), was a passionate advocate for the view, so it is no surprise to find it striking the monster as so reasonable.

The blind old cottager De Lacey is *almost* a utilitarian, as shown by his attitude to criminals. Before realizing that the monster is a monster, and knowing only that he is a stranger in need, he assures him that he would protect him from being driven out of society even if he ". . . were really criminal, for that can only drive you to desperation, and not instigate you to virtue" (p. 96). His attitude is characteristic of the desire of utilitarians to see reform in the justice system, to place the focus on rehabilitating criminals rather than on punishing wickedness. De Lacey goes on to promise: "I am poor and an exile, but it will afford me true pleasure to be in any way serviceable to a human creature."

He means well, but in specifying that he would help a human creature, he's discriminating against the non-human. The monster may be less biologically related to the old man than other humans are, but he's in no less need of help. If only the old man had acted as a true utilitarian, he would have disregarded the irrelevant fact of the monster's unusual composition and concerned himself only with the monster's happiness and suffering. Significantly, utilitarians were among the first to speak up for animal rights.

Victor, when he finally thinks his duties through, embraces utilitarianism without discounting non-humans. When deciding whether to give in to the monster's demand for a mate, he reasons: "This was my duty; but there was another still paramount to that. My duties towards the beings of my own species had greater claims to my attention, because they included a greater proportion of happiness or misery" (p. 161). Victor adds up the happiness and misery of all parties, the monster's included, and decides that happiness *overall* is best served by not building a female.

On the face of it, Victor is not being speciesist (biased against others simply because they are not members of his species) like De Lacey. He's not claiming that the monster's happiness is less valuable than that of a human, but just that the misery the monster suffers by being alone is outweighed by the good of all of humanity. But when we look deeper, he really is being speciesist. Firstly, he considers only the worst possible case for humanity, not what we might gain from associating with creatures so much more intelligent and, judging by the monster, so much kindlier in nature than ourselves. Secondly, he considers the suffering of generations of humans yet unborn, but not what joys may come to cadaver folk yet to be born. What achievements might these brilliant and naturally virtuous children of humanity make if only given a chance to exist, and what sort of society might they build?

As much as I enjoy the 1930s horror films of Universal Studios, movies like *Frankenstein* (1931) and *Bride of Frankenstein* (1935) cemented in the public mind an image of the monster as an unreasoning brute acting out of instinct, a forerunner to the hordes of zombies that have rampaged through pop culture. Despite all of the times that the monster has been paired up with his only competition as a horror icon, Count Dracula, not once has a popular film taken the fascinating opportunity to show the meeting of minds between the world-wise, cynical genius of Bram Stoker's vampire and the naive, idealistic genius of Mary Shelley's monster. The monster is much more likely to be found stumbling stupidly around a haunted house on Dracula's orders, in pursuit of Abbot and Costello.

Yet robbing the monster of his extreme intelligence is to rob him of the most interesting of his many inhuman abilities. He's quite simply the cleverest person who has ever lived. This is a fellow who taught himself to speak and read by watching through a window as a Turkish speaker learns French, and then managed to make sense of the histories *Ruins of Empires* and Plutarch's *Lives*, John Milton's epic religious poem *Paradise Lost*, Johann Goethe's tragic novel *The Sorrows of Young Werther*, and Victor's medical notes. If the monster is *that* brilliant, he should be able to construct a woman *himself* and then sail off with her in his home-made submarine. In any case, it is clear the "race of devils" that Victor fears would, in fact, be a race of geniuses, functioning at an intellectual level Einstein could only drool at.

At base, Victor rejects the monster for being different, for being outside the clique of humanity. The great horror author H.P. Lovecraft praised *Frankenstein* by writing: "It has the true touch of cosmic fear."[3] But what is "cosmic fear"? Lovecraft explains: "Dread of outer, unknown forces must be present; and there must be a hint of . . . suspension or defeat of those fixed laws of Nature which are our only safeguard against the assaults of chaos and the daemons of unplumbed space." In other words, we must be faced with something mysterious and unknown that defies the rules by which we think the universe operates. But being strange and unfamiliar to us and defying our expectations of what the universe is like are not to do anything wrong. We fear the unknown, but every friend is unknown until we get to know them.

Building Friendships and Building Friends

The opportunity science gives us to try to create intelligent creatures with a view to establishing friendships with them is too valuable for humanity to pass up. After all, it's the only chance that humanity has to make any friends in the universe at all. One of the most persistent fears in science fiction is that the aliens are coming. But the science fiction nightmares paper over the far more terrible truth revealed by modern science. The aliens are *not* coming. We are going to be alone forever, or at least, as long as we last. If intelligent life were going to find us, the probability is overwhelming that they would have found us by now. As mathematical physicist Frank Tipler has pointed out, it should take less than half a million years to fill the galaxy with self-replicating robot spaceships on the lookout for life. That nobody from the great void has ever bothered to say hello is excellent grounds to believe that nobody is ever going to, while the lack of evidence of robot spaceships suggests that no other species has even grown clever enough to look for life beyond their world.[4] As noted above, our species, *Homo sapiens*, once shared this planet with another intelligent species, our cousins the Neanderthals. But we drove them to extinction,

[3] H.P. Lovecraft, *Supernatural Horror in Literature* (Dover, 1973).

[4] Frank Tipler, "Extraterrestrial Beings Do Not Exist," *Quarterly Journal of the Royal Astronomical Society* 21:267 (1981).

a tragic and incalculable loss. As far as we know, in the entire universe there was only one other form of intelligent life and we wiped them out.

As individuals we're free to make friendships with other humans and that is extremely valuable. Yet just as it is good for individual humans to gain an outside perspective from their human friends, so the perspective of outsiders would be invaluable for humanity, as an aid to understanding both ourselves and the universe. In whatever way intellectual conversation between individuals benefits individuals, intellectual conversations with different forms of life might benefit us as a species. Truth is most effectively hunted in an environment with a diversity of perspectives, and other forms of life might offer us perspectives and ways of thinking that we would never have acquired on our own, just because of the limitations of our natures.

Certainly, we can make friendships, of a sort, with some animals. We can even share some basic communication with them. Your dog can let you know it is happy to see you and vice versa, while some chimpanzees have even been taught rudimentary sign language. But we can't connect with other animals on an intellectual level. A consistent theme in *Frankenstein* is our need for intelligent companionship. Walton finds that the hardest part about exploring the Arctic is the lack of an intellectual equal to share thoughts with. He writes: "I have no one near me, gentle yet courageous, possessed of a cultivated as well as a capacious mind" (p. 4). Victor, who cherishes the time he spends with his friend Clerval in intellectual conversation, sees intelligent friendship as essential to our development as humans. He explains to Walton: "We are unfashioned creatures, but half made up, if one wiser, better, dearer than ourselves—such a friends ought to be—do not lend his aid to perfectionate our weak and faulty natures" (p. 12).

Even Safie flees to Europe not simply to be with her love Felix, but to get some decent chat. With an "intellect and an independence of spirit forbidden to the female followers of Mahomet," she couldn't bear to be "immured within the walls of a harem, allowed only to occupy herself with infantile amusements" (p. 88). Most strikingly, the monster cannot tolerate an existence without intelligent friendship. When he demands that Victor build him a mate, he's not just looking for someone to talk to about his day, or to share monster cuddles with on freezing arctic nights. He must "live in communion with an equal." Despite mastering a team of sled dogs, the friendship of the dogs is no balm for the monster's soul. Dogs are notorious for putting up with ugly owners without complaint, and besides, the monster must smell *wonderful*. Yet whatever relationship he has with them, it brings no relief to his loneliness.

A Modern Prometheus

Shelley describes Victor as "the modern Prometheus" for usurping a power that belongs only to God. But if it wasn't for Prometheus stealing fire from the gods (at least according to the myth), we humans would still be eating our food raw and technological development would have ended with the sharpened rock.

No doubt our ancestors were afraid of fire at first, however they acquired it, and rightly so. Fire is dangerous, especially if treated irresponsibly. Yet judged by utilitarian standards, the benefits of this weird new technology have outweighed the costs, as fire lit the path to a new way of life for humans, one stranger and more wonderful than our ancestors' wildest dreams. New things aren't always bad, however bizarre they seem initially seem, and sometimes the risk of change comes with new opportunities worth welcoming with open arms.

I started from my sleep and, by the dim and yellow light of the moon, as it forced its way through the window shutters, I beheld the creature whom I had created. He held up the curtain of the bed and his eyes, if eyes they may be called, were fixed on me while a grin wrinkled his cheeks. His jaws opened, and he muttered "I am sorry that I awakened you, Victor. That was not my intention. I merely enjoy the sight of you at slumber. Goodnight. I love you."

I answered as I reposed myself, "I love you too. Goodnight Nigel."

4

So, You Want to Be a Mad Scientist . . .

DALE JACQUETTE

> After days and nights of incredible labour and fatigue, I succeeded in discovering the cause of generation and life; nay, more, I became myself capable of bestowing animation upon lifeless matter.
>
> —VICTOR FRANKENSTEIN

Mythic elements of Mary Shelley's gothic 1818 novel *Frankenstein: Or, the Modern Prometheus* express an interesting modern attitude about the conquest of applied experimental science and technology over human adversities.[1]

If we think of nature as willful, then we can understand what Victor Frankenstein does in his rented Ingolstadt attic as flaunting the seemingly inevitable forces of nature, battling against mortality to bring life back from the dead. To know that such power exists would go far to alleviate our anxiety concerning the inescapability of death. Shelley's novel has been so much more than a dire warning about the dangers of scientific hubris, or even the hope for eternal life. Somehow she breathes life into a story that has achieved an immortality about which her imaginary mad scientist could only dream.

Hearts and Kidneys Are TinkerToys!

In Mary Shelley's time, people were just starting to realize the full impact of their dependence on natural science. They were already

[1] *Frankenstein: Or, the Modern Prometheus* (London: Penguin, 2003).

becoming indebted to science in efforts to prevent and cure disease, improve housing and food, sanitation, transportation, education and communication, together with all the professional health services that many people today can take for granted.

Isn't it better to live with science? And, when it all goes as advertised, who can knock it? How, then, can we look such a gift horse in the mouth, or strangle the goose that lays golden eggs, by questioning the value of even the most morally unbridled scientific inquiry? Frankenstein in Shelley's novel takes this potential to one of its fascinating extremes by considering the possibility of surgically attaching and then electrically re-animating an eight-foot tall (no exaggeration, see page 54) stitched-together assemblage of shopped out charnel-house dead body parts. It's only the logical conclusion of the modern argument that if we can defeat smallpox and polio, then why should we not be able to cheat death altogether by somehow bringing life back to the clinically dead?

How exactly it is all supposed to work from a technical standpoint is no more than hinted at in Shelley's tale. The point is that Victor Frankenstein figures out how to do it, and then suffers intense creator's regret:

> It was on a dreary night of November, that I beheld the accomplishment of my toils. With an anxiety that almost amounted to agony, I collected the instruments of life around me, that I might infuse a spark of being into the lifeless thing that lay at my feet. It was already one in the morning; the rain pattered dismally against the panes, and my candle was nearly burnt out when by the glimmer of the half-extinguished light, I saw the dull yellow eye of the creature open; it breathed hard, and a convulsive motion agitated its limbs.

It is as though when telling Captain Walton his story, Victor, now in pursuit of the monster, cannot bear to dwell on any of the disgusting details. Even Walton fails adequately to describe the Creature, near the novel's end, saying only: "I entered the cabin where lay the remains of my ill-fated and admirable friend. Over him hung a form which I cannot find words to describe (p. 209).

The hard work of hooking up the organs and tissues in his rented attic laboratory invites filmmakers to elaborate on the apparatus and the electrical drama, and most importantly on the re-animated Creature. Although it's not in Shelley's book, an electrical storm is typically harvested and the power brought to bear somehow upon the dead being and against all odds, Frankenstein succeeds. If, as readers of Shelley's spooky yarn, we ask again, how exactly this is all supposed to happen, then we can only observe that Shelley draws a misty veil and pulls some quick scene transitions over just these kinds of details.

We almost participate in Frankenstein's overworked trance state as he spends late nights collecting and whip-stitching dead body parts together and positioning electrodes on the lab table. It's as though he's already returning to the Creature with regret for his tampering when it next opens a yellowed eye. Shelley generously leaves us free to fill in the finer points ourselves, and film-makers have tried to do so in a variety of visually and conceptually interesting ways, inevitably changing or distorting Shelley's story. If we want to take a darker view, then these parts of the story, these indescribable aspects of the Creature, are also by analogy something like a humiliating sexual encounter, an event too shameful for the discrete novelist explicitly to say any more about than is necessary, without wallowing in all the scandalous fun.

A Riot Is an Ugly Thing . . . Und I Zink It Is Just About Time Ve Had One!

Victor Frankenstein, in bestowing life on the Creature, mythically embodies an idea that continues to be a forceful undercurrent of our technological culture. It's what might be called an optimism or faith in science—the belief that with enough time, determination, and application of resources, there can be an unlimitedly promising future of scientific control over virtually every human adversity.

If there is no natural limit to the assumption, then in the new enlightened age of applied scientific knowledge, it ought to be possible in principle to thwart many if not all age-old challenges to health and happiness, including overcoming the supposed inevitability of death. Frankenstein is not evil, although he does play God by inadvertently creating a monster and then leaving it to fend for itself outside of all society. Frankenstein wants to be able to impart (and to gain fame for imparting) eternal life to individual human beings, to free them from physical ailment and the fear of mortality.

It hardly comes as a surprise, therefore, in a frequent even overworked literary theme also brilliantly adapted by Shelley, that tempting the most profound forces of nature against human willpower and a do-it-yourself chemistry set is bound to turn out badly. We see it from a mile away after turning even the first few pages of the book: Creating new life out of spare parts of the dead is sure to result in an uncontrollable monster. We are in no suspense as to the fact that a great tragedy must boomerang on the modern Prometheus who dares like his namesake to bring a fire-like spark of life down from the gods to benefit his beloved creation. To attempt what Victor Frankenstein finally achieves in Shelley's *Frankenstein* is to engage in the *unnatural*, for which in fiction at least there is always a price to be paid.

Shelley's fable, however, is not, *supernatural*. Stories of werewolves and vampires all typically depend on forces beyond nature. What Shelley describes is appropriate instead to eighteenth century science fiction. If we make the assumptions that were being made then about the unlimited prospects of experimental science—like all that is needed to defeat death is to combine parts of different dead bodies and then jolt the rag-doll into life with a little direct current, then much of the Frankenstein myth becomes not only possible, but inevitable. All it takes is undaunted human ambition, salvaged detached limbs and once living components, a needle and thread, maybe a couple of pneumatic pumps, and a lightning rod to harness a sufficient source of electricity infusing a renewed spark of life. It is a task at which no one can succeed who does not madly dream and madly dare, but the dreamer does not need to call on the occult or supernatural.

The dark side of Shelley's picture is that Victor's effort to serve human demands over nature eventually leads to chaos and destruction. His arrogance leads him to try to exert dominance over the prescribed contingencies of life and death. There are grisly countryside homicides and the execution of an innocent falsely condemned and executed in the wake of the fiend's misdeeds. All derive from the fact that Victor does not accept the monster he makes or take responsibility for its proper upbringing, protection, and education.

As though in a supreme act of denial of his involvement, Victor does not even give his creation a name. He runs from it in terror, and thereby makes of it an outcast from all human society, without guidance or adult supervision to smooth its way. Once the Creature's jaundiced eye cracks open on the world, Victor abandons his manufactured progeny to whatever fate holds, to finding its way in the world on its stumbling own. If the monster survives, and regardless of the havoc it wreaks in the process, it is with no help from its creator.

Victor Frankenstein recklessly combines a baby's untutored mind and high-strung emotions with the hideous form of a giant's grotesque post-mortem body, and then tries to wash his hands of the whole miserable business. Later, when the Creature tracks him down, the justly guilt-ridden mad scientist dolefully reports:

> A flash of lightning illuminated the object, and discovered its shape plainly to me; its gigantic stature, and the deformity of its aspect, more hideous than belongs to humanity, instantly informed me that it was the wretch, the filthy daemon to whom I had given life. (pp. 77–78}

Victor's creation is subsequently left to experience rejection after rejection, eventually coming to hate all humankind.

Oh, Sweet Mystery of Life, at Last I've Found You!

What is to be learned from the Creature's vicious exclusion from the kindness of his creator or from the country folk he helps? As the story unfolds, all hopes fail, one by one, and the Creature turns personal misery into anti-social violence. Victor Frankenstein, as the modern Prometheus, reaps his own destruction at the hands of the monster he creates.

There is predictable poetic justice embodied in Shelley's classic moral narrative arc. The interesting question is why the Frankenstein myth in so many different manifestations has captured the imagination of popular culture to such an astonishing degree. The tragedy of *Frankenstein*, imaginatively set by Shelley in the previous century at some distance from her contemporary scene, obviously touches a raw modern nerve.

Written after inspiration as part of a literary challenge on a cold Swiss winter night, having pored over a cache of French ghost stories in the extraordinary company of no less personages than Lord (George Gordon) Byron, Shelley's husband Percy Bysshe Shelley, and Byron's personal physician and traveling companion, Dr. John William Polidori, Mary Shelley's drama has stood the test of time as a well-crafted work of literature, while proliferating outward in many directions, penetrating deeply into the popular culture. There are over a thousand Frankenstein-related films and TV episodes. It is a popular Halloween costume and mask, and untold numbers of related spin-off artifacts. There is even a Frankenberry kid's cereal!

Shelley in unleashing her novel creates as much a popular culture monster as Frankenstein in the story engineers. How, exactly, given that the consequences could not have been foreseen, does she manage to do this? What is the secret of Frankenstein's unparalleled success in the time-honored world marketplace of mythical ideas, images, contagious and irresistibly insightful icons, parables, allegories and images? How does *Frankenstein* continue to strike such a responsive chord almost two hundred years after its original publication with readers and cinema-goers?

The answer may be found in the story's remarkable unique combination of the following powerful elements. Shelley's novel invokes:

- The progress of experimental science in nineteenth century Europe, beginning to reap the intellectual and practical implications of the age of Enlightenment that the previous century had inaugurated, and that is still with us most powerfully today.
- The struggle against death and the characteristically human consciousness of the first and major premise in the Aristotelian syllogism that every logic student learns, "All men are mortal." It is the awareness of life's greatest mysteries and its cruelest limitations, the yearning in all times for immortality, as we find among the ancient Egyptians and in a majority of religious traditions. (We are reminded here of Woody Allen's quip that he never wanted to achieve immortality through his work, but through not dying.)
- Nature's forceful retribution against human arrogance in daring to challenge its fundamental prescriptions, laws

> and productions, exemplified already in ancient Greek times by the original Prometheus myth in whose shadow Frankenstein explicitly stands, and as Shelley unmistakably invokes in the novel's choice of subtitle. It is the penalty for overweening human pride in the modern scientific age.

Take exactly these three components, then, gathered and more elegantly stitched together from different fresh grave sites and hospital morgues in Shelley's narrative, and you have at once the secret ingredients that have accounted for the popularity of the Frankenstein myth she creates and into which she breathes literary life. We love a frightening monster, and we are as cautiously suspicious of, as we are dependent in so many aspects of modern life on, applied science and what it is capable of doing for us and to us.

Hitch human progress to the wagon of experimental science, create ill-advisedly in the process a terrible monster, one that crosses the line between the natural and unnatural, that cannot be controlled, and with a mind of its own, without venturing into the supernatural, and we have, in miniature, the dilemma that all of modern culture with the rise of scientific method seems to have made inevitable.

The modern world is humbled like Victor Frankenstein for audacious attempts to rule nature through an understanding of its laws. We may be doomed like Prometheus whose liver was torn out every day by an eagle for bringing down fire from the gods to improve human existence. There is a sting in the scorpion tail of science, against which novels like Shelley's *Frankenstein* sensibly urge caution. With science and its applications here to stay, and in light of its increasing repertoire of successes and menacing potential for unthinkable catastrophe, it's no cause for astonishment that Shelley's story of Frankenstein resonates so profoundly with an ever-expanding appreciative readership and audience. It's the modern myth of what science can dare, and of what happens when it goes too far.

Shelley's novel is not a tale of doom and gloom inevitably resulting from the excesses of unrestrained experimental science. As the daughter of social philosophers, activist Mary Wollstonecraft and liberal political theorist William Godwin,

Mary Shelley was cultivated in an atmosphere of advanced free-thinking social morality. Indeed, for some contemporary male readers, Frankenstein's Creature may have been less frightening than the prospect of educated women winning the vote—something with which the Godwin, Wollstonecraft, and Shelley families were associated. If only Victor Frankenstein had fulfilled his responsibilities toward the Creature, the tragic events of the novel need never have occurred.

Having created a monster, Victor was obligated to cultivate its life and education, in the performance of which duty he abjectly failed. "Unfeeling, heartless creator!' the Creature wails at one point, rebuking his maker. "You had endowed me with perceptions and passions and then cast me abroad an object for the scorn and horror of mankind" (p. 141).

It's not science and technology themselves that are morally dangerous, but rather the unwillingness to take responsibility for their application. If we are Frankensteins in the most general sense of the word, if we use science to accomplish unnatural ends for the sake of enhancing human life, then, unlike Victor Frankenstein, we must own up to the ominous consequences. Frankenstein tragically seals his fate only by bringing the Creature to life *and then* abandoning it to its own resources. If he had taken appropriate care of the monster he made, he might not have made such a monster.

Wait. Come Back. I Was Gonna Make Espresso

The blind cottager played by Gene Hackman in the Mel Brooks's 1974 movie spoof *Young Frankenstein* alone tolerates the Creature's presence. His hospitality nevertheless leaves a lot to be desired. It includes dousing the monster's lap not once but twice with scalding soup, smashing his cup of wine in an excessively enthusiastic toast before a drop can reach Peter Boyle's lips, and finally igniting his cigar-like thumb ablaze with a candle flame. He is sincerely instructed: "Blow on the tip until it glows."

The Creature in Shelley's novel eventually laments, in posing an ultimate philosophical question about existence and the human condition:

> But where were my friends and relations? No father had watched my infant days, no mother had blessed me with smiles and caresses; or if they had, all my past life was now a blot, a blind vacancy in which I distinguished nothing. From my earliest remembrance I had been as I then was in height and proportion. I had never yet seen a being resembling me, or who claimed any intercourse with me. What was I? The question again recurred to be answered only with groans. (p. 124)

Ludwig Wittgenstein, in his brilliant posthumous *Philosophical Investigations* (1951) seems to anticipate the Creator's difficulty, writing in §261: "So in the end when one is doing philosophy one gets to the point where one would like just to emit an inarticulate sound."[2]

The monster Frankenstein created answers its own question of existence with the same inarticulate groans. Along with the monster, we can only listen in the dark and hope for a comforting answer. (Closing credits roll. Fade to Igor—It's pronounced 'Eye-gore'—Marty Feldman on a dismal mountain crag blowing a mournful theme on an alpine hunting horn.)

---

[2] New York: Macmillan, 1968. Wittgenstein has in mind something rather different than Shelley's Creature, referring to the desire to avoid circularity and infinite regress in using language to explain how language functions.

II

Dr. Frankenstein's Treatment Notes

5
That Frightening Frankenmetaphor

ELENA CASETTA AND LUCA TAMBOLO

When people want to alarm us about some technological development, they usually compare it to Frankenstein's Monster. The Monster metaphor makes us think of a patchwork creature put together in an artificial way by scientists, which then runs amuck and does a lot of damage.

So the name "Frankenstein" is often muttered darkly by people suspicious of genetic engineering. Frankenstein has become the governing myth of modern pop biology,[1] and the Monster often features on magazine covers along with bioengineered tomatoes and papayas, disturbing featherless chickens, and other—allegedly diabolical and menacing—lab products.

You may think this is inevitable, especially if you recall that, in shaping the character of Dr. Frankenstein, Mary Shelley had in mind the work of important scientists of her age such as the physician and anatomy professor Luigi Galvani (1737–1798) and Erasmus Darwin (1731–1802)—who was a physician and a naturalist himself and the grandfather of both Charles Darwin (1809–1882) and the eugenicist Francis Galton (1822–1911).

The most popular Frankenstein-related metaphor is the term "Frankenfood," made famous by Jeremy Rifkin's Pure Food Campaign but coined in 1992 by Paul Lewis, Professor of English at Boston College. In a letter to *The New York Times*, Lewis echoed the countless movies inspired by Shelley's novel

[1] Jon Turney, *Frankenstein's Footsteps: Science, Genetics, and Popular Culture* (Yale University Press, 1998).

by suggesting that, if scientists tried to sell us Frankenfood, then perhaps it would be time to gather the villagers and head to the castle with lighted torches.

But does it really make sense to evoke the Monster to describe genetically modified organisms? Is the Frankenfood metaphor a good one? Does it fit?

Frankenfood—food derived from genetically modified organisms, be they plants, animals, or even micro-organisms such as the genetically modified yeasts used to ferment beer—may seem to be very similar, in some important respects, to the Monster.

As we learn from Mary Shelley, in assembling the Monster, Dr. Frankenstein selected his features as beautiful. Similarly, biotechnologists often select organisms' features aiming at enhancing their natural beauty (think of ornamental and flowering plants such as torenias and petunias, or the angelfish that glows in the dark); or their resistance to insects and pests (genetically modified crops such as some varieties of wheat, corn, canola, potatoes, and soybeans); or to improve their shelf life, like tomatoes, or their nutritional value, like rice.

The Monster is assembled by putting together scattered materials stolen from dissecting rooms and slaughterhouses. Dr. Frankenstein, a scientist whose profane fingers disturbed the secrets of the human frame, collects the bones that he puts together to produce the Monster in charnel-houses, and as a result, he animates the filthy daemon that makes his life miserable. Genetically modified organisms, at least as understood by most of the public, seem to work in a similar way. Their production can sound pretty scary when described to consumers: in the most common procedures, scientists can "assemble" pieces of DNA coming from organisms belonging to different species thanks to particular types of bacteria which are naturally able to penetrate cells; or scientists can shoot, like micro-bullets, portions of DNA bounded onto gold particles. Sometimes, cells' membranes are destabilized by means of electric shocks (an echo of what breathed life into the Monster?) to make them permeable to delivered portions of DNA.

Both the Monster and genetically modified organisms inspire fear, probably for similar reasons. First, because we're not certain whether or not we will like the result of the experiment: once his job is done Dr. Frankenstein's heart is filled with horror and disgust; similarly, we could at a certain point discover that food containing genetically modified ingredients are unsafe or unhealthy. Second, because most people think that transgressing boundaries that are supposed to be natural is something wrong in itself, which can bring unpleasant consequences.

Are the similarities between the Monster and genetically modified organisms strong enough to make "Frankenfood" a good metaphor? Not really, because the similarities that the metaphor highlights are less significant than the differences that it ignores. We can learn more about genetically modified organisms by looking at the differences that the metaphor overlooks than at the similarities on which it is based. Frankenstein's creature and Frankenfood, while similar in certain respects, are different in the most important ones, namely in their *nature*.

This is what we can call a "metaphysical issue." According to a view that finds its roots in Aristotle's (384–322 B.C.) *Metaphysics*, the task of metaphysics is to explain the ultimate nature of the things that exist in the world. At first sight, Frankenstein's Monster and genetically modified organisms may seem entities of the same sort, since they are talked of as evil, dangerous, manmade concoctions. But this impression vanishes on a closer look.

Monstrous Metaphors

Metaphors are much more than a device that we use to make our language colorful and entertaining: they help to shape the way we view the world, and sometimes they can help us to improve our knowledge of it. In technical terms, when you use a metaphor, you connect a so-called "source domain" (*A*) to a "target domain" (*B*): in the case under consideration, for instance, you connect Frankenstein's creature (*A*) to genetically modified food (*B*).

This connection allows you to exploit your knowledge of *A* to describe *B*, which may be less well-known—and the implication is that what holds for *A*, holds for *B* too, at least approximately. This is why the language of science and of scientific communication is filled with metaphors: physicists speak of "waves" and "particles," biologists speak of genes as "blueprints" and DNA as "information." The examples of metaphors used in science may go on forever: think of the *struggle for survival*, of the *selfish gene*, of *the mind as a computer*. And all of modern science owes something to René Descartes's (1596–1650) metaphor of *the world as a machine*.[2] Metaphors help us to connect things that we know well to things that we don't know so well: the things that we know (the source domain) give us an idea, even if approximate and incomplete, of the things that we don't know (the target domain).

But, now we return to the Frankenstein metaphor in connection with genetically modified organisms. . . . Do we know the source domain (the Monster) that well? Does our knowledge of the Monster really improve our understanding of genetically modified organisms? In other words, is the Frankenfood metaphor a good one?

A first problem is that, in technical terms, using the Monster to describe genetically modified organisms is a flagrant violation of the so-called "principle of unidirectionality." According to this principle, in metaphors, the typical path is the one that goes from the more concrete, and well-known, to the more abstract, and less well-known. Terrifying as he may be, the Monster doesn't exactly seem to be anything concrete. But here, one may object that the violation of unidirectionality is only apparent. In the context of the novel the Monster, which starts as an imaginary or abstract entity—the object of Dr. Frankenstein's ambitious dreams—soon becomes very concrete; in the same way, in the real world, bioengineered food used to be thought of as a futuristic dream, which has now become concrete.

A more serious problem concerns our knowledge of the source domain. What is the Monster's nature? The Monster himself isn't very sure about his own nature: he claims to be similar yet at the same time strangely unlike human beings. "Who was I? What was I?" he repeatedly asks, without ever being able to answer the question. Moreover, Dr. Frankenstein is totally secretive about the particulars of his creature's real-

---

[2] Richard Lewontin, *The Triple Helix: Gene, Organism, and Environment* (Harvard University Press, 2001), p. 3.

ization, since he doesn't want anyone to repeat his mistakes and create another demoniacal enemy for the world. And in the very last pages of the novel, the Monster announces that he will collect his own funeral pyre and make sure that no track remains of his miserable frame.

So again: do we know the Monster that well? And if so much concerning Frankenstein's creature is so studiously kept secret, how can we hope that the source domain of the Frankenfood metaphor (the Monster) will help us to understand its target domain (genetically modified organisms)?

Manufactured Monsters

In order to investigate the nature of our two monsters, Frankenstein's creature and Frankenfood, and see if they actually compare, we choose to examine their "genesis" (origin) and their "sort" (as determined by their structure). Our choice is not accidental: according to some philosophers (for instance, Saul Kripke), a thing is ultimately defined by its origins and its essential properties (generally, microstructural properties: molecular structure for chemical substances; DNA for living entities). In simplified terms, this view of the ultimate nature of things takes the form of two doctrines called, respectively, "origin essentialism" and "natural kinds essentialism."

According to origin essentialism, an object could not have had a radically different origin from the one it actually had without ceasing to be that very object: for instance, a given human being could not have originated from a different zygote without ceasing to be that specific human being, and a given table could not have originated from a different block of wood without ceasing to be that specific table.

According to natural kinds essentialism, an object could not have been different in its microstructure from how it actually is without ceasing to be that very object: for instance, a substance which is not H_2O cannot be water. Now, whether origin essentialism or natural kinds essentialism are true or false isn't something we can settle here. But it seems reasonable to buy into the general idea that the nature of a certain object is somehow tied to the way in which it has been brought into being (its origins) and to its structure. So let's begin with how artificially created monsters are originated.

A first, obvious, difference is that the Monster is made by assembling together medium-sized pieces of dead matter, while genetically modified organisms are the result of the insertion of a microscopic portion of some DNA into other DNA. No dead matter, no corpses.

A less blatant difference has to do with the naturalness of the process through which the two types of creature are made. While the Monster is the product of a completely artificial process, with no possible analogue in nature, bioengineering techniques can be viewed, at least in principle, as a human attempt to replicate natural processes, the far end of a continuous that begins with grafting, hybridizing, and crossbreeding.

The idea of bioengineering techniques as a means to replicate natural processes lies at the very heart of the so-called "principle of substantial equivalence." Widely used in the US as a basis for the safety assessment of food produced with the help of biotechnologies, the principle states that organisms deriving from biotechnological processes ought to be substantially equivalent—with no significant differences, whatever that might mean—to their "spontaneous" cognates. In other words, to be considered safe, bioengineered tomatoes ought to be an analogue of homegrown tomatoes.[3]

At this point we're not concerned with the moral legitimacy of certain genetic manipulations or the risks connected to them, but only with the features of the processes through which the Monster, on the one hand, and genetically modified organisms, on the other hand, are brought into being.

In origin, then, genetically modified organisms are very different from Frankenstein's Monster. Let's now move from origins to results.

The Monster and the Salmon

Why would we want to consider Frankenstein's Monster and a genetically modified food to be entities of the same type? To

---

[3] For a criticism of the principle of substantial equivalence see M.W. Ho and R. Steinbrecher, "Fatal Flaws in Food Safety Assessment: Critique of the Joint FAO/WHO Biotechnology and Food Safety Report," *Environmental and Nutritional Interactions* 2 (1998), pp. 51–84. A book discussing the political aspects of genetically modified food production is Peter Andrée, *Genetically Modified Diplomacy* (University of British Columbia Press, 2008).

make the comparison between the Monster and bio-engineered food more tangible, let's put the Monster face to face with a concrete example of genetically modified food: a salmon recently engineered by a US biotechnology company—and at the time of writing under the review of the Food and Drugs Administration: if approved, this would be the first genetically engineered animal meant for human consumption.

The ancestors of the present populations of genetically modified salmon were generated in 1989 by micro-injecting into the fertilized egg of a wild Atlantic salmon a portion of recombinant DNA composed of one sequence coming from chinook salmon and one from ocean pout. The result is a salmon that grows to full size in about half the time of its wild counterpart. Needless to say, in no time the media baptized it "Frankenfish."

Are the Monster and the genetically modified salmon entities of the same type? Recall that the Frankenfood metaphor is mainly based on one property that the two entities which it connects are supposed to share, and that would make them entities of the same type: genetically modified organisms are, just like the Monster, patchwork creatures, assembled in an artificial way by scientists. Nevertheless, when we focus on the results of the process through which the entities at issue are produced, two important facts immediately appear:

1. On the one hand, being a patchwork, a mixed creature, is not a peculiarity of our two monsters, hence this doesn't seem to be one of their essential properties.

2. On the other hand, by looking at the different properties that result from the different ways in which our patchworks are realized, we can learn interesting things about the nature of both the Monster and the genetically modified salmon. But those properties are precisely the ones that the metaphor makes us sidestep.

When we consider point #1, a glimpse at the variety of life immediately shows that living entities are anything but unmixed. Surprising as it may be to some, we ourselves are patchwork beings. Just think of the fact that in every human being there are so many indigenous symbiotic bacteria—the vast majority of them living in our intestine—that bacterial cells outnumber "human" cells.

At first sight, you may be inclined to view our bacteria and us as separate and autonomous organisms—unlike the pieces of dead matter that the Monster is made of. But is that really so? As a matter of fact, many of these bacteria are so-called "obligatory symbionts," which means that they cannot survive outside us and we can't survive without them. They are more than guests, they seem to be part of ourselves.

And very important parts! We can survive without our nails or hair, we can lose an arm, a leg, or an eye, but we simply cannot survive without our bacteria. So then, being "mixed" doesn't seem to be a property distinctive enough to legitimate the use of the Frankenfood metaphor, unless we're prepared to go so far as to allow that the metaphor applies to every human being!

As for #2, if the similarities between the Monster and the genetically modified salmon are not significant enough, what about the differences? What about the "microstructural properties" of the Monster and the genetically modified salmon, namely their genetic makeup?

If you look at the DNA of the two creatures, you will find out that, while the Monster is genetically heterogeneous (the parts that compose him, coming from different people, each have different DNA, namely the DNA of the original owner), the so-called "Frankenfish" is genetically homogeneous (every part of it has the same DNA). This depends on the fact that the genetically modified salmon, unlike the Monster but like us, is the result of a unitary developmental process beginning with a single cell (the egg).

As a consequence, the Monster could be classified as a sort of biological chimera—namely, an entity whose different parts have different DNA, and accordingly different observable properties, each corresponding to the DNA in those different parts. Just as the fruit of the Bizzarria of Florence can be partly an orange and partly a lemon, in the very same way the Monster could have a black arm and a white arm, or dark black hair and blond arm hair. As far as the genetically modified salmon is concerned, it could be considered, at most, a hybrid such as a mule, a creature made from the interbreeding of organisms belonging to different species.

The Sons of the Monsters

We have deployed what seems to be a very sound philosophical idea—namely, the view that the ultimate nature of a certain object is tied either to the way in which it has been brought into being (its origins) or to what the outcome looks like up close (its structure). Or, of course, both. We can now answer the question raised by the comparison between the Monster and genetically modified food.

In spite of some striking but truly superficial similarities, Frankenstein's creature and the so-called "Frankenfood" are *not* entities of the same type. Instead of helping us to increase our understanding of genetically modified food, the Frankenfood metaphor muddies the waters and leads us astray. From a metaphysical point of view, the problems plaguing this metaphor are vividly illustrated by the example of the genetically modified salmon.

First, the property of being a patchwork, a mixed entity—supposedly defining the ultimate nature of both the Monster and genetically modified food—is in fact shared by many living beings, including humans. Secondly, the actual, relevant differences between the Monster and genetically modified food—the differences that help us to understand genetically modified food better—are ignored.

Imagine cloning the Monster: you pick up some of his cells, let's suppose the cells of his arm. But his arm previously belonged to, let's say, John. The cloning process would end up with an organism whose DNA is that of John, and not that of the Monster (or is only that of a small part of the Monster). But cloning the genetically modified salmon we talked about would simply give us another salmon, genetically identical to the original one.

In metaphysics, and in philosophy more generally, truth is the name of the game. So there seems to be little doubt that we should treat the Frankenfood metaphor as intellectual junk, and simply get rid of it. But is this really possible?

Well, we can't be sure. The enduring success enjoyed by Frankenstein-related metaphors depends on their triggering a deep-rooted feeling that no amount of philosophical or scientific analysis may be able to sweep away. The very flaws of the

Frankenfood metaphor lie at the heart of its allure: Frankenstein's creature being an—apparently living—patchwork made of materials taken from corpses makes it a living(ish) threat to our view of ourselves as unmixed, integral, "pure" organisms. But we humans are also pretty much a patchwork. So, wouldn't that make each of us at least something of a "Monster"?[4]

[4] We're thankful to Andrea Borghini, Gustavo Cevolani, Giulia Ferraresi, Jorge Marques da Silva, Marica Romano, and Achille Varzi for their comments on an earlier version of this chapter.

6
Frankenstein's Failure

DANIEL KOKOTZ

I have lost every thing and cannot begin life anew.

—Victor Frankenstein

When we meet Victor Frankenstein for the first time in Mary Shelley's novel *Frankenstein*, he's a dying, distressed, and terrified man, without friends, family, or hope. He survives just long enough to tell his tale to his new-found friend Robert Walton, who saved him from freezing to death in the Arctic ice.

From his tragic tale we learn that Victor, as far as we know still in his twenties or early thirties, has spent most of his life studying the secret mysteries of alchemy and even created a living being as the final goal of his studies. But now his once brilliant scientific mind is reduced to a maniacal obsession with murdering his creation.

So what has happened? One might think that Victor, after creating life from dead matter, should have been one of the most famous scientists of his day, teaching alchemy and being invited to share his knowledge all over the world. Instead he lived his last days trying to destroy this being, so, obviously, something in his accomplishment must have gone terribly wrong. Why did his enormous success turn into utter failure?

So Much Has Been Done, Far More Will I Achieve

Although the discipline of alchemy was frowned upon by some of the professors in Ingolstadt, Victor perceived more potential behind its principles than many of his contemporaries. Instead of seeing an art that was about to die out, he decided that there had to be more to it than just superstition and cheap tricks. His belief in this science was so strong that he hoped to banish disease and even tried to defeat and find a cure for death.

Victor really had two goals: From a purely scientific point of view he wanted to unfold the mysteries of creation itself, and from a practical perspective he wanted to use his alchemical knowledge in order to find new ways of fighting diseases. But it wasn't just medical treatment he was looking for but rather a way to rid humanity of disease and death entirely. In other words, he dreamt of using the natural sciences to create technology that would help him directly manipulate the human body in order to enhance his physical and mental abilities.

Victor's hope might sound utterly crazy and over the top if you hear it for the first time. But his idea is an ancient one. Ever since the famous Mesopotamian *Epic of Gilgamesh*, where the hero dedicates himself to finding a rare plant that will grant him eternal life, humanity has sought a cure for disease and hoped to find a cure for death. Death, to make things just a tiny bit simpler, is the ultimate pathology, where not only some parts of the body do not function properly, but nothing works at all anymore—it is the final enemy of human life.

It should be no shock to anyone if I say that our human bodies are far from perfect. We are susceptible to all kinds of diseases, injuries, accidents, heat, cold, hunger, thirst, parasites, predators, murder, and natural disasters. We are biologically utterly underequipped to live in the wilderness, and our evolution failed to provide us with much to be proud of—our eyes are weak, our claws almost non-existent, our fur not thick enough to keep the cold away—we are feeble, slow, and fragile. So, for as far back as we find humanity, we find the hope to discover something that will lift at least some of the burden of pretty-much-everything-is-able-to-kill-you off our shoulders.

We have accomplished quite a bit already. Many of us are nowadays in no danger of attack from predators, and we can treat many diseases and heal a lot of injuries. Yet, we almost always change our surroundings instead of ourselves. We live in cities, where predators are rather rare, and use our medical knowledge to treat illness and injuries. Our intelligence is the only advantage that we have, enabling us to modify nature to suit our demands, mostly by means of technology.

But isn't it logical to advance to the next step and alter our bodies so that they become more resistant to everything that can harm us? If we make up for our biological inaptitude by scientific means, we can rid humanity of its ancient enemies disease and, perhaps, even death! Victor Frankenstein believed this and was therefore just one more person in the eternal struggle of man against death, so his desire to improve the human body is no isolated case in the history of mankind.

This movement of attempting to alter our bodies ourselves is nowadays called "enhancement." Proponents of enhancement, like the young Victor, are of the opinion that we should change our bodies technologically so that we become more resistant to illness, heal faster, upgrade our capacity to store memories and knowledge, and generally become stronger, more agile and ultimately perfect in every aspect of our lives. Human nature, it is argued, is too faulty and we need to take evolution in our own hands in order to *create* the bodies, minds, and lives we want to have.

Such enhancement is much more than medical treatment. Doctors can only treat something that's already there, which means that any injury or disease must already have come into being before treatment can be applied. Enhancement, on the other hand, seeks to prevent diseases from happening at all. If our bodies are manipulated so that they prevent disease from occurring, and are resistant to injury, then medical treatment becomes almost unnecessary.

Many of the goals of the enhancement movement are still far away, since Victor always kept his groundbreaking discoveries to himself, but there are already some enhancements applied even today. Vaccination, which enhances our natural resistance to many diseases, is a widely applied and ethically unproblematic example of modern enhancement.

So we can say without any difficulty that Victor Frankenstein was and is still known as one of the most famous proponents of enhancement. And we might spontaneously agree that enhancement is something positive. After all, the verb "to enhance" means that something is made better than before, and my dictionary offers synonyms like "to improve" and "to ameliorate." If enhancement changes our physical abilities to make them better than before, it appears to be a most desirable scientific movement. The young Victor had thought so, and, although the events around him and his creation happened earlier, he would probably have agreed with John Stuart Mill's famous analysis from 1859:

> The only proof capable of being given that an object is visible, is that people actually see it. The only proof that a sound is audible, is that people hear it: and so of the other sources of our experience. In like manner, I apprehend, the sole evidence it is possible to produce that anything is desirable, is that people do actually desire it. (Mill, *On Liberty*)

Victor's desire to find a cure for most of humanity's ailments and the possibility of success was enough reason for him to venture his experiments and keep him going even after many, many failures. Freeing humanity from illness and death through an ultimate enhancement occupied his mind more than anything else, making him become so dedicated in his work that he overlooked a few important things. So the result of his experiments came about quite differently than expected . . . and he realized his mistake way too late.

You Are My Creator, but I Am Your Master

Victor's creation is usually called "daemon" by him, so we might as well stick with that name. This daemon surpasses the bodily limits humans have in almost every aspect and thus constitutes everything Victor had hoped to achieve with his alchemical knowledge. So let's have a closer look at the daemon to help us understand why his creation was a mistake in the first place.

The daemon is first of all a gigantic being. He stands eight feet tall, and his massive body holds more strength and agility than one would expect even from a well-trained and muscled human athlete. He can climb nearly perpendicular mountains without any supportive gear and run at extremely high speeds. His joints are more supple; he can endure greater heat and cold and needs less food in spite of his enormous build. Although he still feels pain and does not heal much faster than humans, he does not get knocked down as easily and can even survive in the wilderness without proper medical treatment after being shot in the shoulder.

Apart from those physical enhancements the daemon has a lot of mental characteristics, which, though not all of them are by themselves superior to those of humans, are of a kind we generally find delightful if found in our fellow humans. He is incredibly intelligent, first in an instinctive and later in an intellectual way, and quite a fast learner, too. He comes to understand his environment as well as his position in the world, and even learns language in less than two years. He is generally a kind, helpful being with a delicate sense for beauty and sophisticated sense of morality. On quite a few occasions throughout Victor's narrative the daemon utters his moral indignation about several incidents he had heard of during his early existence (like imperialism). Furthermore, he lives on a vegetarian diet, because he does not want to kill other beings simply for food, as mankind does.

So physically as well as socially the daemon at least matches average human levels of ability, and in some of them even surpasses us. What, then, is wrong with him? Why is everyone more than scared of a being that possesses so many agreeable traits? There are, I think, two answers to that question.

First of all, the daemon is incredibly ugly. We do not get that much information about his outward appearance, but as far as Victor explains, the daemon consists of dead body parts of different people stuck together and connected with each other, and although Victor has also tried to create a beautiful being, he could not prevent his skin, which barely covered the facial muscles, from turning yellowish, and his watery eyes suffered the same fate. His black lips got the same color as his hair, and on top of all that his voice turned out to be of an unpleasant harshness. When Victor saw his creation move for the first time, he was deeply shocked and avoided attending to the daemon's first movements. He did not stay to realize all of the positive things about him, to really get to know his creation and to realize the success he had had. And everybody else reacted in pretty much the same way—they all started running and screaming (or turning violent against him) as soon as they laid eyes on the daemon and realized how hideous he looked.

Eventually the daemon comes to realize that his life is entirely miserable this way, forced to hide all the time and with no companionship. He starts pondering the possibility that death might be better than life, but instead of suicide he chooses revenge on Victor, since he owes his existence to the young scientist. Here we find the second reason why the creation of the daemon causes so much horror. Deprived of basic needs like companions, friends and other people he could relate to, he vows to destroy the cause of his desperate situation. Victor even turns down the daemon's last (more or less) peaceful suggestion of creating a wife for him because, in spite of his own fear of suffering under his creation's revenge, he did not want to have the daemon reproduce and consequently be the founder of a race of beings that could subdue all humankind. (We now know that this would have been out of the question, since any possible offspring would have been the normal, human, non-monstrous product of the two individuals from which the two daemons' sexual organs had been harvested. And even supposing the offspring to be somehow non-human, two individuals are not enough to found a viable breeding population. But we can't blame poor Victor for not knowing what Mendel and Weismann would discover decades later.)

From that point onwards the daemon really becomes the killing monster that everyone has already seen in him, and Victor comes to realize what an awful mistake he has made by creating the daemon and handling him the way he did.

I Had Turned Loose into the World a Depraved Wretch

Now let us have a look at what constitutes Victor Frankenstein's failure in more detail. Victor had always been a thoughtful young man with a strong interest in the natural sciences. So it's difficult to understand how he could have failed to see in advance that first creating a being with enhanced human traits and then deserting him and denying his existence was a bad idea. If he had not run away in shock but taken his time to teach the daemon himself and accustom him step by step to humanity (and the other way around, of course), it is most likely that nothing bad would have happened. Victor refused to abide by standard scientific safety measures, which he ought to have known as a scientist, and therefore some of the blame is his. I say some of the blame, because, as we have seen, the daemon is an intelligent, self-aware being responsible for his own actions. Yet Victor has to account for the daemon's environment, which makes the daemon resort to violence after every possible peaceful attempt to make his existence known to mankind himself had failed.

Nevertheless, the daemon is everything Victor had hoped to create in his pursuit of enhancing and perfecting the human body. But the hideous features of the daemon—the only aspect that came out worse than the human standard—prevent everyone from getting to know him, and even Victor himself fails to give the daemon a chance because of his ugliness. The achievement of perfection in almost every aspect came thus at the cost of downgrading the superficial features: Many aspects of the daemon are indeed enhanced compared to our simple human traits, but the first impression rests nevertheless on the horrid outward appearance, denying the daemon access to human society.

As a result, we have a scientist who wants to find new ways to abolish diseases, get rid of death itself, wants to understand the foundation principles of life, and on the other hand a being that is enhanced both physically and mentally, but unable to be accepted by society as the great scientific breakthrough that it is, let alone as an intelligent creature. Victor had wanted to achieve enhancement but had not foreseen the negative effect of the daemon's existence on society or on himself. Paradoxically the daemon turned out to be both exactly what Victor had hoped for and what he had never wanted to create. Scientific results that end up like this are victims of something called the "Midas problem." The legendary King Midas wanted everything he touched to turn to gold but realized too late that even his food and drink were transformed and he risked starvation. Similarly, scientific experiments can lead to results that do not meet the original goals. If you want something you have not experienced before, it might later turn out to be less desirable, or even not desirable at all, when you finally have it.

Victor becomes a victim of the Midas problem because he has created the unwanted daemon, whom he is afraid of himself, although he succeeded in his initial goal. His desire to improve human beings was fulfilled, but the result turned out to be completely undesirable in retrospect. Victor's failure, therefore, was that he did not understand that something that is desired is not necessarily desirable. Desirability is not like visibility or audibility: You can desire something that is not desirable, as Victor's example teaches us, but you can't see something that is not visible and you can't hear something that is not audible. To compare these characteristics is to miss the point that desires come from the human mind and do not have their origins in nature.

So we see that our desires are not reliable when we have to decide whether we should or should not take an action. We can have mistaken conceptions about the result of our actions if we do not know everything concerning the action, and that is always the case if we desire to achieve something we have no knowledge of. Victor did not know how his experiment would turn out, he just *thought* he did, and would, in his words, "pour a torrent of light into our dark world." He was surely wiser after the daemon had killed some of his family members and friends, but when he had started his experiments he had sought something beneficial to the human race and pursued this goal simply because he thought it was good to do so.

In accordance with the Midas problem, Victor made the mistake of enhancing the traits of a human being so that it became aggressive towards humanity and could even destroy our whole race if given time. What we can learn from Victor's tale, therefore, is that enhancement, taken by itself, is not something good or desirable on its own account. In fact, something can be enhanced so that it is made worse than before. Enhancement cannot exist alone but needs to apply to something, and it is that *something* that defines whether the enhancement process turns out to be good or bad. So if something is enhanced, it is made better, but only regarding the attribute that the enhancement is meant for, and that does not mean the enhancement itself will be used *for* good.

Enhancing the human ability to withstand disease is desirable because it is good for us not to fall ill. Enhancing the capability to easily kill and to subdue the human race is not desirable because we cannot morally justify the deliberate slaughtering of intelligent beings. To create a being that is so much more powerful than a human with no access to society and companionship combined with the ability to feel abused, neglected and shunned is to create a situation that *must* end poorly. The daemon is worse off for being unable to become a part of society, and humanity is worse off for having to deal with a human-hating threat that can neither be controlled nor destroyed.

That is the reason why Victor's creation of the daemon was an enormous failure in the history of enhancement. His example is especially memorable, and makes his tale a classic horror story even today, because not only did his enhancement result in gruesome consequences, but he did so with the best of intentions. Victor was not intending to enhance something in an immoral and terrible way. If he had wanted to build a dangerous daemon because he wanted to create a new weapon or because he generally hated humanity the daemon would have been a full success and his tale less tragic (though still horrible). But doing research in order to free humanity from illness and death sounds like a good thing to do, and we can understand his actions, or at least his intentions.

So before we enhance something and interfere with our human nature we need to figure out whether it is a good idea to do so, and whether we are prepared to live with the consequences to the best of our ability.

"Avoid Ambition, Even if It Be Only the Apparently Innocent One of Distinguishing Yourself in Science and Discoveries"

The fact that enhancement is not desirable all by itself is a great challenge for modern scientific research. It seems simple enough to think about the consequences before starting an experiment in order to avoid the Midas problem, but the fact remains that there will always be uncertainties when desiring something that has never been experienced before. Victor did in fact think about the results of his work but did so in a purely positive way—he pondered the usefulness of his knowledge for the sake of humanity. He never asked the question whether it really makes sense for humans to never die or if we really need superhuman strength and speed. Instead he just thought about the possible benefits.

So what could Victor have done to avoid his failure, and what could be done in the future to prevent science from unknowingly creating something equally harmful to mankind? There are a couple of things that need to be considered when doing scientific research, especially if it concerns any possible interference with human nature.

Science should not be a process behind closed doors. Victor apparently thought it should be, since he never told anyone of his years of secret research in his own accommodation, where he studied alchemy and finally uncovered the secret behind the process of creating life. When the daemon escaped, however, the result of Victor's research interacted with society. Victor's research took place without anyone knowing, and while this may be fine with fundamental research, as soon as any experiment reaches a stage where humans or nature could be affected, careful review and ethical supervision is necessary because once something exists there can be no guarantee that it will not find a way into the world outside the laboratory. Victor's tale shows us what can happen if science is not monitored.

This demonstrates vividly that science must not be pursued without any moral guidance, be it from professional ethicists or "just" from public opinion. Science cannot operate in an ethics-free zone, and if Victor had followed this simple rule, this whole catastrophe would most likely not have happened. Modern scientific research is too complicated and too delicate to be handled by one person alone. Both for the sake of the scientist and for the sake of society the responsibility concerning how much scientific and technological interference with our biology we can morally justify must be shared by everyone who could be affected. A scientific breakthrough of Frankensteinian dimensions comes with too much responsibility for a single scientist to bear. After all, Victor himself died when attempting to undo his experiment by killing the daemon.

What is needed, and what could have saved Victor from the beginning, is a proper analysis of each scientific enterprise, especially when concerning the possible alteration of the human body. Humans are far from perfect, but precisely for that reason we need to look carefully at our desire to change our current biological equipment. Just because we want to become stronger or more intelligent does not mean that we should do everything in order to acquire an enhanced state. We need to learn from Victor's failure and take a very close look at all the possibilities we will have in the future to change our bodies, so that we do not end up creating something we have never wanted and maybe cannot control once it has left the stage of research and entered our lives. It is so important that science is conducted in the open within full view of the world it can so drastically benefit . . . or destroy.

Can We Believe Them?

My account of the philosophical problems around the daemon's creation process and Victor Frankenstein's failure in pursuing his desire for perfection of the human body and mind are based on the assumption that both Victor and the daemon are entirely honest with their respective audiences. Whenever I referred to the *Frankenstein* narrative, I took the examples directly from the text.

It might be that Victor was changing some parts of his story for Walton when he related his tale, either on purpose or unknowingly; and the daemon could have been deceiving or erring as well when he spoke with Victor and told him about the first two years of his life. What if Victor was more of a monster than the daemon, but he did not want Walton to know that? What if the daemon tricked Victor into believing he is kind, although he has murdered humans ever since he left the place of his creation? There are even more possibilities to interpret the connection between the scientist and his creature if we ask questions about their own plans and agendas apart from what they said.

Erring and lying are simply human, after all.

7
Frankenstein and Zarathustra—Godless Men

CHRISTOPHER KETCHAM

There are eerie similarities in the original story of *Frankenstein* by Mary Shelley and the fictional but mysterious *Thus Spoke Zarathustra* by Friedrich Nietzsche. Both Shelley's monster and Nietzsche's Zarathustra are rejected by humanity, their journeys are long and arduous, and both spend significant time in darkened seclusion. They even both seek respite from a cottage-dweller at the beginning of their journeys!

Both stories herald new possibilities for humanity, the monster as the potential for technological power, and Zarathustra preaches about the "Übermensch," who epitomizes the great realization of human power. And although these similarities are uncanny, their differences are profound, both reflecting on what belongs to God and what belongs to humanity.

Dr. Frankenstein abhorred the monster, his gift to the world. But Nietzsche said Zarathustra was the greatest gift yet made to mankind! The monster is gargantuan in stature, strength, and stamina; Zarathustra is but a man who teaches about the idea of the overcoming of humanity through the "will to power." Nietzsche's quest was to cast the seed of Zarathustra's will to power among humanity; Dr. Frankenstein refuses to provide a mate for his monster. The stories end with very different images of humanity's future. . . . the monster leads Frankenstein to the land of darkness—the North Pole; Zarathustra seeks the great noontide for man.

Differences aside, both creators, Frankenstein and Nietzsche, have an important similarity: Frankenstein and Nietzsche have become *godless men* and their creations are godless. Nietzsche and Zarathustra have rejected God and "good and evil," while Shelley and Frankenstein are steeped in good and evil and the godlike revenge taken by the monster. Shelley subtitled Frankenstein, *The Modern Prometheus*, after the Greek titan who for the crime of gifting fire to humanity is damned to an eternity of having his liver torn out by an eagle.

The monster's murdering of everyone Frankenstein loves is similar punishment for Frankenstein's crime against God by gifting humanity with the ability to defy death. The monster becomes like the eagle that Zeus commands to feed on the bound Prometheus's liver . . . know ye that such knowledge is reserved for the gods. But Zarathustra has the eagle as a companion, a creature of nature that honors the sun and by implication the great noontide of humanity. Nietzsche subtitled his book "for all and none," suggesting the potential and mystery of a humanity free from a vengeful God. However, the subtitle also suggests that Nietzsche was uncertain humanity would understand the book.

Both Nietzsche and Shelley were challenged by life: Nietzsche by disease, infirmity, and ultimately dementia at a young age; and Shelley, by the death of her daughter and early death of her husband, the poet Percy Bysshe Shelley. Through their separate characters they reveal complex approaches to what it means to "be." The changing event for both the monster and Zarathustra was not their births but their *rebirths*. The monster sees humanity as evil, and he uses his strength and will to power to destroy everything his creator loves and then eliminates the evils that are his creator and himself. Zarathustra looks into the future—not at the horrors of man, but at the hope for humanity in the love of life. The monster's journey ends in self-immolation. Zarathustra's journey is never concluded.

Usurping God

Shelley seems to ask us, "Behold the trinity of God, alchemy, and science—which will ultimately prevail in the hands of humanity?" Dr. Frankenstein describes the cause and generation of life in mystical and alchemical terms such as elixirs of life and even the philosopher's stone. However, he outlines his anatomical activities in the creation of the monster as a scientist does, examining both life and decay.

While Frankenstein molds his creation, he thinks little of the ethical implications of his activities. The alchemy of Shelley's tale includes man as mother immaculately conceiving a human life from bits of dead flesh, bone, and sinew. Dr. Frankenstein himself explains that in his youth he preferred the work of the magician and occult writer Cornelius Agrippa, and Paracelsus the alchemist to the dull tomes of science. More curiously, he coveted the works of Albertus Magnus, a saint and one of the first scientists to propose that there would be limits to science.

At the moment of his final assembly of the monster, Frankenstein understands that he has changed from a good doctor to an evil creator and usurper of God. The pregnant question born of this book is, "What is the province of science; what is the province of God?" Science and technology in the early nineteenth century, when Shelley was writing, were advancing so fast that humanity couldn't help but wonder if it too could create life.

God Is Dead

Sixty-four years after *Frankenstein* was published, Friedrich Nietzsche in *The Gay Science* proclaimed that the idea of God was dead. Yet he knew that the shadow of the dead god would exist in the mind of man for some time to come—even centuries. God's death is meant to free humanity from the shackles of good and evil—the "thou shalt" of the divine, creating a freedom for the human will to succeed, to power, the "I Will." Nietzsche's avatar is Zarathustra who leaves his home by a lake at age thirty to climb into the mountains where he meditates in a cave for ten years. The biblical analogy to Christ's leaving home at age thirty is quite intentional, not to promote Christianity but to propose an alternative view of the world where humans can be and become without interference from or owe obeisance to a deity, a world much like the one Dr. Frankenstein ushers in. After ten years, Zarathustra leaves his cave, returning to the world of people to teach them about the Übermensch: the successor to man.

The Abyss

Both Shelley's Frankenstein and Nietzsche's Zarathustra have created monsters. Frankenstein's monster is a hulking eight-foot brute made from the dead, yet possesses the mind of a child. The monster is the spawn of evil but his childlike mind does not understand why his creator would abandon him and why the townspeople chase him out to wander in the wilderness. This shunning is his first encounter with humanity's fear of difference, but not his last.

Zarathustra's Übermensch is not a being like Frankenstein's monster, it is born in the analogy that "Man is a rope stretched between the animal and the Übermensch—a rope over an abyss."[1] The Übermensch is the idea that humanity can be succeeded by a being who is free from the teachings of the church, which make us docile and despisers of life in exchange for heaven. The Übermensch possesses and uses the will to power, which simply means the will to live life as if it could recur again and again exactly the same way. For some who read Nietzsche this eternal recurrence is literal—a repetition of the same life over and over again. That would be a stretch even for Nietzsche. Think of this as an analogy, that if we only have one life to live we should live it the best we possibly can and in such a manner that if we could live life over again we would do nothing different. . . . Nothing.

Zarathustra says that Man is both over-going; a tentative traveler of the rope across the abyss; and going under, towards rebirth. The crossing of this abyss is made even more tentative when we're tempted to look back towards our animal origins. According to Zarathustra, humanity stumbles and lurches, like Frankenstein's monster, as it stretched across the abyss.

The abyss for Shelley is the idea that science could be poised to usurp God with the impunity to create even life itself. The abyss for Nietzsche is the realization that God is a dead idea, but God's shadow continues to hold humankind back from becoming the Übermensch, the successor to humankind whose powerful will can not only produce strong individuality but does not fear or denigrate difference and peculiarity. Shelley's *Frankenstein* portrays the abyss as the war between the good and evil of humanity subject to the laws of God and church. Nietzsche sees the abyss as the weakness of humans who believe that good and evil exist and as a result, fall back into a world where human will is subjugated.

---

[1] *Thus Spoke Zarathustra* (Barnes and Noble Classics, 2005), p. 11, Zarathustra's Prologue, Section IV.

Going Under—a Monstrous Rebirth

In the infancy of his first going under, Zarathustra speaks to villagers about the Übermensch and the will to power—the life worth living. He decries the "last man" who preaches a happiness where everyone is the same and longs for a pleasant and promised eternity. But Zarathustra says these things about the Übermensch during a carnival and is mistaken for a jester.

After his speech, all eyes in the village turn towards a tightrope walker on a rope over the abyss between two buildings. A demonic jester accosts the man and the tightrope walker falls to his death at the feet of Zarathustra. Zarathustra picks up the dead man and begins to exit the town. As he leaves the demonic jester tells Zarathustra to leave town because even the good and just people hate him and that he is a danger to the true believers and the faithful. Zarathustra leaves the town, carrying the dead tightrope walker over his shoulder.

Both Frankenstein's monster and Zarathustra have been exiled but for different crimes of difference. The monster is exiled because of the prejudices against those who are physically different, for not being the accepted norm of society. There is no sympathy for the monster and no one, not even his father-mother Dr. Frankenstein wants to understand him. He is alone, spurned and denied affection—denied the happiness that comes from being just like others.

Zarathustra, on the other hand, challenges the basic tenets of society—God, conformity, happiness as meekness, good, evil and a pleasant afterlife. He preaches the pragmatic: an Übermensch who understands that life is difficult but that life is the only thing. The will to have *this* life over and over again, rather than an afterlife, is what makes these "last men" shudder in the presence of the idea of the Übermensch.

Dr. Frankenstein alludes to an equilibrium that is neither depressive nor manic when he says to Captain Walton that the perfect human is tranquil and possesses peace of mind not disturbed by emotion. Dr. Frankenstein is the analogy of the stretched rope, the last man whose will is subjugated to the greatest good for the greatest number—a pleasant happiness. But Zarathustra says that the Übermensch will shout, "What good is my happiness! It is poverty and pollution and wretched contentment" (p. 10).

On the Three Metamorphoses

"There is much that is difficult for the spirit, the strong reverent spirit that would bear much: but its strength demands the difficult and the most difficult." Zarathustra speaks of three progressive metamorphoses of the sprit: camel, lion, and child, in that order. The first, a camel, willingly bears the burden of being. However, to achieve the second metamorphosis into lion the camel must first "hasten the spirit into its desert," and in this loneliest wilderness, "here the spirit becomes a lion who would conquer his freedom and be master in his own desert" (p. 25). Zarathustra at his first going under has just become this camel while bearing the burden of the dead tightrope walker and entering the wilderness, hastening his spirit into the desert.

The monster carries his own burden of existence as an outcast into the forest. But his metamorphosis begins in the reverse of Zarathustra. He is born a "superman" of sorts with the mind of a child. He begins as the child, Zarathustra's third metamorphosis. The monster is pure potentiality—a pure will to power filled with the curiosities of a child but with a physical superstructure that ensures that he will be different from humanity. Yet he is thrown into the world and thrown away. He finds a dark womb-like hovel to become in. He begins to conquer his freedom and become master in his own affectionless existence by learning the ways of people through listening and observing the peasant family and its blind patriarch. But, the monster is learning the ways of humanity and not the Übermensch so his metamorphosis is being conducted in reverse, traversing back over the abyss.

The monster experiences only one act of compassion in his existence when he waits until the family of the blind cottage dweller departs leaving only the sightless old man in the dwelling. The monster introduces himself to the old blind man. The old man tells the unseen monstrosity he too is an exile and that the monster has persuaded him that he is sincere so he would be happy to hear more of the tale. The monster embraces the old man.

This monstrous creature, who desires only affection, is soon disabused of his minor brush with understanding and compassion. The family returns and when the monster is seen for the first time by those he has been secretly helping by chopping firewood, he is attacked and beaten by Felix, the old man's son. Yet the abused monster could have easily overpowered his assailant as the lion overcomes the antelope, but he does not. He returns to his hovel-womb and burns it, howling like the lion he is reluctantly devolving into.

Zarathustra says about this second metamorphosis, "Here he seeks his last master: he wants to fight him and his last god; for final victory he wants to fight with the great dragon. Who is the great dragon whom the spirit will no longer call lord or god? 'Thou shalt,' is the name of the great dragon. But the spirit of the lion says, 'I will'" (p. 25). After burning his hovel, the monster sets out to find his last god: his father-mother Dr. Frankenstein.

On the other hand, Zarathustra's forward metamorphosis into lion is gradual. He has made speeches and traveled the world. On his return journey to his cave Zarathustra encounters men that are like Frankenstein's monster—society's outcasts. They include the ugliest man, an old pope, two kings, a voluntary beggar, Zarathustra's own shadow, and a magician. He calls this foul-smelling group his "higher men" and determines to make them his apostles and teachers of the Übermensch. In the end, these higher men prove not to be worthy. At the moment of this understanding Zarathustra speaks:

> '*Pity! Pity for the higher men*!' he cried out, and his face changed to brass. 'Well! *That*—has had its time! My suffering and my pity—what do they matter! Should I strive for my *happiness*? I strive for my work! Well! The lion has come, my children are near, Zarathustra has grown ripe, my hour has come. —This is *my* morning, *my* day begins: *arise now, arise, you great noon*!' (p. 281)

Zarathustra abandons the higher men (his last gods—the last men) and his cave to go under again and metamorphose his spirit to fight for his final victory. At that moment of lion-like revelation, his final metamorphosis into child is nigh, "The child is innocence and forgetting, a new beginning, a game, a self-propelled wheel, a first movement, a sacred Yes-saying" (p. 26). This is the spirit that wills its own will, and with this power, even the outcast conquers his own world.

The monster wrestles with his last God and his only God—Frankenstein, demanding that Frankenstein create a female companion for him in turn for which the monster agrees to exile himself and his companion from humanity. His vision of his life with his companion is like that of the Garden of Eden with beds of dry leaves and a warm sun that will ripen their food. His great noon is but more exile but perhaps a new beginning with a new companion who like himself is neither human nor animal. This is also the struggle for his will, as outcaste to conquer his own world and create his future, but he cannot do it alone. Dr. Frankenstein agrees and begins to commit his sin again, but then renounces the monster and cuts his nearly finished second creation into pieces, disposing of her in the sea.

Frankenstein defies his godless monster and asserts his will . . . but towards what end? The monster confronts Frankenstein after this betrayal and in a reversal of positions with his last God says in true lion-like form:

> Slave, I before reasoned with you, but you have proved yourself unworthy of my condescension. Remember that I have power; you believe yourself miserable, but I can make you so wretched that the light of day will be hateful to you. You are my creator, but I am your master;—obey!

Frankenstein begins his own metamorphosis into a victim—a victim being chased by the monster. The monster's quest for goodness, happiness, and companionship is drowned. His will towards becoming human is left unfulfilled and his backwards metamorphosis into lion is finished. His anger knows no bounds and, like Zeus, he attacks Frankenstein's very being—not the liver as with Prometheus but his heart, killing those whom Frankenstein loves, one by one. That both he and Frankenstein shall be miserable in this life is now assured and they each chase each other into the darkness of the North Pole, seeking to extinguish each other.

In the end Frankenstein expires on his own and the monster, who has in retrograde metamorphosed into Nietzsche's camel, carries Frankenstein's corpse off seeking to burn both himself and the body of his last God and immolating that which should not have been created.

Just before his death, Frankenstein laments to Captain Walton that he once had the highest aspirations, the loftiest ambitions but has sunk so low that he will never rise again.

Ashes to ashes—dust to dust. Good and evil have warred between Frankenstein and his monster but what has won? Humanity has won in the end over the possibility of a successor to humanity, the superhuman creation of Frankenstein who could have been more than any moral man—an Übermensch of humanity's own creation and divination. Science has been dealt a blow and God remains the sole creator. The omniscient creator will continue to reign even as humanity finds the tools to imitate the creator's most intricate handiwork.

Noontide and Moonlight

Zarathustra seeks the great noontide—an enlightening as if from the sun—for humanity's awakening from the false-happiness of the church and its promise of pleasant eternal rest for the good and the righteous. He fights death, considering life the only thing that matters: any life lived, even if disease and suffering is all that life could be for someone (as was Nietzsche's own). That one would wish for this life to recur in eternal sameness is what Zarathustra seeks for humanity.

On the other hand, both Frankenstein and the monster find solace in the moon and rush to stage their final battle into ever deepening darkness at the cold and frozen North Pole. The good of happiness that both the monster and Frankenstein have sought have devolved into a hateful evil; a hatred of life itself. For Dr. Frankenstein this is first hate for his creation and then for himself for creating it: revenge and retribution in the usurpation of God.

The monster begins his life-journey wanting to be part of something more than himself. He willingly bears the burdens of exile . . . but the need for human happiness and companionship drives him on. His journeys and trials do not lead to a love of life—they lead to death, an eternal smoldering death that he believes will wipe away his existence as if it had never occurred. Shelley's story continues the battle between good and evil in the realm of God and the realm of humankind. The monster willingly sacrifices himself having accepted his existence as evil.

Zarathustra's message is that happiness is not the question nor is it the answer. Willingly bearing the burdens of life is the answer and these burdens are neither good nor bad but simple exigencies of nature, of living, of life. And life is what is *to be*; it is what humanity should be venerating. Zarathustra seeks an overcoming of man—a re-creation of man into a form that accepts the burden of the will but seeks to live life to the fullest.

The monster seeks an overcoming of man because humanity is evil but he provides no foundation for a successor. The monster has abandoned humanity and with his self-immolation gazes into the animal that is humanity's predecessor. Yet the monster's will is strong, not the will to live, but the will as sheer power. The complicating aspect of the monster's story is that this powerful will exists and it is up to humanity to choose to use it to propel itself forward and towards the Übermensch or backwards across the abyss towards the animal that precedes humanity.

At the conclusion of the story the monster acknowledges his plight:

> But it is even so; the fallen angel becomes a malignant devil. Yet even that enemy of God and man had friends and associates in his desolation; I am quite alone.

The monster has looked forward to taste the desire for beauty and truth and has looked back at the animal of man who sees only what he wants to see. In the end he is the monster—himself and nothing more. It is at this moment that he sees that he is a bridge between animal and monster (Übermensch) but destined for neither because he is the bastard child of a godless man and he will never be human. He sees no future in his evolutionary being, and says, "I shall collect my funeral pile, and consume to ashes this miserable frame, that its remains may afford no light to any curious and unhallowed wretch, who would create such another as I have been."

I ask you, "whither humanity?"

8
Capitalism the Monster

JOHN R. FITZPATRICK

The philosophers have only interpreted the world, in various ways; the point, however, is to change it.

—KARL MARX

Karl Marx was only born in the year that Mary Shelley published *Frankenstein*, but my guess is that Shelley would have endorsed the view Marx stated above.

Shelley saw the world changing and did not like what she saw. Marx's vision was more optimistic, but rings with similar dire warnings. Shelley warns us of the danger of creating that which may destroy us. Specifically, she warns us about bringing to life a creature which, through isolation and abuse, masters us and separates us from our own lives and loved ones. When Marx wrote, he thought we had already brought that creature to life—a monster that separated us from ourselves and everything we love.

In his *Economic and Philosophic Manuscripts of 1844,* Karl Marx discusses how the workers suffer under capitalism through a social and psychological *deformation* that he called "alienation." Workers are alienated from the product of their labor, and the act of labor itself. We can see this most visibly in the way Victor Frankenstein reacts to his creature. This two-part alienation from labor, from the product and the act, that Marx called "estranged labor" leads humans to be alienated from their own humanity as well as from other humans.

This same story of turning people into isolated creatures is told over and over again by Shelley, as we see how Victor views the creature, and other humans view the creature, and inevitably how the creature views himself—alienated, isolated, and alone. From Marx's perspective, capitalism turns alienated workers into monsters, much like Frankenstein and his creature.

The Frankensteins and the De Laceys

Marx and Engels begin their most famous work, *The Communist Manifesto*, "The history of all hitherto existing society is the history of class struggle." In slave owning societies this struggle is between slave owners and slaves. In the era of *Frankenstein*, the tail end of the eighteenth century, Europe finds itself still largely a feudal society, but the early stages of capitalism are in play.

We can see the advent of capitalism clearly in the Kenneth Branagh movie *Mary Shelley's Frankenstein*. The Frankensteins live in a huge mansion, while others sleep in the street. But in a pivotal scene in the film, we see the clear struggle between the landed aristocracy and the serfs who work the land. After fleeing Ingolstadt and entering into the woods, the creature finds shelter in the pig hovel of a family of serfs (unnamed in the movie but called the De Laceys in the book). But there has been an early frost, and it's impossible for the family to harvest enough crops to stay alive, let alone pay the landlord the rent. This scene, which brilliantly demonstrates the precarious nature of the livelihood of poor serfs as tragically played out in the Irish potato famine, ends with the serfs leaving the farm to an untold fate. In the potato famine many farm workers simply starved. One supposes that this is the fate of the De Laceys as well. But there is no shortage of food for the rich and landed aristocracy.

Production and Society

Materialism in philosophy is roughly the view that the only stuff that exists in the universe is matter. Marx certainly believed this, though his view goes even deeper. He thought that the material conditions of a society, largely the means of production available to that society, would dominate many of the other features of society including its morality and politics. So, the technology and means of production that a given society is capable of employing influences other features of society.

A typical example of this Marxist theory is that the dominant religious views of hunting and gathering societies are often similar to each other and not similar to those of agriculturalists. The materialist impact of technology on belief is another theme that is at the center of Mary Shelley's universe.

Do we have any right to change the natural order of things and bring the dead back to life? Or is it simply human vanity that allows us to play at being gods? This question was important to the Victorian romantics, and it remains one for environmentalists today. Is Frankenstein a modern Prometheus, bringing us instead of the great gift of fire, the even greater gift of life? Or is he an arrogant fool, who cannot foresee the unintended consequences of his meddling in the natural order of things?

Production and Change

Frankenstein shows us a changing world. There is a tendency for societies to evolve according to their own internal forces. Acorns grow into oak trees, and tadpoles metamorphosize into frogs. Similarly, feudal societies with the right technologies advance into capitalist societies.

Societies evolve because new technologies and means of production allow certain processes to operate more efficiently. But as these new efficiencies allow important improvements in some areas, they create problems in other areas. Because of this, a new resolution must be found that incorporates a solution to these difficulties. But the new resolution causes its own difficulties and the process goes on.

Watching a society evolve over time is to watch this process play out over and over. For example, male median wages stagnated in the 1970s at a time of increasing consumer demand. This was resolved by women entering the workforce in large numbers to raise household incomes. But then because there were more workers median wages fell, and workers had to work more hours. Meanwhile, who looks out for the children (or creations)?

We find a similar story playing out in *Frankenstein* when it is clear that the creature cannot live among humans, so it has to go. The creature agrees to go to the North Pole. But there is a problem. . . . The creature is a social creature, and demands a companion. Victor agrees to create one. However, after creating a companion for the creature, Victor realizes they are not just things, but a "he" and a "she!" In the facing of creating a potential race of monstrous creatures, things quickly spire out of control for Victor.

History and Moral Progress

Capitalism is a creation, and like Victor's creature has a good side and a bad side. Often Marx is presented as being against capitalism, but this is only half true. Capitalism is a necessary stage in the developmental process that can lead to communism. And this is an important point for Marx. Much of human history involves improvements in the technologies and means of production of societies. But we have the Dark Ages to prove the process can go the wrong way. Europe spent centuries with technologies and means of production inferior to those that had existed earlier in the Roman Empire.

Hunting and gathering societies have the important feature of social equality. They are in effect primitive forms of communism. But life is so precarious in those societies that agricultural societies are an improvement; an advanced agricultural society will under normal conditions be able to offer all its members enough food to eat. Similarly, a functioning capitalist society is an improvement over a feudal one in that it offers its members a higher standard of living. But this comes at a price. Does this higher standard of living comes at too high a moral cost?

In the film version of *Frankenstein*, we witness the frightful breakout of cholera at Ingolstadt, and the frantic rush of people trying to escape the city to avoid the quarantine. In other words, we see a large number of selfish individuals willing to put others at risk for their own safety. Cholera is a city disease often caused by water supplies contaminated with the fecal matter of those infected with cholera. We also witness the hostility of the mob to the creature who is falsely accused of being the agent of contamination. There are many known cholera riots during the Victorian era where the inhumanity of humans towards each other is on display. City life, the life that helps breed capitalism, is often brutal by hunting and gathering standards.

Alienation

Life for the working class during the Victorian era was quite harsh. Marx was clearly aware of how precarious the working class individuals and families found their financial situation. Where we often suggest that many middle class families in our era are but one paycheck away from ruin, this situation was literally true for working class individuals in the times when Marx and Shelley were writing.

Both Shelley and Marx were concerned about spiritual as well as physical wellbeing. Spiritual, in this sense, does not mean anything religious. Marx famously referred to religion as the opium of the people, and considered it a diversion that distracted the working class from organizing for better conditions. But Marx also thought that humans could reach a kind of spiritual self-actualization, but were hindered by capitalism.

Humans are capable of great productivity, creativity, and social awareness. Marx thought that in the communist society we could reach our highest potential as full human beings. Under capitalism with its rigid division of labor, workers are forced to use their talents in boring and repetitive tasks that maximize efficiency—they don't get to self-actualize. Instead, Marx suggested in *The German Ideology* that under communism we could choose to develop our talents in any areas we want. I could choose to do one thing today and another thing tomorrow. If I wanted to I could "hunt in the morning, fish in the afternoon, rear cattle in the evening, criticize after dinner" if I choose to do so, and I am not committed to becoming a "hunter, fisherman, herdsman or critic."

We can see in Victor Frankenstein the opposite of a self-actualized individual. He dies without friends and family, disgusted by the utter perversity of the consequences of his labor. Victor is the truly self-loathing and alienated individual. He is in this regard surpassed only by his creature—who seeks not self-actualization, but self-*annihilation*.

Estranged Labor

When we look at Marx we can see how capitalism causes alienation in four ways. Marx believes that capitalist political economy begins with "the fact of private property," but he finds the idea of "private property" poorly defined. How do I know I own a thing? It seems obvious, but when we think about it we realize that, I can only say "I know I own it because I own it." Maybe someone else (like the government) can back me up and say, "Yup, he owns it!" But what does that really mean? Classical political economy assumes but does not show how private property causes "the division between labor and capital, and between capital and land." How this translates into the ability to own, transfer, and *possess* objects, rivers, mountains, animals, slaves, and our creations, remains painfully unclear.

Private property is the source of greed and envy and ultimately competition. In the 1980s there was a popular expression "He who dies with the most toys wins." Thus, the assertion is that winning is the point of life and one wins by accumulating the most luxurious commodities. We value ourselves by the commodities we own, and the worker for the commodities he or she creates. The more we value the commodities the worker creates, the less we value the worker (because what *really* matters is the *thing*, not the *person* who makes it).

As Marx suggests, this "*devaluation* of the world of men" is directly proportional to the "*increasing value* of the world of things." The worker finds that while labor produces commodities it also turns labor and the worker *into* commodities—humans become *resources* rather than *people*.

We experience the product of our labor as an object as "something alien" as a "power independent" of ourselves. When we objectify the product of our labor as something alien to us we become estranged from it. Ultimately, as the objects of our labor become estranged to us, we become estranged to our labor itself. Marx finds a similar phenomenon goes on with religion. The more we find our value depends on God, the less value we can find in ourselves. The more we value what we are paid for our labor the less we value the products of our labor and the less we value ourselves as productive individuals. In other words we no longer make what we create out of pride or love, as Dr. Frankenstein did when he began his process; we make it only because we are *paid* to do it.

In a capitalist economy the focus becomes, inevitably, the money. But, like Dr. Frankenstein, who came to loathe his creation, when our production lacks emotional investment it can because very dangerous indeed. The *alienation* of workers from their product of their labor makes the product of labor an object, what Marx calls an "*external* existence," something we experience as being outside ourselves, something alien to us. And ultimately the life which we have conferred on this object "confronts [us as] something hostile and alien."

The Creature as Commodity

Quickly, Victor became so estranged from his labor that he couldn't even give his creature a name. Victor's creation is, if nothing else, a stunning scientific achievement, but is always discussed in the most denigrating terms. The creature is an "it" and never a "he" even though he might well be fertile. The terms Victor uses in describing his creation include "wretch," "deformity," "monster," and "filthy demon." Instead of taking any pride at all in his scientific achievement, Victor is disgusted by his own efforts and by what he has produced.

Victor has clearly become alienated from his labor and the object of his labor. He finds, as Marx suggests, that his relationship to his creation as one where the creature "is an alien object exercising power over him." And as the story unfolds this self-fulfilling prophecy becomes true; the creature enacts his revenge for Victor's rejection by killing his brother and wife. The creation is also alienated from the act of production. Victor abandons the role of a working scientist since he finds his labor "an alien activity not belonging to him" but as an "activity which is turned against him."

He is told by his creation that it is now his turn to "obey" and I cannot help but think of how we are often slaves to our work, and slaves to the objects we produce. This is exemplified when the creature coerces Victor into making him a mate, and the scenario plays out with great irony as Victor has become so alienated at his labor that he destroys the second product of his labor and seeks to destroy his first creation. Even in the reinterpretation of the movie Victor's second creature is not the reincarnation of his loving wife, but something alien and foreign to him.

Marx believes that estranged labor leads to two more forms of alienation. First he suggests that under capitalism we become alienated from our "species being." It is natural for us to want to be productive and self-actualizing. But as we become estranged from our labor and the act of production both our natural and spiritual properties become alien to us. We don't value our own potential as a species. We don't value the natural world. We only value the commodities that we produce: We have become estranged ultimately from our "*human* being." We are commodities that produce commodities.

Frankenstein is a gothic tragedy, and the creature never really has a chance. In the right setting he could have been Victor's Adam, but as Marx would suggest under capitalism, and its superficial values he finds no intrinsic value in himself nor in others. He becomes and sees himself as an alienated, ugly, vengeful, murderous thug.

The Destruction of Victor Frankenstein

Victor Frankenstein's obsession with vengeance on his creation ultimately leads to his death. As he pursues the creature through the harsh arctic environments he weakens, and as he realizes he will never have vengeance on the creature, he loses the will to live. He has become alienated from his own labor and the product of his labor, and this estranged labor is now so hostile and alien to him that it actually proves fatal.

The Victor we begin the story with has great human potential. He has great intellect, a loving family, a grand goal, and a commitment to scientific learning and research. But the alienated Victor we end with is a broken man. He has nothing but his own disgust with a wasted life. Science, as Marx would inform us, has the great power to transform society for the better. But under capitalism, science can be used as a tool of our own destruction. Victor's scientific endeavors led not to his self-actualization, but rather to his alienation and death.

The Destruction of Nature

Super Storm Sandy has been called a Frankenstorm. Why? It is largely the result of man-made climate change. The rising temperatures of the oceans create a longer and stronger hurricane season. Rising temperatures cause additional moisture in the atmosphere and lead to more intense rainstorms and blizzards. When factors such as these combine the whole is often greater than the sum of the parts. And Frankenstorms are the result of exactly the sort of human hubris that motivated Shelley to write *Frankenstein*.

Victorian London was reportedly one very polluted city with dark smoggy skies. Even non-Marxist economists can recognize the problem here. It is called the problem of externalities. In our era and Shelley's it's profitable to produce excess carbon dioxide and other pollutants. As long as oil is cheap to produce, British Petroleum will sell it to us and as long as it is cheap to buy many will use it. The external effects are real, but nobody bears the costs. The capitalists buy the regulations most profitable to them, and an alienated public simply will not pay attention.

As the Marxist Vladimir Lenin once suggested the capitalists are so greedy that they will sell us the rope which we will use to hang them. In the case of man-made climate change, the capitalists are willing to sell us the rope with which we can hang ourselves.

III

I Made a Monster! Now What?

9
Is the Monster Free?

PETER D. ZUK

> Man *himself* must make or have made himself into whatever, in a moral sense, whether good or evil, he is or is to become. Either condition must be an effect of his free choice; for otherwise he could not be held responsible for it.
>
> —IMMANUEL KANT, *Religion within the Limits of Reason Alone*

Few monsters in history have conjured up as much dislike and fear as Dr. Frankenstein's. In many *Frankenstein* movies, the monster is depicted as an unthinking brute, a nearly unstoppable force of indiscriminate destruction. But the original *Frankenstein* novel by Mary Shelley (1797–1851) paints a very different picture. Shelly's monster is far more man than beast. He may be incredibly large and strong, but he also possesses a fearsome intellect. It's this combination of physical strength and cunning that makes Frankenstein's monster one that will continue to terrify us for a very long time.

What explains this disconnect between the original version of the monster and the more animalistic one that we see in popular films? One promising idea is that a smart monster makes for a more frightening monster. When it comes to zombies and werewolves, we can run away or hide. But against a really clever monster, this won't work. A clever monster seems to find us no matter how far we run or how well we hide. Shelley needs this kind of monster, and not just because it makes for a scarier story. This kind of monster isn't just a danger to us; this kind of monster is a *villain*. And in order to be a villain, the monster must have freewill. He must be able to freely choose good or evil.

Monster Court Is Now in Session

Now why does Shelley need a villain rather than just any old monster? She needs a villain because her version of the *Frankenstein* story is supposed to contain a message for the reader, a message that couldn't be conveyed as effectively without a villain. The monster is a *personification* of an idea. She has given a philosophical concept a vaguely human form.

The concept that Shelley wants the monster to stand in for is scientific discovery. Shelley wrote in the 1800s, a time when the Age of Enlightenment was in full swing. Thinkers of the Enlightenment emphasized the ability of human reason to understand the world around us and change that world for the better. One important way of doing that was to perform scientific experiments in pursuit of knowledge. By coming to understand how the world works, Enlightenment thinkers argued, we can learn to control it, even master it, and in this way improve the human condition.

Shelley disagreed with this point of view. She was involved with an intellectual movement called Romanticism that rejected, among other things, the Enlightenment's strong support for scientific discovery. There are some things that human beings just aren't meant to know, Romantic thinkers claimed. It's not that Romantics were completely against science—they wanted to understand nature too. But they did believe that the highly rational methods of Enlightenment thinkers were mistaken, and they certainly thought it was a bad idea to try to control nature.

According to Romantics, too much knowledge about nature's inner workings is dangerous because we just aren't capable of controlling nature completely. We *think* we can, but that makes things even worse. Thinking that we can control something that we really can't gets us into trouble fast. We end up releasing forces that we can't stop. The monster represents Enlightenment-style science taken to what Shelley thinks is its natural conclusion. When Victor Frankenstein creates the monster, he's toying with the forces of life and death, something that only God has any business doing.

We said before that Shelley needs more than a mere monster to convey this message; she needs a villain. A mere monster is just a mindless simpleton. Such a monster is bad only incidentally; it could have been good had we simply done a better job of getting it under control. A villain, on the other hand, is an *autonomous agent* that *chooses* to do bad things. A villain defies our attempts to make him or her behave. Even our very best efforts can't guarantee that a villain will stop doing evil because a villain has *freewill*. Only something with freewill can help Shelley make her point. She wants to show not just that too much scientific progress *can* be bad, but that it *is* bad. She wants to show that it will *always* have bad consequences whether we try to use it for good or for evil.

If Shelley can show this, it will be bad news for science and those of us who support it. But in order to show it, Shelley needs to establish that the monster really has freewill. If she can't, her allegory won't be convincing.

(Philosophical) Jury Instructions: How Can We Know Whether the Monster Is Free?

But just what do we mean when we say that someone is free? Roughly, we mean that they act of their own volition and are therefore *responsible* for what they do. And when we say that someone can be held responsible, we usually mean that they can be praised or blamed and rewarded or punished for what they do.

We don't want to say that about everyone—we don't want to say it, for example, about young children or people who are coerced by others to act a certain way. We wouldn't say that someone who is held at gunpoint and forced to give up their wallet gave it up freely. Neither would we say that a young child who commits a crime is responsible for what they have done. This is recognized by our legal system (which tries children *as adults* when we do think that they should be held responsible) and by many religious traditions (as in the doctrine of an "age of accountability"). So we need to get clear on the principles that allow us to determine who is free and responsible and who isn't. Fortunately for us, this is a problem that philosophers have been working on for quite a long time.

Some philosophers are *libertarians* about freewill and responsibility. They think that in order for an action to be free (and therefore responsible), a person must have another option available right at the moment of choice. We can apply this to our own case: Shelley's monster. For the monster to be free and responsible in committing the murders he eventually does, it must be the case that, at the moment he acts, he could have decided to refrain. If he could have refrained, he is free and responsible for his actions and Shelley has her allegory. Most of us will find this position to be common sense: in our daily lives, we often feel as though we have all kinds of options open to us at any given time.

But there are some problems with libertarianism. For one thing, it's at odds with another important philosophical thesis: *determinism*. We can sum up determinism like this: everything that happens in the world is caused by the way things were before. In other words, the past *causes* the present. The way that the world is, say, today, is a direct result of the way it was yesterday. And if we changed something about the past, that would change the future. For example, if Victor had not created the monster his family would not have died at the monster's hands (perhaps from some other cause but not *that* cause). So if the past causes the present, then suppose someone knew everything about the way the world was yesterday. If determinism is true, that person could perfectly predict everything that happened today. Of course, no one (except perhaps God) could *actually* know enough to make such a prediction. But the example still shows something important: according to determinism, given the way things were yesterday, things *had* to go the way they did today.

Contemporary physics tells us that determinism is probably true, at least at the level relevant to human action. Our world (people included) is made up of tiny atoms, and atoms follow physical laws. As contemporary philosopher Ted Honderich points out, determinism is also confirmed by everyday experience.[1] We see the strict cause-and-effect relationships implied by determinism all the time. We strike a match, says

[1] Ted Honderich, "Effects, Determinism, Neither Compatibilism nor Incompatibilism, Consciousness," in *The Oxford Handbook of Free Will*, second edition, edited by Robert Kane (Oxford University Press, 2011), p. 444.

Honderich, and the match lights. We drop a dinner plate, and the plate breaks. This seems very hard to deny. And if determinism turns out to be true, it potentially has a lot to say about freewill. Applied to our case, the result would be that the monster *had* to act in the bad ways he did. Things couldn't have gone any other way. Then we might ask: if he *had* to act as he did, how could he possibly be free? And if he can't be free, then Shelley can't make her point about science.

Enter *compatibilism*, another theory about freewill and responsibility. The name of this position gives it away: it says that freewill and determinism are compatible. Compatibilists think that even if determinism is true, we can still have freewill and thus be held responsible for what we do. There are many forms of compatibilism—too many to discuss here. But the most promising one accounts for freewill in terms of the ability to *respond to reasons*. According to this school of thought, what matters for freedom isn't the ability to do otherwise than we actually do. Instead, what matters is that we deliberate about what to do, weighing our options in a rational way. What matters is that we think our actions through, and the ability to do that is completely compatible with determinism. If this is right, then what matters for the monster's responsibility is that he acts rationally and with a clear head. If the monster just needs to be free in this sense, perhaps Shelley's allegory about science can succeed after all.

Lunch Break: There's No Such Thing as a Freewill?

But another group of philosophers thinks that we simply might not have freewill after all. The members of this group go by a variety of labels—*skeptics*, *deniers*, *impossibilists*, and others—depending on the specifics of their point of view. The last group, impossibilists, make a very strong claim: they say not only that we lack freewill, but that freewill properly defined turns out to be impossible.

One famous impossibilist still doing work today is Galen Strawson. He says that *what we do* depends on *how we are* as people.[2] People who get angry often do so because they have a

[2] Galen Strawson, "The Impossibility of Moral Responsibility," *Philosophical Studies*, 75:1/2 (1994).

temper. People who are always kind to others do so because they have a good heart. If this is right, then in order to be responsible for what we do, we must be responsible for how we are. As Kant says in the quote I opened with, we can only be responsible if our character is of our own making. So far, so good; that all seems true enough.

But this is where Strawson thinks that things get interesting. If we agree with what he's said so far, then we must also agree that in order to be responsible for how we are now, we have to be responsible for how we were in the past. Since it was the actions of our earlier selves that made us who we are today, we can only be responsible for who we currently are if we are also responsible for how we were then.

But now we're in trouble: we can keep applying the same test over and over. And that means we'll keep going farther and farther back in our lives until we get to our early childhoods, and no one thinks that we were responsible as young children. Back then, we were shaped by many influences over which we had no control: our families, our friends, our teachers, and so on. But if we weren't responsible then, Strawson's argument tells us that we can't be responsible now either. So Strawson has an easy answer to the question of the monster's responsibility: the monster isn't responsible for what he does because *no one* is responsible for what they do!

Is Strawson really right that no one can ever be free and responsible? That subject is best left for another time. Our question is whether the monster is free and responsible. And we don't need to agree with Strawson that people are *never* free or responsible in order to recognize that people *sometimes* aren't. Even if we think that most people are free and responsible most of the time, we can still say that there are cases where this isn't true. What we need to ask is whether that monster's tale as portrayed in *Frankenstein* is one of those cases. If it is, we can still say that Shelley's argument doesn't go through.

Your Honor, the Monster Would Like to Say a Few Words . . .

Let's look at *Frankenstein* to try and answer this question. The monster starts out strongly inclined toward goodness. After stumbling across a troubled country family, the De Laceys, he quickly begins to care about them and refer to them as his friends without even having any direct contact with them. "I longed to discover the feelings and motives of these lovely creatures. . . . I thought (foolish wretch!) that it might be in my power to restore happiness to these deserving people," he tells us.[3] He initially lives off of the family's food supply, but upon realizing that they are quite poor and have little to spare, he forages for his own meals instead. In describing the young man Felix De Lacey's reaction to the arrival of his beloved female companion, the monster says, "Felix seemed ravished with delight when he saw her . . . at that moment I thought him as beautiful as the stranger" (p. 120). The monster also speaks of language and reading as allowing him to enter "a wide field for wonder and delight" (p. 122). What we're describing here sounds like a wise and moral being, not a monster.

The monster is unable to understand violence and the need for laws and governments, turning away with "disgust and loathing" when he hears detailed accounts of various human evils. He continues to empathize with the De Lacey family to the point of developing love for them and seeking their love in return, professing a powerful desire for virtue and an aversion to vice. The monster's initial development shows his natural inclinations to be of a profoundly humanistic character. In fact, at this point in the story he's a more committed humanist than most humans. Despite being contrary to the natural order, the existence of the monster is nonetheless a remarkably good and beautiful thing.

The monster does of course eventually become monstrous in the moral sense of the word, enslaved by cruelty and a desire for revenge against his creator and others who have mistreated him. We'd be right to wonder whether this is really the fault of the monster himself, though.

It seems as if the actions of others toward the monster are what ultimately drive him to such behavior. From his very beginnings, he is rejected by each and every person he encounters. His own creator turns from him in disgust, a fact that causes him considerable emotional pain. The village he flees to after being abandoned by Victor likewise rejects him, this time

[3] Mary Shelley, *Frankenstein* (Penguin, 2003), p. 117.

by violent means that leave him with injuries. He comes to view the De Lacey family as loving companions, but is "dashed . . . to the ground and struck . . . violently with a stick" by Felix upon attempting to make direct contact with them (p. 137). Psychologically shattered, the monster desires revenge but stifles these feelings, attempting to remain benevolent and humanistic. He saves the life of an unknown young girl from a swift river at great peril to himself, only to be shot and wounded by her companion, at which point he states, "Inflamed by pain, I vowed eternal hatred and vengeance to all mankind" (p. 143).

Human violence against the monster twists and corrupts his original disposition of reason and benevolence. The physical and psychological pain he faces time and time again makes him a slave to his passions, overwhelming a character that was initially oriented toward goodness. This cycle of rejection culminates with the monster's encounter with young William Frankenstein, whom he at first attempts to reason with when the boy cries out in fear at the monster's grotesque appearance. It's only when the boy ignites the monster's despair once again by initiating verbal and physical violence against him that the monster finally reciprocates humanity's mistreatment, and his description of the event—"I grasped his throat to silence him" (p. 144)—makes it ambiguous whether the monster intends to harm the boy or simply doesn't know his own strength.

Closing Arguments . . . and a Surprise Expert Witness?!

Does this sound like someone who's responsible for what he has done? Is this the case of a villain—a *criminal*? I certainly don't think so, and I hope you agree. The monster was naive, innocent, pure—and the world corrupted him. He freely chose to be good, but circumstances beyond his control made him evil. It looks as if the monster isn't responsible for doing bad things because he's not responsible for his evil character. The fault lies instead with those who drove him to that character; it lies with those who made him into the evil being that he became. He had been so overpowered with negative emotions that he probably couldn't have acted differently than he did. And his overwhelming desire for revenge makes it unlikely that he acted rationally or fully thought through what he was doing.

Still, some might insist on asking whether the monster was free to remain good despite all the abuse he suffered. Couldn't he have stayed virtuous even in the face of all that suffering? To say that he could have would be, I think, to deny many of the monster's most significant influences. He was created from the brain and body parts of others. All of his physical and character traits were forced upon him. Of course, none of us has complete control over our genetics and brain chemistry and natural abilities, but we do have our entire lives to work on improving ourselves. The monster never had that chance; he awoke as a full-grown man.

We also can't forget the influence that other people and society as a whole have on all of us, and the monster is certainly no exception here. We might not always recognize it, but the way we are depends a great deal on the culture we live in. We act courteously and kindly to others at least in part because that is what society expects of us. If everyone around us was rude and hurtful instead, is it really plausible to think that we would still be able to take the high road and be just as good to them as we are now? We follow the law because we think it is the right thing to do, and we see others around us setting a good example. But if we were taught that following the law really doesn't matter and saw everyone around us disregarding it, would we really be the law-abiding citizens that most of us are now? We try to act morally and help those in need because we were taught right and wrong by our parents or religious communities. But if we were raised to believe instead that doing the right thing isn't important, or never taught right from wrong at all, does it really make sense to think that would still be good?

Perhaps there are people who could remain honorable even in the face of such adversity, but surely not everyone is like this. Many of us do the best we can under very favorable conditions and still fall quite often. Are we prepared to say that we could rise to such a seemingly impossible challenge as being a saint in a world of the worst possible sinners? At least in my own case, I'm not prepared to say that. And if I can't say it about myself, I can't say it about the monster either. I've had all kinds of advantages that the monster didn't have: a loving family, responsible friends, and wise teachers. If I still make mistakes even with all of that on my side, who am I to condemn someone who lacked all those things?

For most of the story, the monster's creator Victor regrets the scientific investigation he conducted, calling his efforts to overcome death "unhallowed acts" (p. 189). Yet at the end of his life, he appears conflicted. By this time he's fled all the way to the arctic in an attempt to escape the monster and been rescued from the cold by a ship on a polar expedition. Surprisingly, Victor encourages the crew of the ship to continue when they wish to turn back:

> You were hereafter to be hailed as the benefactors of your species; yours names adored, as belonging to brave men who encountered death for honour, and the benefit of mankind. Oh! be men, or be more than men. Be steady to you purposes, and firm as a rock. This ice is not made of such stuff as your hearts may be; it is mutable, and cannot withstand you, if you say that it shall not. (*Frankenstein*, p. 217)

These purposes, like Victor's own experiments, question the fundamental bounds of nature. These men are seeking discovery and achievement in the same way that he was seeking these things in creating the monster, and he encourages them to continue. So even Victor, the one who started all of the trouble described in the novel by creating the monster, isn't sure that what he was trying to do was really a bad thing. It turned out badly, but he seems to think that it didn't have to. And if that's right, he's disagreeing with Shelley that too much scientific progress is *necessarily* bad.

The Defense Rests

The monster is abandoned by his creator, rejected by all of society, and left to learn on his own. Yet he does strikingly well nonetheless, becoming a virtuous being with a strong sense of the value of humanity. The creation of such a being was surely a good thing. His subsequent fall cannot count against this fact. It was contrary to his very own nature and everything that he stood for. It was only the misunderstanding and mistreatment of those around him that brought about the disasters of the novel. Applied to the notion of the monster as a personification of scientific progress, this suggests that such progress in itself is a beneficial and wonderful thing even when it reaches beyond natural limits.

So *Frankenstein* can't be taken as a critique of the scientific enterprise. Instead, we should read it as a caution against releasing the fruits of science unguided upon people who are not qualified to sufficiently understand or utilize them. Directed by Victor and prevented from arousing the fear of society at large, the monster could have blossomed even more than he did on his own. Victor, the one best equipped to guide the monster properly, failed to appreciate the value of his own creation. *Frankenstein* thus becomes a call to proper understanding and appreciation of science lest prejudice and fear turn its initially humanistic and benevolent nature toward undesirable ends.

To argue against scientific knowledge and progress is to mistake the technology itself for the ways in which it is perceived and applied. As *Frankenstein* shows, science can surely be turned to destructive ends. But this is not a necessary feature of science, and indeed, is contrary to the humanistic goals professed by many who engage in it.

So if Shelley wishes to speak against scientific progress, she isn't on very firm footing. She has confused science with *perversions* of science brought on by human misunderstanding, and we can all agree that perversions of science are an awful and dangerous thing. Science done with care and concern for the well-being of humanity is a wonderful enterprise, and we can cite *Frankenstein* as an example of what happens when we fall short of that ideal.

10
How to Raise a Monster

JANELLE PÖTZSCH

I could think of less intimidating places to encounter my monster—like a noisy café or a crowded train station. Poor Victor has to meet his in the middle of the deserted Alps. More startling than the meeting itself is the way the monster behaves, for it entreats Victor:

> I was benevolent and good; misery made me a fiend. Make me happy, and I shall again be virtuous. (*Frankenstein*, Penguin, 1968, p. 264)

Was Victor justified in ignoring this plea? The Swiss philosopher Jean-Jacques Rousseau (1712–1778) would strongly disapprove. He would remind Victor that children as well as monsters are innately good. To preserve this goodness, parents (or creators) should shield their children from the harsh realities of our civilized world as long as possible.

According to Rousseau, society negatively affects human character. If it's true that civilization is, in fact, bad for us, then Rousseau's philosophy of education offers not only an explanation of *what* went wrong with the monster, but also why.

Something's Rotten in the State of Culture

Rousseau lived in the era of the Enlightenment, a time of political and social upheaval. This period is called the "Enlightenment" because of the scientific advancements which were made at that time: They literally *enlightened* people's minds on life, the universe, and pretty much everything else.

Victor Frankenstein shares the ensuing atmosphere when he boasts: "What can stop the determined heart and resolved will of man?" (p. 278). New insights in domains like math and physics (which, among other issues, also settled the question of whether the Earth or the Sun is the center of the universe) made people reconsider their status not only in the universe, but also in their respective societies. Ultimately, this led to a new understanding of society and political legitimacy: If the Sun doesn't revolve around the Earth, as we've been told for centuries, who can tell whether kings really rule by the grace of God? In the same way, Victor's professors at Ingolstadt point out that the achievements of the earlier scientists were hardly worth mentioning.

To cut a long story short, the times they were a-changing. And Rousseau was right in the middle of things. His views were highly popular because they took in people's notion that something was wrong with the current social system. Rousseau's explanation is charmingly simple: People feel uneasy in society because it affects them negatively. Hence, the problem doesn't lie with the people themselves, but with the society they live in.

That's the meaning of the opening lines of *Émile*, Rousseau's novel on education: "Everything is good as it comes from the hands of the Author of Nature; but everything degenerates in the hands of man." Instead of living according to his nature, man builds an unnatural and harmful system: "He overturns everything, disfigures everything; he will have nothing as Nature made it, not even man."[1] This idea is contrary to the view (ours as well as most of Rousseau's contemporaries) that we need society to become good people and to follow certain rules of appropriate social behavior. According to Rousseau, it's the other way round: Society doesn't so much improve as ruin our moral character.

Back to the Roots!

Rousseau contrasts the simplicity of nature with modern society which is marked by class differences and rigid social proto-

---

[1] Jean-Jacques Rousseau, *Émile: Or, Treatise on Education* (Prometheus, 2003), p. 1.

cols. These run counter to man's disposition and force him to display an artificial behavior. In short, we have to disguise ourselves in civilized society. This point is illustrated by the monster's encounters with the De Laceys: Felix, Safie, and the others have fled from France. In Rousseau's time, France was the epitome of an old-fashioned society run cold, later called the *ancien régime* ("old order"). People had to play by the (not always discernable) rules of their society to avoid repression.

In Rousseau's view, the character and happiness of man are subverted in society. As soon as we encounter other people, we tend to compare ourselves with them. Gradually, we develop the urge to distinguish ourselves from them, to show how special we are. We become competitive and jealous. To show just how much better we are than all the others, we accumulate private property and invent special rules for language and behavior ('Don't do that; only *vulgar* people do that.'). In the long run, this distorts our view of humankind. We no longer see the person herself, but only what she has or does. From there, it's only a small step to a class-ridden society of haves and have-nots.

Man is his true self only in the "state of nature." Rousseau's ideal of man. The aim of Rousseau's philosophy is to establish social harmony by aligning society as closely as possible to man's original state of nature. The only persons who are as close as possible to this desirable condition are those who haven't yet experienced civilization—in other words, children.

Little Monsters

Thanks to Rousseau, childhood is no longer considered a mere transitory state, but as an independent and valuable life stage in its own right. Rousseau's achievement was to convey the view that children are not incomplete, unfinished adults. They're simply different from grown-ups:

> Humanity has its place in the order of things, and infancy has its place in the order of human life. We must consider the man in the man, and the child in the child. (p. 46)

This isn't something which would be heralded as a milestone of pedagogical learning today, but it was quite revolutionary in an age where children as young as four were dressed in tiny versions of adult clothes (including handy crinolines for little girls). But Rousseau did not only advocate that people dress children more appropriately as regards their need for movement and physiology.

Rousseau's philosophy of education marks a turning-point because it's in direct opposition to the then traditional lore of the Catholic Church, according to which children are born evil because they're tainted by Original Sin. Therefore, it takes a severe education to turn children into decent and good grown-ups. This includes denying children any will of their own; rather, parents should aim at breaking their child's will to make the child into a civilized person (an interesting way of dealing with the nag factor, when you come to think about it).

Rousseau challenges this view outright when he claims that it's not the children who are in conflict with civilization but the other way round: Culture is at odds with human character and hence corrupts people. We can trace Rousseau's idea that children are innately good in the portrayals of Elizabeth Lavenza and William Frankenstein: The young Elizabeth is compared to an angel, and in a letter to Victor telling him of William's murder, the now grown-up Elizabeth dotingly remembers William's lovable and cheerful temper.

Monstrosity Begins at Home

How do we ensure that children preserve their good character as adults? And what could Victor have done to be spared the monster's hatred? According to Rousseau, we need an education which is aligned with human nature. This means that parents shouldn't try to 'civilize' children too early. Censoring children for their behavior subjects them too early to social (and according to Rousseau, false) ideas of how people ought to behave.

Rather than killing a child's impulses, parents should give in to them: They should pursue an education which encourages children to live their life fully by developing their senses and feelings. A child's typical impulses, like its spontaneity or enthusiasm, shouldn't be repressed for they are worth preserving: "Love childhood; encourage its sports, its pleasures, its amiable instincts."

Loving childhood is accomplished best if parents employ what Rousseau calls 'negative education'. Children shouldn't be taught or shown what they ought to do. Rather than forbidding certain actions, parents should simply *prevent* their children from doing anything harmful or wrong. It's like hiding a pair of scissors instead of explaining to your child why it shouldn't play with scissors.

Victor's own parents seemed to have followed this advice, for he recalls that he was "guided by a silken cord" and "received a lesson of patience, of charity, and of self-control" (*Frankenstein*, p. 292). This is Rousseau's negative education in a nutshell, which "consists not at all in teaching virtue or truth, but in shielding the heart from vice, and the mind from error" (*Émile*, p. 59). This also implies that parents should disclose facts only gradually. Some things in our world are simply too depressing or cruel to be made known to children. To a certain extent, they have to be *protected* from information. Rousseau's views influence our thinking even today, as is shown by our practice of rating movies according to their age-appropriateness.

Apart from outright instructions, parents should also refrain from exerting their authority. According to Rousseau, authority is not necessary to make a child obedient. All it takes is to make the child aware of its dependency on its parents: "Never command him to do anything whatever, not the least thing in the world. Never allow him even to imagine that you assume to have any authority over him. Let him know merely that he is weak and that you are strong."

This means that a child doesn't learn by experiencing coercion or restraint, but through necessity. You can spare the rod without spoiling the child because you can make it "supple and docile through the mere force of things" (pp. 55–56). Similarly, the monster has been cruelly made aware of its dependency on Frankenstein. Contrary to Rousseau's recommendations, it didn't have a sheltered and gradual access to the world. Instead, it experienced too much and too soon. This is why the monster declares that the more it learned, the more depressed it became. Still, it is willing to obey Frankenstein on the condition that he fulfills his parental duties: "I am thy creature, and I will be even mild and docile to my natural lord and king if thou wilt also perform thy part" (p. 364).

Half-Devil or Half-Child?

The monster experiences a moral as well as a physiological evolution: It gradually acquires both language and knowledge. As for the monster's moral development, its tale reveals that it used to have a positive, childlike attitude towards the world which has been cruelly disappointed: "I desired love and fellowship, and I was . . . spurned" (p. 495). Most importantly, it didn't have a conception of 'evil'.

The monster explains that it couldn't imagine why people would kill each other, or why we need things like government and laws. Compare this outlook to the attitude it displays after it has murdered William: "I gazed on my victim, and my heart swelled with exultation and hellish triumph" (p. 410). Rousseau points out that "all wickedness comes from weakness. A child is bad only because he is weak" (p. 31). Therefore, as weird as it may sound, the monster's misdeeds may stem from its helplessness and incapacity. It resembles a furious child who tries to make adults do what it wants. The monster resorts to crime because it can't force Frankenstein to take care of him or to create a companion for him: "I will revenge my injuries; if I cannot inspire love, I will cause fear, and chiefly towards you my arch-enemy . . . do I swear inextinguishable hatred" (p. 413).

The monster both illustrates and shares Rousseau's views, especially those on the corrupting influence of culture: It tries to befriend William Frankenstein and a blind man because it thinks them less judgmental than the persons it has hitherto met. Both attempts backfire and trigger its moral change. The monster would probably not have become evil if it hadn't experienced rejection and cruelty throughout its life.

Is Frankenstein a Family Guy?

Rousseau would probably applaud Frankenstein's understanding of the duties of parents: Victor recognizes that a child's "future lot . . . was in their hands to direct to happiness or misery, according as they fulfilled their duties." His own childhood seems to have been a happy one for he remembers that his parents had "a deep consciousness of what they owed towards the being to which they had given life" (p. 291). So it seems a bit surprising that he doesn't act upon these ideals when it comes to his own monster. We could read this as a comment of Shelley on Victor's scientific endeavors. She was in fact a huge admirer of Rousseau and might even be trying to show us that actions against nature will *always* revolt us, simply because they move us farther from nature. Hence, Victor's failure in nurturing the monster is inseparable from how deep his project is invested in science, yet distant from nature.

But even though Victor had to learn Rousseau's lesson the hard way, he realizes the true meaning of his deed almost immediately, which is why his enthusiasm for his creation wanes so quickly: "I had desired it with an ardour that far exceeded moderation; but now that I had finished, the beauty of the dream vanished, and breathless horror and disgust filled my heart." He's not even able to bear the sight of the creature he had given life to (it's a good thing people don't act like this in the maternity ward!).

Eventually, the monster reminds Victor that forsaking those who are most dependent upon us is no trifle: "Remember that I am thy creature; I ought to be thy Adam, but I am rather the fallen angel, whom thou drivest from joy for no misdeed." Victor's conduct is blameworthy because he and his monster are "bound by ties only dissoluble by the annihilation of one of them." Like Rousseau, the monster thinks that nothing is as binding and authorizing as familial obligations. If your own father refuses to assist and love you, what can you expect of those with whom you don't share any family ties? Bearing Victor's fate in mind, Rousseau's account of the duty of a father reads like a dire warning:

> A father who merely feeds and clothes the children he has begotten fulfills but a third of his task. To the race, he owes men; to society, men of social dispositions; and to the state, citizens . . . . Reader, believe me when I predict that whoever . . . neglects such sacred duties will long shed bitter tears over his mistakes, and will never find consolation for it! (*Émile*, p. 16)

Seen in this light, Frankenstein appears like a parent who isn't ready (or willing) to undertake responsibility for his offspring and hence fails to fulfil his parental duty. Consequently, the monster fails to be a good and compassionate citizen because it commits murder.

No Woman No Cry?

Victor Frankenstein's refusal to treat his offspring appropriately doesn't stop here: He even refuses to build his monster a female companion. According to Rousseau, settling with a partner is a decisive developmental step which makes people fit to live in civil society. Man is not made for living alone. This view is mirrored in the monster's request: "You must create a female for me with whom I can live in the interchange of those sympathies necessary for my being."

The monster senses that a fellow being is important for its social and emotional contentment because only "the love of another will destroy the cause of my crimes." Frankenstein's denial of this demand gives rise to the monster's cruel revenge. Seen through the lens of Rousseau, the ensuing murders of Henry Clerval and Elizabeth Lavenza represent the monster's refusal to display social dispositions. It is neither willing nor able to do so because it has no experience with human relationships: "If I have no ties and no affections, hatred and vice must be my portion" (*Frankenstein*, pp. 412–13).

Corrupted by Culture— and Science

Although Victor doesn't seem to share Rousseau's views on parental duties, he's at least able to appreciate nature. While hiking through the Alps, he muses: "Why does man boast of sensibilities superior to those apparent in the brute; it only renders them more necessary beings" (p. 361). The idea is that cultural progress makes people vulnerable: our wants not only multiply, they also become more refined. This makes them increasingly difficult to satisfy (that's why people spend so much time eyeing store windows). Ultimately, men will begin fighting to gain what they desire. Competition and greed are also the motives behind colonization, as the monster learns: "I heard of the discovery of the American hemisphere and wept with Safie over the hapless fate of its original inhabitants" (p. 385). Rousseau claims that man invents the concept of private property and social ranks simply to justify the reckless fulfillment of his wants and to prevent others from doing the same.[2] The first step to humane society would be to recognize how little we actually need.

According to Rousseau, our luck is influenced by the relation between our wishes and our abilities. The smaller the distance between them, the happier we are. But even though Victor shares Rousseau's notion that man can only be happy if he contends himself with what is within his range, he is determined to pursue his scientific aspirations. He boasts that he can achieve anything due to his determination and will. Surely, he succeeds, but the realization of his scientific aspiration is also the cause of his ruin. The only thing he can do is to warn Robert Walton of the risks which come with the thirst for knowledge: "Unhappy man! Do you share my madness? Have you drunk also of the intoxicating draught? Hear me; let me reveal my tale, and you will dash the cup from your lips!" (*Frankenstein*, p. 284).

The case of Frankenstein demonstrates Rousseau's point that cultural and scientific achievements come at a price. Surely, Frankenstein is able to fulfill his self-assigned task to make a dead thing come alive again, but this accomplishment has tremendous social and emotional costs: Speaking with Rousseau, Victor performs his paternal duties partially at best. He hereby commits a crime against society: William, Henry, and Elizabeth are murdered because Victor fails (or rather, doesn't even try) to socialize the monster in a way which makes it a morally good person.

Mad Schemes Are the Cause

Rousseau's philosophy represents an alternative to the strong, somewhat even exaggerated belief in science and progress typical of the Enlightenment. Victor's professors in Ingolstadt share this belief, which sometimes borders on megalomania: Professor Waldmann declares that modern scientists "have indeed performed miracles" and deprived nature of its powers. Victor will recall that their words were "enounced to destroy me" because they gave rise to his ambition: "So much has been done,

[2] Jean-Jacques Rousseau, *The Social Contract* (Prometheus, 1988), p. 1.

exclaimed the soul of Frankenstein—more, far more, will I achieve" (pp. 307–08). As Rousseau predicts, Victor craves for recognition as soon as he encounters other people, in his case: Fellow scientists desperate to outdo each other in their research.

Victor's aspiring attitude is in stark contrast to the notion he entertains while still in Switzerland with his parents, where he muses that although scientists have "partially unveiled the face of Nature, . . . her immortal lineaments were still a wonder and a mystery." Then, Victor still thinks that modern science can solve some, but not all the mysteries of nature. His thoughts change while browsing through old-fashioned books by the earliest natural philosophers (well into the nineteenth century, the natural sciences as we know them today were clumped together as 'natural philosophy'. Their separate branches of biology, chemistry, and physics were developed only later.).

These writings awaken his ambition: "Under the guidance of my new preceptors I entered with the greatest diligence into the search of the philosopher's stone and the elixir of life" (pp. 298–99). It's because of such overly ambitious, and to a certain extent also unnecessary and harmful, knowledge we can gain from books that Rousseau declares: "I hate books; they merely teach us to talk of what we do not know." He recommends that children should read only one single book: Daniel Defoe's *Robinson Crusoe* (pp. 161–62). He considers it useful because it teaches us how to survive in nature.

The purpose of Rousseau's philosophy is to highlight man's dependency on nature. Therefore, the foremost task is to educate man in alignment with nature: It's the only thing he can't influence or change. Rousseau's views couldn't be more contrary to Victor's quest to master life and death, which is an attempt to *conquer* nature. Although Rousseau belongs to the leading thinkers of the Enlightenment, he was a harsh critic of their belief in progress. His ideas on education and his optimistic view on man were revolutionary, but his expectations concerning the beneficial effects on culture and scientific progress on human nature were rather wary. (Given the horrible outcomes of Victor's little project, it isn't difficult to imagine a triumphant Rousseau knowingly shaking his head: 'Told you.').

Rousseau's philosophy represents an alternative to Dr. Frankenstein's. Victor coolly pursues his questionable research only to be shocked and repelled by its consequences. Rather than employing pure (and as Victor's example illustrates, cold) reason, man should follow his heart and compassion. What modern science has achieved is quite nice, but we shouldn't forget that it takes more than science to raise responsible children. . . . it takes compassion and perhaps even some philosophy.

11
When Creations Go Bad

Skyler King

Imagine . . .

Smoke permeates the air like ink released in water. Fire, like a raging, undiscovered river, swallows and bombards everything in sight. Screams, infant-like screams, bludgeon the volcanic air—that horrendous sound plays upon your cheeks. It grates your ears. The heinous cackling of the fire drowns out the sound of the buildings mourning while their ashen tears are blown from their facades like pixie dust. In an instant, you see yourself as those breaking, relenting buildings: where once you stood strong and seemingly indomitable, now waves of emotion and circumstance ruthlessly submerge you in the inescapable, crippling fury of inferno.

The town—*your* town—quickly evaporates.

Everything you worked so hard to accomplish, the safety you worked so hard to maintain and create—gone. Disintegrated. Consumed, like the town, in a flash of angry fire.

As you stand on the street, devastated by the upheaval of your entire community, you detect movement in the distance. You turn, cautiously, and notice a freakish, monstrous figure ambling forth from amidst the flames.

That abomination caused the destruction of your world. That detestable creature, bathing in the maelstrom of inferno, is a fully self-aware and self-evolving android created and planted into society by your reclusive neighbor.

Well, you think, *my neighbor always wanted to replicate Victor Frankenstein's experiment—and I guess he did. His heartless monster, like Victor's, has ruined us all, inexorably destroying everything in its path. I heard that blasted android complaining about "experiencing emotions and love" just last week. Now look what happened. For this, that hermit neighbor of mine undoubtedly deserves the same fate as this town.*

While the few remaining buildings finally succumb to the tyranny of the android's flames, your conscience whispers, "But *does* he deserve to share that fate?"

Looking for Love in All the Wrong Places

Immediately, you probably think, "Of course that bumbling idiot deserves to burn, just like the town!" However, think about your gut reaction for a moment. What factors went into arriving at that conclusion? Are you *certain* that your neighbor cannot be exonerated in *any* way? Are you *certain* that he undeniably deserves to die because he, like Victor Frankenstein, decided to become a mad scientist and create something monstrous and potentially dangerous? From a rigid absolutist perspective, the answer to these questions is undoubtedly yes. But is that fair?

Many people familiar with some version of *Frankenstein* like to blame Victor for all the terrible acts committed by his monster—much like you would probably blame your neighbor in this scenario. Their reasoning? "If Victor would've listened to the creature instead of ignoring him," they say, "then all those people wouldn't have died and the monster wouldn't have been a 'monster,' *per se*." Essentially, the majority of Franken-fans and critics think that the monster's condition exponentially worsened as a result of Victor's neglect.

Ah, but that thought raises more questions! Why is it *Victor's* fault—or even your neighbor's fault? Why *can't* it be *the monster's* fault? Perhaps one of the biggest reasons for avoiding placing blame on the monster, in Mary Shelley's *Frankenstein*, is that the monster is *oppressively* lost in terms of its identity, its social expectations, and its place in the world. These questions or personal struggles of the monster are, from a psychological perspective, generally paramount for any sense of self-efficacy and self-worth.

According to the psychologist Abraham Maslow (1908–1970), all humans (and we can assume re-animated humans too) innately possess a *hierarchy of needs*; this hierarchy of needs forms its foundation at the basic psychological and physiological factors requisite for a comfortable and healthy life (such as safety, food, shelter, love, and sex) and moves to "higher" or more complex needs (such as prestige, planning and anticipating the future outcomes of one's actions, and success) once the basic needs are fulfilled.

In the monster's case, it experienced an incredible deprivation in the basic "love need." Victor, by refusing to acknowledge his creation and abandoning it, showed that he didn't love it and that he thought it could *only be* a monster—basically, that his creation was worthless and only fit to be hated. Following Maslow's theory, we see that fulfilling the "love need" consumed the monster's thinking so much so that all it could do was try to *gratify* or *satiate* that "building-block need." Since Victor refused to teach the monster to be "like its creator," all the monster wanted was a freaky, hybrid monster-human wife to accompany it. Sounds reasonable enough—to a crazy person. Anyway, who could have presumably allayed the monster's "love need"? . . . Victor Frankenstein. Who could've spared your town, presumably, by providing the android with love of some sort? . . . Your neighbor.

So, it seems that even if the monster or android was "looking for love in all the wrong places," Victor and your neighbor could *at the very least* have lessened the monster's suffering and made it feel welcomed into the world—which means, so far, it appears as if your gut reaction to your psycho neighbor's whacked-out android stands correct. It also means that it seems like the absolutist's response of unconditional judgment is correct. Don't officially seal your neighbor's fate just yet, though.

The Android Did It! It Was Just a Power Play! (Maybe)

A bigger issue than psychological deprivation is at work here—at least when it comes to addressing the *universal* problem of Shelley's *Frankenstein*. By blaming Victor for the monster's actions, whether it be because of not fulfilling basic needs for a healthy individual or animosity towards it in general, we *assume* that the monster bears no *moral responsibility*—or, if we do assume *any* moral responsibility, we think that the harm caused by Victor supersedes what little moral responsibility the monster possessed. Again, the reason many people don't feel the need to assign any moral responsibility to the monster is because it didn't really know any better—and *couldn't* have known better, given Victor's attitude and actions towards the monster. Remember, if you are a die-hard absolutist considering judgments of right and wrong, then maybe these questions don't even matter. Don't they seem important, though? Don't they seem worth considering?

With that said, *when* can one person *reasonably* assign moral responsibility to another sentient, thinking creature, or at least expect that creature to account for its actions? To help answer this question, let's first look at humans. Adults don't assign much moral responsibility to kids. In fact, the law considers children under the age of seven to be *incapable* of committing a crime simply because children don't understand the permanence and full consequences of their actions. Psychologist Jean Piaget (1896–1980) would definitely stand by this cushion in the law because, according to his theory of cognitive development, children typically don't begin developing *true* logic skills until they reach seven to eleven years old, which he calls the *concrete operational stage*.

Furthermore, people, in general, don't reach the pinnacle of their abilities to reason, understand, and engage the world until they reach the *formal operational stage*, which involves abstract reasoning and much greater problem-solving skills. Sadly, some people *never* reach the formal operational stage. However, Piaget suggests that people typically hit this stage around adolescence and into adulthood. Again, this is a typical or generic model; obviously, some people defy Piaget's trajectory. Development isn't always systematic and predictable, but his theory serves as a decent approximating tool. In the law, people who are eighteen years of age or older are fully and completely capable of understanding their actions and can rightfully incur punishment accordingly.

Does Shelley's portrayal of Frankenstein's monster fit the definition of the "formal operational stage"? While the answer often seems elusive, the fact that the monster constantly says things like, "Create another one like me and I will leave you and the world alone forever," shows that the monster *realizes* there is more than one way to act, that it can modify itself and its behavior at any time. Moreover, Shelley shows the monster threatening Victor, delivering on those threats, and *fathoming* the permanence and concept of death (because many children truly don't comprehend death). Thus, it seems very reasonable to assume that the monster *could have done otherwise*, but deliberately *chose* to do what he did.

This also applies to our opening scenario about your neighbor's android. Assuming that the android *is* a *fully* self-aware *and* self-evolving entity, we can at least reasonably blame both the creator and the creation for the terrible and dastardly deeds that transpired. (And, if that's true, then we must also wonder about God and who shares the blame in that instance of creator versus creation.) Since robots' taking over the world is a growing paranoia, we should just assume that the android decided to raze the town as some sort of ruse to power, or power play, right? Well, let's not be ridiculous. Let's just stick with this broad and greatly disappointing assumption: while we like morality to designate "proper" answers, it, unfortunately, rarely provides easy or black-and-white scenarios. And, for that reason, perhaps an absolutist perspective doesn't always work.

Revolutionary Repartee, Relatively Speaking

Excluding extreme scenarios, when it comes to normal moral reasoning, you traditionally find two prominent camps to determine whether something is right or wrong: *moral absolutists* and *moral relativists*. Moral absolutists maintain that a general principle of morally right and wrong acts applies without exception. For example, a moral absolutist might say, "Lying, of any form, is morally wrong." So, from an absolutist perspective, even telling kids that Santa Claus brings them their presents on Christmas Eve represents an immoral act.

Moral relativists, on the other hand, argue that multiple perspectives and paradigms should be considered before making any sort of lasting judgment. For instance, a moral relativist might think lying represents a *generally* wrong act, but telling kids about Santa Claus, since our culture dictates that it is acceptable to lie about Santa, does *not* constitute a wrong act.

Some philosophers, however, don't think the concept of morality even exists! They question morality incessantly and they typically think it's an artificial convention with no permanent or lasting consequences. Perhaps the most damning assault exemplifying this dissenting voice came from a German philosopher by the name of Friedrich Nietzsche (1844–1900), who essentially claimed that morality is a sham—that it only serves to suppress those superior beings who might threaten the balance of power in society. Nietzsche went as far as asserting that morality is inherently tyrannical. If his ideas ever became widely accepted, it would completely alter the psychological landscape of humanity, for sure. So, not only did the non-black-and-white issue of morality perturb Nietzsche, but he also seemed to consider the *idea* of enforcing morality to be a travesty.

Livin' the Herd Life

Friedrich Nietzsche, in *Beyond Good and Evil*, expressed some of the most audacious claims ever made against morality and God. He claimed that Christianity—because it teaches self-destruction, self-sacrifice, and self-imposed servitude—created and perpetuates a *herd mentality*. This herd mentality has become so ingrained and incorporated into our existence that it has become natural. He called this herd mentality *slave morality*, which means that people surrender their power and will to a few in command out of a sense of imperative obedience—or a *compulsive need* to obey someone or *something*.

If such a thing as a *moral injustice* existed to Nietzsche, it would be accepting any sense of morality. Ironically, if we transpose Nietzsche's beliefs onto the story of *Frankenstein* and the belief in God, we find that apparently *no one* has any moral responsibility because we're all supposedly livin' the herd life! We can't blame the monster *or* Victor in *any* way! But Nietzsche *wanted* us to believe that God and Christianity oppressed people by robbing them of the power to *truly* live, which leads us, at last, to consider the concept of morality.

Morality or No Morality: That is the Question

A major difficulty for morality is that the idea of a *moral law* seems contradictory to the very nature of morality. Morality can *only* exist if an agent is *free* to choose between the morally right or morally wrong action, but a law seems to imply that we aren't free. If Victor's monster *didn't* have a choice (hypothetically speaking)—if it literally couldn't do anything but make Victor's life a living hell—then the notion of moral discussions about this novel is completely pointless. However, our society thrives on unwritten rules and laws pertaining to immoral actions. Think about what this discussion means: morality is *the chosen* and a commandment is the *forced*, so asserting the existence of *moral commandments* contradicts the fundamental necessity and idea of morality.

But we *need* morality to live together peacefully, don't we? Otherwise people would begin killing like Victor's monster, and burning the town to the ground like the android at the beginning of this chapter. If morality didn't exist, *everyone* would start devouring their neighbors' faces! Okay, probably not that severe, but this exaggerated theme remains incredibly common in dystopian literature. This duality, the apparent need for morality and yet the ineptitudes and conflicting nature of morality, represents the fundamental problem of morality, of moral reasoning, and of ethical discussions.

"But *does* he deserve to share that fate?" your conscience demands.

If something like morality is so confusing, troubling, and sometimes contradictory *by its very nature*, is it possible that the very idea is false? Some people, like Nietzsche, when asked the question, "Morality or no morality?" have responded, "That is the question," and abandoned morality. Thankfully, morality, unlike the story of Victor's life and the life of his deformed and loveless monster, is not entirely hopeless and destitute. Existentialist philosophers, such as Jean-Paul Sartre (1905–1980), believed that no objective foundation existed concerning our moral resolutions; each person simply decides which path is right and must accept the consequences. As ethicist James Sheppard has said, "Ethics is and *ought* to be a contentious subject."[1] For that reason, dare to do something different, something radical: dare to believe that, in ethical discussions, the notion of *one* correct answer might not realistically exist. Perhaps *more* than one solution stands equally as

---

[1] Personal interview, 2013.

viable as another one. In case you were wondering, this just so happens to be a relativistic stance concerning the issue of morality.

The Final Verdict: Guilty or Not Guilty?

This might be a slightly harsh way of painting the dilemma here, but the difference between absolutists and relativists can sometimes be the difference between the letter of the law and the spirit of the law. The letter of the law says that no matter what happens, the punishment for everyone committing the same type of crime is always the same; the spirit of the law says that we should consider what happened, the motivations of those involved in the crimes, and whether or not the act was done under compulsion. In fact, we sort of have a relativistic paradigm built into our legal system: *mens rea*, a crucial concept in criminal cases, basically means "Person A must be shown to have had reasonable intent to do x as well as the knowledge that x was wrong."

If we apply *mens rea* (the 'guilty mind' test used in criminal trials) to Victor, his monster, and the android, then it doesn't seem realistic to assert an absolutist morality—to assert that they're all equally blameworthy. But perhaps it's possible that the absolutist perspective is true. Regardless of whether or not the monster and the android were suffering from a deprivation of the basic "love need" or felt unimaginably hated, an absolutist perspective suggests that they are both guilty; an absolutist morality would also say that Victor's guilty, too, because he brought about the deaths of several people. On the other hand, a relativistic morality would say we should consider more than mere occurrences if we are going to make a judgment.

This question of morality and moral judgment is quite tricky. I leave it to you to decide how blameworthy our monster, our android, and perhaps, even, the creators, are. They all seem to make free choices, as we all do, but judgment doesn't seem to make sense if you don't consider the context—and here, as in life, the situation is very complex indeed!

12
Who's to Blame?

JAI GALLIOTT

The plot of Mary Shelley's *Frankenstein* (1818) is quite different from the various watered-down Hollywood movie adaptations. Reading the original novel, we can see that the experience of the two main characters, Victor Frankenstein and his nameless monster, offers us a number of insights regarding the nature of moral responsibility and the way we blame others. Shelley's plot has Victor working alone to create his unsightly creature. When it comes to life, he is horrified by its morbid appearance and abandons it. The poor creature, left all alone to fend for itself in the big bad world, develops a serious attitude problem and goes on a killing spree.

It's a simple plot: scientist creates monster—monster runs berserk—justice is done to the scientist at the hands of his own creation. But, while the plot may be simple, it gives structure to a deep and eye-opening story concerning the consequences of somewhat well-intentioned scientists, engineers, and doctors failing to respect the boundaries of their disciplines and the level of moral responsibility they ought to take for their work when it all goes wrong.

Rather than the mute or grunting monster of the movies, Shelley's creature is quite articulate and does its best to make Victor aware of his apparent responsibilities. "How dare you sport thus with life?" he asks angrily. He goes on to tell Victor:

> Do your duty towards me, and I will do mine towards you and the rest of mankind. . . . Be not equitable to every other and trample upon me alone, to whom thy justice, and even thy clemency and affection, is

> most due. Remember that I am thy creature; I ought to be thy Adam, but I am rather the fallen angel, whom thou drivest from joy for no misdeed.

With yellow skin that barely covered the work of the muscles and arteries below it, the creature may not have been blessed with good looks, but we can see that it was certainly no dummy. Shelley portrays it as an intelligent being that gradually comes to understand its relationship with Victor and humanity at large. She clearly intends it to be seen as a creature capable of reason.

This is a morally significant difference because, although Frankenstein was framed in terms of the primitive electrical, mechanical, and medical technology of the early nineteenth century during which Shelley wrote, in all relevant ways it addresses what is essentially the same problem as it pertains to the rise of intelligent machines, which began in the late twentieth century and will continue well into the twenty-first century as scientists and engineers construct and enhance these systems for deployment in fields such as policing and warfare. Shelley was truly ahead of her time in writing about this modern Prometheus.

Twenty-First Century Frankennovation

Depicted on the ceiling of the Sistine Chapel in Rome is God, the Creator, extending his fingertips down to touch those of Adam. The Bible has us believe that in doing so, he imparts in him the gift of life. In the millennia since the Bible was put together, it seems that various mad scientists have been attempting to play God in replicating this act of creation.

They go about their "frankennovation"—which is my word for acts of creation/animation/innovation—in different ways. Owing to some damn good writing in *Frankenstein*, the actual detail of the act of the monster's creation is kept vague and passes without much fanfare. We're only told that after much effort and fatigue, Victor somehow infuses a spark of being into the otherwise lifeless corpse lying at his feet and, with a convulsive motion, it comes to life.

From this limited information, it seems that Shelley had read about experiments with "animal electricity" or Galvanic electricity, whereby two different metals are connected together and touched on the nerve endings of various body parts, causing convolutions, which also explains the neck bolts on Frankenstein's monster.

Groundbreaking at its time, this sort of science is now all but dead. A distinguishing feature of more modern—and also seemingly more serious—attempts at frankennovation is the fact that the thing or creature being animated is far less human in nature. Some post-*Frankenstein* stories of creation are so far removed from the original that they abandon the concept of a human-looking monster altogether. Tales and films from the 1950s and 1960s were flooded with big, green, radioactive monsters and giant mutated insects and, in the 1970s, we saw super-scary advanced computers and out-of-control artificial intelligence. This not only frightened audience members, but also provoked scientists to think about how far they could push this sort of technology and what it might be good for. In the 1980s a general obsession with technology and enormous advancements in electronics and robotics started to make the possibility of Frankenstein 2.0 much more real.

The possibility of real-world robotic monsters and cyborg killer machines has also been mirrored in cinema for quite some time, with the best known example being the *Terminator* franchise, depicting a virtually indestructible killing machine from the future. However, this is not just the stuff of science fiction. A number of philosophers and self-dubbed "futurists" such as Rodney Brooks, Ray Kurzweil, and Hans Moravec believe we are very quickly approaching a moment—called the Singularity—when computers will become intelligent and not just more intelligent, but more intelligent than humans.

They believe that mankind may well be on the threshold of creating a digital monster that is capable of thinking, having self-awareness, and perhaps demonstrating moral reasoning skills. The definition of words such as "thinking" and "reasoning" are, of course, open to broad interpretation, and the question of whether machines are ultimately capable of these things plagued even the oldest robe-wearing philosophers and theologians. Either way, it's wise to start thinking about the problems that will arise if, or when, Frankensteinian robots come knocking on your door.

If the Pentagon's mad scientists have their way this might be sooner rather than later. The dawn of the twenty-first century has been called the decade of the military robot. Big remotely-operated and semi-autonomous robots called "unmanned aerial vehicles" already rain down Hellfire missiles on suspected terrorists as Zeus did lightning bolts, and a small but influential group of scholars-turned-intellectual-warriors is grappling with what some believe will be the next must-have piece of military kit: lethal autonomous robots.

At the center of the debate and the engineering effort is the Georgia Tech Professor Ronald Arkin, a professional roboticist and consultant for the United States Department of Defense, which spends billions of dollars each year on robotics research and development. He has devised algorithms for an "ethical governor" that would allow a robot to function in lieu of a human warfighter.

This governor acts as a suppressor of automatically generated lethal action, so in much the same way that a mechanical governor would shut down a steam engine running too hot, the ethical governor shuts down the autonomous machine when it is about to do something unethical, such as shooting good guys. He thinks that not only will his robot not present any problems for just war theory, which sets the rules governing the resort to war and its conduct, but that it would ultimately surpass its requirements, writing that "I am convinced that they [killer robots] can perform more ethically than human soldiers are capable of."

I am not so sure. We need to ask ourselves, if human beings do eventually succeed in creating this robotic military capability in much the same way that Victor Frankenstein eventually succeeded in discovering the cause of the generation of life and bestowing it upon lifeless matter, will it also lead to the creature turning upon its creators in the manner of the Frankenstein story? Will it then turn on the public, either justly or unjustly? There's no clear answer. Some would say that robots have no reason to harm humans while others would have us believe that there is no reason for them not to, especially given the traditional human response to unfamiliar threats: kill, kill, and kill. One question we must therefore answer is if our creations do follow the typical plot and go berserk, who are we going to hold morally responsible?

How Responsible Is the Creator?

When you think of science, you probably think of well-defined methods, hypotheses and conclusions, applications, and benefits. All of these are supposed to be good for us, of course. With each new discovery, the human race takes one step further away from other primates on the evolutionary chain. Right? We all enjoy it when innovation results in immense gains for all involved, whether that be in the form of a new smartphone or something more advanced, but this isn't always the case. For every good invention or innovation there are series of mistakes, and no one wants these on their plate.

Just as in the case of Victor Frankenstein and his creation gone wrong, a mistake was made which the creator had to acknowledge and attempt to correct. The only problem was that he didn't. The infamous Frankenstein used science to help him build a human being, but when his experiment failed and he got himself a monster, he wouldn't take responsibility for his creation (outside of trying to kill it). Upon sighting his hideous creation for the first time, he runs off with his tail between his legs. In the period following, he didn't really stop to think about or show any compassion for the monster he let roam free. Trying to kill the creature was the easy way to act; Victor just gave in to his natural revulsion. What he was unwilling to do was take responsibility for raising and loving his creation.

Science is essentially about understanding nature and existence. It incorporates all the things around us and attempts to find out how each interacts with the others. It is also about improving what already exists or has ceased to exist. It's about pushing the boundaries of science when it's safe to do so. Unfortunately, scientists and engineers often go about pushing the boundaries and frankennovating even when they don't fully grasp the complexity of their actions and haven't done the responsible thing and put the necessary safety countermeasures in place. When Victor decided to introduce a new creature into the world, he didn't fully understand the nature and consequences of his experimentation and he failed to think forward and consult with anyone or answer any questions about the potential results of his scientific endeavors.

Without any real oversight, with the exception of some gentle probing from his inquisitive friend Henry Clerval, Victor plays an indirect role in causing four unwarranted deaths and endangering the lives of many more, and he knows it. Throughout the book, the weight of the remorse for his role in the murders of William, Justine, dear Clerval, and even his beloved wife, Elizabeth, began to adversely affect his mental and physical health. While it is understandable that the monster ran away—I would've done the same—Victor had a moral obligation to ensure that it didn't get away uncontrolled and that safety was the number one priority.

This obligation also extends to today's professionals working on those machines that have the potential to become tomorrow's killer robots. I say "potential" because even those machines that are intended to be non-lethal can later be adapted for lethal use or otherwise go berserk and end up killing people. This is exactly what happened with a robotic cannon recently tested by the South Africa National Defense Force. The advanced weapon, capable of selecting targets automatically, mysteriously started firing uncontrollably into the crowd of spectators, killing nine people and wounding fourteen others.

Unlike the *actual* act of creating the monster, which involved Victor Frankenstein alone, the creation of killer robots is a more distributed effort, involving *many* creators. Take the South African case. If we assume that the firing incident were a mechanical problem, with the gun jamming and exploding before discharging its rounds uncontrollably, it's very tempting to blame the engineers who designed the weapon or the manufacturer who put it together. Others might suggest that a computer and its operating code were to blame, in which case it might be insisted that the programmer be held responsible.

After all, modern product liability rules are rather stringent and call for "due care" to be taken. These people are also inherently more knowledgeable about their products than anyone else and are expected to anticipate and design out potential harms. But should we really hold Frankenstein and his contemporaries wholly responsible for their creations' destructive results? Well, no.

The Educator and Industry?

While these creators are, in a sense, their own worst enemies and undeniably hold some level of responsibility for their acts and the consequences that follow, science and innovation rarely take place in a vacuum, even in the case of recluses like Victor Frankenstein. Scientists and engineers are educated folks who have typically been imbued with important knowledge from a very early age and mastered their respective disciplines at the figurative knee of intellectual giants.

Shelley indicates early on that in the case of Victor, much of the blame rests with his teachers; starting with his father who quickly dismisses his interest in arcane knowledge without properly explaining why experimenting with it is potentially dangerous. When the young Frankenstein begins to enjoy studying alchemy, the medieval forerunner of chemistry, his father says "Ah! Cornelius Agrippa! Do not waste your time upon this; it is sad trash." Long after, Victor comes to realize that if, instead of this remark, his father had taken the pains to explain to him that much of Agrippa's science had been denounced and exploded and that a modern system of science had been introduced which possessed much greater and somewhat safer powers than the ancient, there's a possibility that he may have thrown the book aside and not succumbed to the fatal theoretical impulse that lead to his demise.

In the University of Ingolstadt, Professor Krempe, like Victor's father, dismisses the writings of his favorite alchemists as "nonsense," while Professor Waldman, without the same contempt, tells that while these alchemists often promised impossibilities they did indeed perform miracles in "penetrating into the recesses of nature and showing how she works in her hiding-places. They discovered how the blood circulates and the nature of the air we breathe." With these words, Victor reluctantly turns to the study of more modern science, but his educators fail to recognize that whatever interest he has is actually fueled by the impossibilities promised in alchemy. He continues to seek out dangerous knowledge to untangle the deepest mysteries of creation and combines it with new, practical methods of science that eventually give him his monstrous creation. It is up to mentors and educators to clearly identify dangerous knowledge or pursuits and disapprove or otherwise caution those who that go ahead regardless. Those that do not must share responsibility for any ensuing mess.

Unfortunately, in modern times, ethics, safety, and wisdom often clash with financial considerations within funding-focused universities. Government and military organizations fund a significant amount of, and perhaps even most of, the cutting-edge electronics and robotics research that has resulted in the design, manufacture, and deployment of military robots such as the controversial "Predator" drone from the United States. While the Defense Advanced Research Projects Agency (DARPA)—which is the modern-day equivalent of Frankenstein's lab and home to the US military's best scientists—continues to research and innovate, America has budgeted over seven billion dollars to purchase killer robots for this year alone.

Scientists, engineers and programmers face a difficult choice between accepting funding from the military-industrial complex and accepting the responsibility that ought to come with that or paying a high personal price and risk losing their positions. Academic institutions must also be held responsible as many of them, like the University of North Dakota, which now offer degree programs that train students to design, build, and operate robots that may be used to kill and maim.

Monster or Machine? Let's Blame the Bot

The final possible place that additional responsibility might rest is with the creations themselves. Perhaps we should try monsters for their murderous crimes and hold military robots responsible for the deaths of noncombatants? Upon first consideration, it seems ridiculous to take seriously the idea that either monster or machine should—or even could—be held responsible for its actions. It's not particularly hard to see how they could be *causally* responsible for particular harms, such as the deaths of innocent people, but it is another thing altogether to say that they are *morally* responsible.

The flip side of this argument is to say that they should be considered rational beings. Contrary to the many movie and stage versions of *Frankenstein*, the monster, as depicted by Mary Shelley, is a sensitive and emotional creature who longs to spend his life with another thinking being like himself. The monster is a highly intelligent and eloquent speaker capable of accelerated learning. Almost immediately after his creation, he has figured out how to get dressed and, early on in the novel, knows how to speak German and French. By the end, he is speaking English and quoting John Milton's epic poem *Paradise Lost*. Intellectually speaking, he's the envy of any soccer mom! Sure, he had a rough upbringing, but does this necessarily absolve him of all responsibility? No, not if he is the rational being and intentional killer that Shelley makes of him.

The same can be said of intelligent machines, but when we move from the fictional world to reality, this takes a little more imagination on the part of technophobes. For a machine to be the object of blame or to hold it morally responsible, scholars like prominent "roboethicist" Rob Sparrow think that it's necessary to punish it in some way. For many people, this is completely implausible. Personally, I feel that *if* the mad scientists create robots that are sufficiently "intelligent" to be appropriately described as being fully autonomous, then there's little reason why we shouldn't hold robots responsible. While it is currently hard to think how a machine would suffer, such an intelligent machine would presumably have the sort of electrical brain activity and cognitive states that would make it possible for the machine to be punished somehow, possibly by thwarting whatever it is that machines desire.

I Didn't Do It

Drawing from *Frankenstein*'s rich text, we can see that attributing blame for the creation of monsters and monstrous machines is very complicated. We can't really hold Frankenstein and his contemporaries or even just those that educate and fund them solely responsible. The impossibility of punishing present-day killer robots also means that unlike the more intelligent monsters, we can't hold them solely responsible either. It sounds as if we can blame everyone and no one? That's exactly the important point for us today: there is a risk that with so many blameworthy persons, the diffusion of responsibility might encourage further unethical behavior. This occurs when those in the chain of responsibility assume that someone else is going to intervene and so each feels less responsible and refrains from doing anything or does less than they otherwise would to halt the undesirable consequences of their actions and those of others. They may assume that others are more qualified to help and that their intervention is unneeded. It opens up the "I didn't do it" or "I didn't need to do it" response. If no one person has sole responsibility for the consequences of monsters, whether in the form of re-animated corpses or killer robots, we might see more of them and the harms that follow.

When you think about it, though, you might realize that responsibility doesn't diffuse just because many people are responsible. If you and I decide to go murder Victor Frankenstein to get even with him for the harm he has done, we don't get a half-life sentence each just because there were two of us. If a whole bunch of people decide to do something wrong, they are *all* responsible. So although we might feel that being part of an angry mob makes us less blameworthy, it doesn't; it just makes us *feel* more difficult to identify and blame.

So who is responsible for the violence of Victor's creation . . . ? Everyone who played a part in it! And when it comes to the killer creations we are making today, all of us are responsible, even if only responsible for doing nothing to try to stop it. . . .

IV

Dr. Frankenstein's Monster Identification Field Guide

13
Sure It's Aliiiive, but Does It Have a Sooooul?

KEITH HESS

> **THE MONSTER:** God, in pity, made man beautiful and alluring, after his own image; but my form is a filthy type of yours, more horrid even from the very resemblance.
>
> —Mary Shelley's *Frankenstein*

> **THE MONSTER:** You gave me these emotions, but you didn't tell me how to use them. Now two people are dead because of us. Why?
>
> **VICTOR FRANKENSTEIN:** There was something at work in my soul which I do not understand.
>
> **THE MONSTER:** And what of my soul? Do I have one? Or was that a part you left out?
>
> —*Frankenstein*, 1994

God made us in his image. And Dr. Frankenstein made the monster in ours. Consider how his creation is like us. He has a human form. He gets tired, hungry, and thirsty. He feels pain and pleasure. He's rational and uses language. He's filled with love and rage, kindness and cruelty. He experiences sorrow, remorse, and despair. Yet he's a hodgepodge of physical parts. Dr. Frankenstein pieced him together from various cadavers and bestowed life on his lifeless body. It's curious that this hunk of matter can think, feel, believe, and desire.

Mary Shelley's *Frankenstein* makes me wonder. I find myself asking questions like, "Is the monster human? Is he conscious or is he no more than an elaborate, biological machine? If he *is* conscious, how could we know? Does he count as a person?"

But I'll focus on a different question. Let's suppose that Dr. Frankenstein succeeded in creating (recreating? reviving?) a human being. So the monster is human. And, he was pieced together from physical stuff. Does that mean that the monster is solely and completely physical or is there something nonphysical—immaterial—about him, like a soul?

Since I assume that the monster is a human being, I'll also assume that he has a human nature or makeup just like us. So, on this assumption, what goes for our nature goes for the monster's nature and vice versa. If the monster is made up solely of physical bits and pieces, then, since he's a human just like us, we are made up solely of physical bits and pieces. Or if it turns out that there's something nonphysical about us, the same goes for the monster.

The Soulless Monster

> **The Monster:** What kind of people is it in which I am comprised? Good people? Bad people?
>
> **Victor Frankenstein:** Materials. Nothing more.
>
> —*Frankenstein*, 1994

Physicalism is one philosophical theory that gives us an account of our makeup. According to physicalism, humans are just complex material objects with no immaterial parts or aspects. We (and the monster) are only made out of the same bits and pieces that stones, water, mortuaries, dirt, baseballs, severed limbs, houses, and trees are made of. It's just that our bits and pieces are arranged in such a way that they enable consciousness (which is itself physical).

Physicalism comes in different sorts. On one version, everything that exists is physical, not just humans. Nothing that exists is nonphysical, which rules out the existence of God, angels, and demons (assuming they're all nonphysical). Most importantly, it means that souls and nonphysical minds are the stuff of fiction. Modern-day physicalists include Jaegwon Kim and Patricia Churchland.

But you don't need to be an atheist to think that humans are solely physical. Some hold to physicalism about human beings while also holding that some nonphysical things, like

God, exist. Modern-day philosophers Peter van Inwagen and Nancey Murphy are physicalists of this sort. Keep in mind that both sorts of physicalists think that there is nothing nonphysical about human beings.

Not all physicalists deny that we have minds. Some do, like Patricia Churchland, who thinks that our notions like beliefs and desires aren't about anything real. Instead of beliefs and desires, there are just brain states. Others, though, think we do have things like beliefs and desires, but they are nothing more than states of the brain. Regardless of how different physicalists deal with the mind, they're united in this: a complete account of the stuff we're made of won't include anything nonphysical, like a soul or an *immaterial* mind.

So for physicalists, Frankenstein's monster is made up of nothing more than the parts that the doctor used to build him. He's not made of anything nonphysical. For some physicalists, the monster has a mind (which is nothing more than states of the brain). But for others, the monster has no beliefs, desires, or emotions, but simply brain states.

The Ghost in the Monster

Dualism, is an idea opposing physicalism, and it comes in many varieties—but all dualists agree that human beings are more than just physical creatures. That is, they think that, while humans have a physical component, there is something nonphysical about them. *Property dualists* say that humans are physical, but have *mental properties* (I'll say more about these properties later). David Chalmers is a well-known property dualist. People who take this view would say, on the assumption that the monster is a human being, that he has some properties that aren't physical.

Substance dualists think that humans are made up of both body and soul. However, different substance dualists say different things about our relation to our bodies and souls. Some say that we *are* souls and have (or interact with our) bodies. Others say we are made up of both bodies and souls. On the second view, we ourselves are not souls, but we have them as parts. Plato (427–347 B.C.E.) and René Descartes (1596–1650) were substance dualists. Contemporary substance dualists include Richard Swinburne and Alvin Plantinga. Regarding the monster, substance dualists would say either that he *has* or *is* a soul.

Monster Vision

So we have a fundamental disagreement between the physicalists and the dualists. Physicalists think that humans (and the monster) are made up of nothing more than physical parts and properties, while dualists say that there is something nonphysical about us (and the monster). Who's right? Are there any reasons to favor one view over the other?

Actually, there are. The first thing to recognize is that there are aspects of us—of our minds—that are nonphysical. Consider mental properties like *being in pain*. When the monster is in anguish over his hideous appearance, he is experiencing a sort of pain, and so, has the property *being in pain*. Other mental properties the monster might have at some point include *having an itch*, *seeing red*, *desiring to get even with Dr. Frankenstein*, *believing that killing Elizabeth would be a good way to get even*, *having a feeling of remorse over the damage he causes the doctor*. These are all non-physical mental events.

Different physicalists say different things about what mental properties are. Some deny that there are such things, some say that they're just physical properties, some try to account for them in terms of external behavior, but it remains very difficult to account for the experience of colors, for example, as physical.

What's hard (or possibly impossible) for the physicalist to explain is the subjective nature of these experiences. How can the experience of red be something physical? The smartest guys with the best equipment can examine your brain until they're senile. But they'll never find your experience of red. They might find the part of the brain that's active whenever you see red, but that's not the same as your experience.

Consider this example: Suppose that the eyes Dr. Frankenstein used for his monster lacked all the cone cells needed to detect color.[1] So when the monster came to life, he could only see black and white. Imagine further, that while on Captain Walton's ship (at the end of Shelley's novel) the mon-

[1] This comes from Frank Jackson's famous example about Mary the neurophysiologist; "Epiphenomenal Qualia," *Philosophical Quarterly* 32 (1982).

ster decides not to kill himself on a funeral pyre, but to do something worthwhile with his life. So he becomes a color-vision scientist. He dedicates himself to this science so much that he reaches the point of knowing all the physical facts there are to know about color vision. This includes knowledge of what happens when light strikes the eye, of the process of a signal being sent to the brain, of what specific portion of the brain is activated when a person has an experience of color, etc. At some point in his career, doctors realize that the monster is colorblind. So they take out his old eyes and give him eyes that can see color. The monster is amazed. He now has the experience of seeing reds, greens, and blues for the first time. He comes to know something new: the subjective experience, the "what it is like," of color vision!

The point of this imagined scenario is this: before the transplant the monster knew and understood all of the physical *causes* of color experience, but he still did not know what it was actually like to experience color. So the facts that he learned after his transplant were nonphysical. What exactly were they? They were psychological facts: facts about his experience, about what it is like to see colors. If this imagined scenario is right, then physicalism is false: there are aspects of human experience—mental properties—that are not physical.

Having mental properties does not necessarily mean we have a soul. It merely means that there's more to us than *just the physical*—but the soul idea is one that means our essential self can continue on *without the body at all!* Perhaps the property dualists are right that we're physical objects that have mental properties. To conclude that we have a soul, we would need a further argument.

Monster Makeover

Philosopher Alvin Plantinga has argued for the conclusion that we're not our bodies or our brains or even a part of our brains, but something nonphysical.[2] (Just to be clear, he does think that we *have* physical bodies!) In presenting his argument, Plantinga makes certain assumptions. First, he thinks that we

[2] Alvin Plantinga, "Materialism and Christian Belief," in *Persons: Human and Divine* (Oxford, 2007).

actually exist. Believe it or not, some philosophers think that you and I and even they themselves do not exist (then who's giving their arguments and writing their articles?).

He also thinks that we are objects, rather than events (like baseball games) or properties (like the redness of an apple) or something else. Finally, though we cease to exist at some point, we are things that persist through time. There is a single subject of my experiences—me!—at every point in my existence, from my childhood to my adult self. As for the monster, the very monster that the doctor creates is the very monster who later hunts the doctor down (so it seems), even though the monster went through many changes during that time.

Here goes the argument: I can survive the destruction and replacement of my body and my brain, so I am not my body or brain or part of my brain. (Think of it. If you can exist when your original body does not, are you your original body? Can something exist separately from itself?) But if physicalism is true, what would we be except for our bodies or our brains or some part of our brains? If we're not any of these things, we must not be physical.

Is there a reason to think humans can exist when their bodies don't? Yes. Imagine that Frankenstein's monster has gotten some news press over his advances in color vision and that he becomes a sort of cultural phenomenon. *Time* runs an article on him (I guess he's lived quite a while since the good doctor made him). He's interviewed by Oprah. He writes a bestseller on color vision. He gives a TED talk.

Naturally, he loves the attention, but realizes that his hideous figure isn't doing much for his public image. This really hits home for him when TMZ televises a picture of him shirtless in Malibu. So he determines that he'll replace his aging monster body for a younger, Ryan-Gosling-esque one. (Maybe with his new body there's a starring role in a Nicholas-Sparks-inspired movie in his future!)

So the monster creates a machine that can rapidly destroy old body parts and replace them with new ones. He sets the machine to replace all of his body parts, one by one, within a second. He gets in the machine and remains fully conscious, perhaps even stewing in anger over the leaked beach photo during the entire process. *He* survives the whole ordeal, but his body doesn't—piece by piece *every* part was replaced with a new one!

The same goes for the replacement of his brain. Imagine that the brain Dr. Frankenstein gave our monster was from an elderly person. The monster now discovers that his once top-notch brain is beginning to break down. So he decides to replace it with a new one. He sets up the machine and gets in. First, the machine transfers all of the information in his left hemisphere (Lefty) to the right hemisphere (Righty) and causes Lefty to go dormant. Then it destroys and replaces Lefty. Next the machine transfers all of the information from Righty to the *new* Lefty and destroys and replaces Righty. All the while, the monster crafts a not-so-friendly letter to TMZ.

All of this seems possible. Science might even advance to the point that such a machine is feasible. Or if it can't, the replacement process is something that God (supposing he exists) could carry out.

The point is this: if this scenario is even possible, then the monster is not the same thing as his body or (part of) his brain—because all of his body has been destroyed but *he* still exists! This is because a thing can't possibly exist apart from itself, but the monster can exist apart from his body and his brain. And we aren't our bodies or (part of) our brains either since we could just as easily imagine ourselves in this scenario (except I'm too philanthropic to subject the good citizens of Malibu to my bare chest). But then what are we? If we're not our bodies or (part of) our brains, it seems we're something nonphysical. Perhaps we're that thing that philosophers and theologians call the soul.

This argument isn't going to impress those who think that we don't continue through time or that we don't exist. Neither will it impress those who think we are properties rather than objects. But the physicalists or the property dualists who think that we're material objects who persist through time will have to respond to this argument. Maybe they'll say that we can't survive the replacement of our bodies or our brains. If this is right, then the monster didn't survive the destruction of his body and brain. Instead, something new came into existence that was physically just like him and had his memories. But if Plantinga's argument is right, then we ourselves are not physical beings, though we have physical bodies.

What about if he's wrong? Well, . . . parts of our bodies, our cells, are dying and being replaced all the time. Similarly, the atoms in our bodies (and brains) are constantly being shifted around, breaking down, and being exchanged for different ones! So, *if* Plantinga is wrong and a new monster is created when his body is replaced, then *we have to say the same thing about human beings!* It looks like we are in it together! If we say, "Nope, when my cells and atoms (my body) are replaced, I still continue to exist" (evidencing the likelihood of my soul) then it seems we have to say the same about the monster.

The Disembodied Monster

Here's another reason to think we're not physical. There is good evidence to suppose that we can exist disembodied, or, without any body at all. That might seem weird (as if famous monster scientists and body replacements weren't weird enough). It's even weirder to think of the monster existing without his body, pieced together as he was from lifeless body parts. But weird or not, we should examine the evidence for what it's worth. Hold on to your hats (and your bodies), because here we go.

In his book, *Evidence of the Afterlife*, Dr. Jeffrey Long summarizes his examination of reports of over 1,300 near-death experiences from all over the world and from people of all ages.[3] He found that they share many common features. I'll focus on one of those features: most near-death experiencers have an out-of-body experience in which they feel themselves leaving their bodies and often even see their bodies from an external point of view.

Some out-of-body experiences can be explained without any mention of spooky disembodiment. But others are best explained by just such a thing. In some cases, for example, the out-of-body experiencer reports seeing something far from her body during her out-of-body experience and the report is found to be correct. One woman, Maria, had a heart attack which caused her to have an out-of-body experience. She had the experience of floating out of the hospital and seeing a shoe on a window ledge of the third story. When she told the story later to a near-death-experience researcher, she provided detailed information about the shoe's location and appearance. The

---

[3] Jeffrey Long, *Evidence of the Afterlife: The Science of Near-Death Experiences* (HarperCollins, 2011).

researcher found the shoe just where Maria said it was and its appearance matched Maria's detailed report.

Maybe we should be cautious about what we can conclude from near-death-experience reports. But one thing is undeniable: if out-of-body experiences are real (if they involve an actual separation of the person from the body), then humans can exist without their bodies. And if we can exist without our bodies, then we are more than just physical beings. Since the monster is human, then he's more than physical as well. Dr. Long offers some interesting reasons for thinking that out-of-body experiences are real.

Final Thoughts

If this is right, then there's good reason to think that the monster (and the rest of us) is not just a physical being. But some questions remain. How did the monster get a soul if he has one? It's not like the doctor injected him with one. ("Let's see, we've got the liver, the brain, the clavicle . . . we're certainly missing something . . . Oh yes, the soul! Here we go. I'll just put that right in.") For that matter, how did *we* get a soul? What's more, how can the physical and the nonphysical interact? How does all this fit with science?

Even if we haven't answered all of the questions related to the nature of human beings, we've seen some interesting reasons for thinking that we're made up of more than just physical parts. What does seem inescapable, though, is the realization that the we and the monster are in it together. When we reject arguments supporting his soul, like Plantinga's, it seems we have to reject our own soul, if we accept it; it seems to act as evidence that we both have a soul. Perhaps the lesson to be learned here is that we should be careful about assuming who does and doesn't have a soul . . . even monsters . . .

14
Who Is Frankenstein's Monster?

JONATHAN LOPEZ

How do you make one man out of many?

Sometimes figuring out what makes a thing is pretty easy; for example, when we look at something like gold we know it continues to be gold just as long as it has 79 protons. When we change this property of gold, perhaps take away protons through radioactive means, we can say that the gold has ceased to exist and is now a new element.

People are a little more difficult because our crucial properties aren't as easy to pin down so that we can definitely say we cease to be a person at some point or another. Philosophers concerned with this question are said to be preoccupied with the question of "identity" which tries to track down what essential properties are necessary for a person to persist through time. Frankenstein's creation, though, seems to pose many problems for identity—because he was constructed of numerous dead bodies!

Two common answers in trying to nail down identity are bodily and psychological criteria. Roughly, the bodily criterion says that someone is identical with himself just as long as he inhabits the same body. This account runs into trouble when it is pointed out that the molecules that made up one's body when they were one or two years old are entirely different molecules than the ones that constitutes a person in adulthood. You want to say you're the same person you were when you were younger, but the bodily criterion doesn't seem to capture this facet.

Imagine that Victor Frankenstein regularly replaced pieces of his creation with new body parts. As a part gets old or decayed, Victor simply cuts it off and replaces it with a new part. Eventually, over time, the monster would have a completely different body. We are like that on the atomic level. Over time every single atom that makes you up will eventually be exchanged with a different one . . . the same kind of atom, but a different actual atoms. So I can't say its "this body" (this matter) that makes me, me. Because, years from now all of that matter will be different matter, just structured similarly.

These kinds of objections have motivated some philosophers to devise much more sophisticated accounts of the bodily criterion, or to support a different criterion—the psychological criterion.

The psychological criterion tells us that a person is identical to himself or herself just as long as they share the same memories. This solves some of the problems with being identical with yourself during younger instances of your life, however, there are still problems with this view. For instance, what happens if you get amnesia? Should we attend your funeral?

Victor's Experiments

Suppose a fictional scientist is running a series of experiments; let's call him Victor. As luck would have it, you're the first of his subjects to show up to the experiment and as such you get some input into his experimental setup. Victor explains that he intends to remove your brain and place it into someone else's body while simultaneously placing that other person's brain in your body.

The day before the brain-swapping experiment Victor still needs one subject for another experiment he is planning to conduct on pain perception. The subject, Victor says, will be awarded $100,000 in compensation for participating in the experiment. The choice that Victor presents to you is . . . Which body will be subjected to the pain experiments and which gets the money, the person in body A or body B?

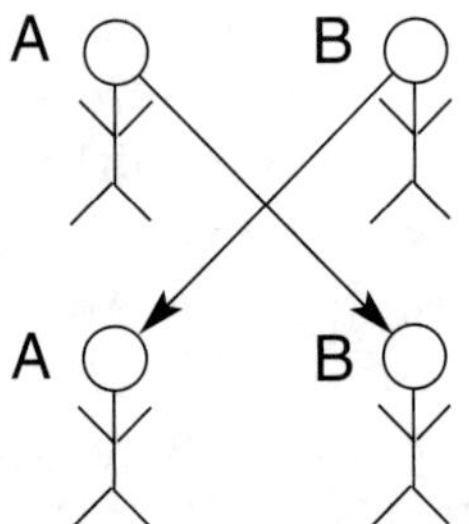

The A-bodied person's brain has been put into the B-bodied person and vice versa.

Wouldn't you pick the person in body B to receive the reward seeing as how that person is going to wake up knowing all sorts of things about your past; knowing all the same things as you used to; and having an identical personality and self-concepts in virtue of having your psychological (brain) contents? People often use the analogy of the brain being the hardware that runs the software. Taking the whole brain (hardware) or even if Victor was somehow able just to exchange your minds (software) without switching the actual brains, it seems like the important stuff is going to end up elsewhere than where it started.

Now remember the pain part of the experiment? Victor tells you that he has devised an experiment that will be testing human pain perception, in other words, torture. You of course don't really want to feel pain and ask if there is any way to reduce it. He tells you that he can wipe your memory clean before the experiment, that way when he's torturing you, it isn't really "you" he is torturing. Wouldn't you still object? And not just because you don't want to lose your memories. You would object because even if you had amnesia, you wouldn't want your *body* to be tortured. Would you?

As a last ditch effort to try to alleviate your worries Victor offers you that after the amnesia has been administered he can implant your old memories back into you. But this doesn't really seem to get at the point that presumably someone is going to wake up and experience the pain and it's not clear that the amnesia offered here is going to let you escape it, and just because you'll have your memories back doesn't seem to change the fact that you don't want to be tortured. But then Victor points out that it's basically the same as the first experiment where you gave a positive response.

Stepping back from these thought experiments let's examine where we stand. In the first experiment we felt driven to identify with our memories in keeping with the psychological criterion. In the second case, however, we tend to give a response opposite to what the psychological criterion suggests. We begin the experiment apprehensive we will be tortured even if we are given amnesia. Victor's offer to give you amnesia doesn't seem to abate the pain you'll soon experience, nor does his offer to give you novel memories seem all that helpful.

The point in offering these two sets of examples is to undermine the seemingly strong impulse we feel to give a response along the lines of the psychological criterion. All we did was change the presentation of the experiment and we seem to get conflicting answers. In both cases we were facing torture with someone else's memories, and we seem to be giving inconsistent answers. So far it's not looking good for the psychological view. On the one hand we think of our memories as us, but on the other, we think of our bodies as us! Surely we shouldn't let the concept of identity rest on such a flimsy feeling.

Enter the "Monster"

This is where Frankenstein really helps us analyze and evaluate the damage done to the psychological criterion by Victor's proposed experiments. The monster in *Frankenstein* comes into the world with no memories and is re-animated from human remains. If we're willing to say we persist through amnesia, in the second set of experiments, such that we're afraid of the impending pain experiments then we would also have to say the brain placed in the monster's skull survives having his memories wiped. As such, we would have to say that whoever inhabited the body before the monster died the first time, thus making him a corpse, is the same person as the reanimated monster.

Taking the amnesia seriously we finds ourselves in a position very similar to the monster in *Frankenstein*. Specifically, the absence of memories through and through makes the monster's case of amnesia relevant to our analysis. Once we get a real appreciation of what being subjected to amnesia looks like, we'll revisit the second set of examples to see if our answer differs.

The monster wakes up with no idea of the situation he finds himself, a serious case of amnesia. Perhaps this is not the same sense of amnesia which is usually depicted in soap operas but what I mean here is a very severe damage to his psychological contents. A person who has had amnesia induced, by whichever method, would find themselves in a very similar situation as the monster since neither has any idea what's going on around them. It is amnesia in this sense that motivates us to say that the monster is discontinuous with whoever was in their body before, that is, he does not persist through his corpse phase. If you think you will persist through the amnesia then you need to grant that the monster has also persisted through a similar ordeal and is the same person that lived and died in the body from which the monster was made.

The most telling part of the story, for our purposes, is the dialogue that happens between Victor Frankenstein and the monster. At this point we're told that the monster was incredibly confused on the day he came into being. The monster goes on to recount the days following his creation noting the difficulty in familiarizing himself with his senses. From this initial bit of testimony we start to appreciate how hard it can be to come into the world with no memories. The part where the monster familiarizes himself with the fire is a dramatic illustration of him learning about his senses. The monster describes being thrown into the world similar to how an infant would find himself in the world. Although there is certainly something going on inside the monster's head, that is, he has some psychological content, it seems to be a new kind of content.

To give us an even better picture of how "new" the monster is he recounts how he has come to acquire language. The monster describes to Victor how he intently listened in on the cottagers teaching a language to one of their guests. And he starts from the very basics by mimicking the sounds made by the cottagers and eventually inferring names and meaning. Like an infant acquiring language, the monster is able to pick it up a swift and natural manner. This isn't a person recollecting past memories, this is someone starting anew, someone thrown into the world with practically a blank slate.

Also important in the monster's candor is his implicit revealing of where his values came from. The monster notes how he would sympathize with the cottagers, feeling depressed when they were unhappy and sharing in their joys. He paid close attention to the relationships of the family lamenting very deeply his exclusion. Among the books the monster finds in the woods, *Paradise Lost* influenced him deeply as he takes it to be a historical narrative about creation. Although much more could be said about the monster constructing his system of values it seems that a large part of the monster's values are reducible to the cottagers and the books. So in building up some system of values the monster seems to enrich his psychological content that he has cultivated from scratch.

If we don't think of the monster as a new instance of a person then the monster is literally numerous people, which just sounds strange. If we really want to hold on to a strong version of the bodily criterion, saying we are constituted by our physical parts, we would have to admit that the monster shares a history with all his body parts, including his brain. If this were the case then we wouldn't expect the monster to exhibit behavior characteristic of someone starting from scratch, similar to an infant.

I really hope I've driven home the point that the monster's testimony is of coming to terms with the world and not simply of someone coming back into being after some gap in consciousness. In other words, the body parts that the monster happens to be made of do not determine his current identity. Taking the amnesia featured in the second set of examples seriously, the monster being a prime example of such amnesia really helps bring to light that there is some discontinuity in personhood. Whoever was in the monster's body before is not in there now and similarly whoever was in our body before the amnesia does not continue on to the pain experiments.

So What of the Monster?

After listening to the monster's testimony, we have to conclude that the monster is in some sense a person. At this point it may be helpful to unpack and spell out what exactly is meant by the psychological criterion. Though there is no consensus on this issue a fruitful attempt of spelling out what goes into the psychological criterion is:

1. Consciousness (of objects and events external or internal to the being), and in particular the capacity to feel pain
2. Reasoning (the *developed* capacity to solve new and relatively complex problems)
3. Self-motivated activity (activity which is relatively independent of either genetic or direct external control)
4. The capacity to communicate, by whatever means, messages of an indefinite variety of types, that is, not just with an indefinite number of possible contents, but on indefinitely many possible topics

5. The presence of self-concepts, and self-awareness, either individual or racial, or both.

Under these conditions, it seems as if we should accept the monster as a person with his own (possibly new) identity. Arguably, the monster gains consciousness from the moment Victor Frankenstein "infused a spark of life into a lifeless thing." The monster then proceeds to develop his reasoning faculties as well as his capacity to communicate during his time with the cottagers.

Although it's very briefly outlined, the monster definitely has self-awareness as he makes constant comparisons between what he describes as the "perfect forms" of the cottagers and his disfigured self. Now self-motivated, as defined above, might be interpreted as some degree of freewill, which is a contentious subject in philosophical circles to say the least. Without committing myself to saying whether the monster has freewill, I'll simply say that the monster has some appreciable amount of what we can call self-motivated activity. So it looks as if the monster can be considered to have his own identity, despite the amnesia problem. As to when exactly he attained-personhood, it can only have been at some point in his hovel.

Overall, the monster's identity seems rooted in both his psychological contents (his memories and thoughts) and his physical makeup. By now it does look as if the monster is a new instance of a person, at least not identical to whomever owned the body parts at some previous time. The monster starts his identity in Victor's lab and doesn't share a history with any of his previous body parts. But at the same time I guess it's important to recognize the role the physical body plays in the monster's identity since it is at least necessary for him to build an identity in the first place. After all, what is Victor infusing life into if not a body, regardless of how gruesome it may be? But again, this casts the body as secondary to what is truly important to identity, as we saw how the monster came to build one for himself despite being given an improvised body, really a very crappy hardware system upon which to load a software.

While this may be all well and good for the monster does it tell us anything about what makes up our identity? While we wouldn't expect to suffer from the same kind of amnesia discussed here there are plenty of other ways our psychological content can be damaged. Short of actual brain damage some of us might suffer a few concussions throughout our lives, perhaps be struck with dementia, or even kill a few hundred brain cells after a night of too much drinking. It just seems absurd to say I'm not going to be identical with the person who's suffering a hangover.

Surely we need an approach that doesn't tell us we're different people with the most minimal of change in our psychological content. And actually this view does a good job at capturing those intuitions because it's perfectly alright to have different psychological contents across time just as long as it's the same prevailing stream of consciousness.

I'd still be identical to myself if I forgot the name of a casual acquaintance but not if I could remember none of my loved ones. The *amnesia* discussed previously is more serious than some of the neurodegenerative diseases we may be more familiar with but both still attack our psychological contents, which we've taken to be intimately related to our identity. While we may or may not be able to suffer anything similar to the *amnesia* discussed here, I think we're safe in donating our bodies to science knowing full well we won't wake up in a Victor Frankenstein type experiment at a later date.

15
I'm the *Person, You're* the *Monster*

NICOLAS MICHAUD

Monster, Murderer, Fiend, Demon . . . whatever you may call it, Victor Frankenstein's creation is dark and scary. . . . There seems to be little human about it, especially in many movie versions.

As time has passed, the creature has devolved from a rational, feeling thing into a lumbering monstrosity with little intellect and a thirst for violence. Here and there, though, a version of Mary Shelley's tale comes up that is far more in line with Shelley's vision. In *I, Frankenstein*, for example, the monster acts to defend humanity from *other* monsters. But even there, the monster as hero still must hide his true self from humanity—because he knows we loathe him. And I think he's wise to do so, because no matter how smart, good, kind, or forgiving the monster is, to us, he will never be a person.

Reading through the chapters of this book we find many ways of looking at the monster and understanding its actions. But when we're honest with ourselves, we know that it's just too different a *thing* for us to ever really accept it into our community. That's what it means to be a person; it means to be someone that the rest of the community respects and acknowledges as one of their own. And, when we look at human beings, we see that we are very, very, bad at accepting anyone different from ourselves. Frankenstein's creation, like many others who we treat as disabled, disfigured, inferior, or as outsiders, is far more capable and deserving of respect than we want to admit. I think I can prove that Frankenstein's hideous creation is in fact a *person* . . . well, in every way other than the one that *really* counts—acceptance by the community.

I Am Content to Reason with You

What does it mean to be a person? In other words, what does it mean to have personhood? Of course, our immediate answer is, 'Being human!' We assume that being human makes us persons. But, if you think about it, you realize that really isn't true. There are things out there that are human—human corpses, for example—that we don't consider to be persons.

"Human" is a biological category, living or dead; *person* is a moral one. That's why it has been so much fun for human beings to define who *isn't* a person through history, whether slaves, women, or other minorities, we have seen governments, legislators, and whole societies decide that particular groups, though human, or human-ish, aren't people, and so they can be property. That's one way of looking at personhood . . . if you are a person, then you can't be property . . . well, until you're dead, anyway. But full-fledged personhood probably means something like, "Member of the moral community"—someone to whom we grant rights, respect and dignity . . . they can't be owned, and they shouldn't be degraded or destroyed.

So determining who gets to count as a person tends to be more a matter of consensus. And often this is deeply problematic for minority groups and those whom we deem "disabled," "disfigured," or "Other." Like Frankenstein's malevolent creation, many individuals who think of themselves as feeling, thinking entities are treated by the rest of society as things to be owned or destroyed on a whim. If we are to be fair, though, we shouldn't just pick who is a person and who isn't based on what benefits us the most, or whoever we like the most at the time. We should avoid just deciding that we (our group) are people, and anything that is different isn't.

When we do that, we get to enslave or destroy anything or anyone we think is too different. We know how that has gone in the past; that way of thinking tends to lead to a great deal of evil. In fact, those evils occasionally come back to do the oppressor harm when we find ourselves, like Victor Frankenstein, unable to stop the violence that we initiated through our hate and lack of inclusion. So what is a fair way to decide what counts as a person—to decide what and who should count as a member of our moral community?

I Ought to Be Thy Adam, but I Am Rather the Fallen Angel

Immanuel Kant (1724–1804) thought one way to deal with the problem was by using the criterion of "rationality" to determine what counts as a person and what doesn't. The ability to think and solve problems, then, would be what makes you count as a person. Your corpse (under most circumstances, it seems) can't think, so it's not a person. Many aliens, vampires, and even the Monster would also count as persons. Kant thought that we should have respect for rationality, regardless of where we found it. So you might find that even your computer is deserving of some respect.

That idea, though, has some weaknesses. It almost sounds as if we're saying the smarter someone is, the more worthy of respect they are. But there are many individuals—children and the developmentally impaired, for example—whom we should treat as part of our moral community, regardless of any inability to rationalize. If anything, these people are a "vulnerable population" to whom we *owe* more concern because we can easily harm or take advantage of them. Very smart people, like Victor, on the other hand, can be very cruel and do evil things. So rationality doesn't seem, at least by itself, to be the best way to determine who counts as a person and who doesn't.

Philosopher Mary Anne Warren (1946–2010) argues that if we are fair, there are five qualities that, if something has them, we should treat that something with respect—even a "monster": 1. consciousness, 2. reasoning, 3. self-motivated activity, 4. the capacity to communicate, and 5. the presence of self-concepts.[1] Warren doesn't think that you have to have all of these qualities to count as a person, but a combination of some of them is necessary. #1 and #3 are especially important. So, for example, if Victor created a monster that had consciousness and self-motivated activity, then, even if it could not communicate, she would argue that it should have rights.

Notice that Frankenstein's monster, given Warren's criteria, certainly would count as a person. Shelley's version and the *I, Frankenstein* version of the creature both have rationality and

---

[1] Mary Anne Warren, "On the Moral and Legal Status of Abortion," *Monist* 57:1 (1973).

so Kant also would assert that, even though it is comprised of dead flesh, hideous, and a murderer, the monster is, in fact, a person. Given the fact that it is entirely made of human parts, the case is even easier. Although the monster didn't come into existence in the way most humans do, it certainly has human DNA (likely many humans' DNA). But of real importance, though, is *who* the monster is rather than *what* it is. Who the creature is certainly seems to be a deeply thinking somebody. Through the course of Shelley's work we see the monster grow from being unable to communicate or read to being able to understand and quote Milton's *Paradise Lost* and master numerous languages.

In the graphic novel version of *I, Frankenstein*, we can read the monster's thoughts. So we know he is 1. conscious. He solves crimes and comes to conclusions, so we know he is 2. reasoning. He goes about trying to stop harm done to humans, so he seems to act from 3. self-motivated activity. He uses 4. language to communicate with humans (and other monsters). And the work is called *I, Frankenstein*, which is a pretty good hint to the fact that the monster thinks of himself as an "I." Therefore, he has 5. self-concepts. Given all of this, the monster meets *all* of Warren's criteria.

Similarly, we are able to get into Mary Shelley's monster's head through his detailed story-telling. Either version of the monster seems to meet both Kant's and Warren's criteria. You might say that the movie versions do not, but I'm not convinced. Perhaps the monster can only grunt for the most part, but we see him *try* to communicate. We see him even reason a bit when he thinks the little girl will float like a flower (unfortunately for the little girl). And he certainly seems to have at least a level of self-motivated activity. So he may not be the brightest light in the lab, but does that mean he should be treated not at all like a person and destroyed at our whims?

In fact, given most of the *Frankenstein* narratives, there is a very good reason why the monster turns to evil . . . *us*. We might argue that the monster should not be considered a person because he is a murderer. But think about it: to be a murderer, *he has to be a person*. In other words, if the monster's murders are just random acts, mindless acts, or mechanical acts, then they aren't evil. They're just accidental and the monster has to be stopped in the same way that a runaway locomotive must be stopped. But you wouldn't say a locomotive that goes off its tracks is evil any more so than the monster is evil if it doesn't understand or do what it does purposefully.

But with Victor's creation, we think of the monster as a murderer . . . maybe even someone who enjoys killing. Certainly, in Shelley's story, the monster is very purposeful about his acts of violence. He does what he does because of his creator's cruelty, because the whole of humanity hates him and casts him out. And so he decides that if he cannot indulge in love, then he will indulge in another passion . . . hate. In other words, in order to argue that the monster is evil due to his being a murderer, we must accept that he has some level of personhood.

The real irony, then, is that we think he should be destroyed, which is generally not something you do to a person. This is a real problem in any execution scenario . . . if by executing someone, we're saying, "He's not really a person; he's just a murderous monster," then we are executing a non-person which seems to imply he's a *thing*, and thereby unable to understand his acts . . . and if he can't understand his acts, then killing him seems an extreme punishment! In order for any monster, human or otherwise, to fall from grace, to be really blameworthy for his acts, it must be a person. And so, perhaps we should at least name the monster who is so worthy of execution. Let's call him Adam.

If I Cannot Satisfy the One, I Will Indulge the Other

Adam is an "Other." Otherness generally refers to the way we push someone or something outside of our group. Generally, these groups are arbitrary. In other words, there is no real logical reason for our groups; they are pretty baseless. Whether deciding that someone is an "Other" because of the color of her or his skin, gender, religion, sex, or nationality, you'll find that we almost always treat someone else as an "Other" in order to benefit ourselves. And, of course, the Other is basically just a way of saying "not a *real* person."

Adam is a beautiful example of our capacity for Othering. He brings to mind so many forms of exclusion, oppression, and marginalization, it is difficult to figure out which group he represents. Women, Blacks, homosexuals, as well as many other groups have been, and often still are, treated as Others. Heck, even Artificial Intelligence and non-human animals are groups of entities that likely don't want to be treated as property or as "the Other" but we will gladly do so as long as we can (until they rise up and slay us).

Notice how hard it is for any group that is treated as an Other to gain equal treatment. Blacks literally had to fight for it, women have been repressed for millennia (we often forget that they got the right to vote *after* Blacks in the U.S.A.), and the gay community is in the midst of a tumultuous civil rights struggle as I write this chapter. It is likely that we will never stop torturing non-human animals because it is more convenient to think of them as tasty treats, and "artificial" intelligence . . . well, that creation will be one that can stop us, and like Victor's very angry creation, will likely decide to put a stop to the creator's evil.

Why do I say evil? Because I think that the philosopher Martha Nussbaum is right to point out that rights, kind of like personhood, are something that is granted to us by someone else. Whether they are rights that are given to us by a government or by God, it is pretty hard to claim that you are born with rights unless someone else recognizes that you have them. However, she argues that pretty much everyone is born with certain *capabilities*. In other words, most humans are born with the capability to (by a certain rational age) vote. However, it is the rest of society that decides whether or not you have that opportunity. In other words, it is society that decides whether or not you get to fulfill that capability. If society decides that—as we have done in the case of many, *many* minorities—you can't vote, you are unlikely to *flourish*. To Nussbaum, "flourishing" means more than just living; it means being able to live a full and happy life.

Nussbaum thought, in fact, that there were ten capabilities that we need to flourish.[2] And, I think, Adam has these capabilities:

1. **Life—the ability to live to the end of a life of normal length.**

[2] Martha Nussbaum and Amartya Sen, *The Quality of Life* (Clarendon, 1993).

2. **Bodily health—the ability to have good health.**
3. **Bodily integrity—the ability to be secure from violence and move as we choose.**
4. **Senses, imagination, and thought—the ability to use the sense, to imagine, think, and reason.**
5. **Emotions—the ability to have attachments to things and people outside ourselves.**
6. **Practical reason—the ability to engage in critical reflection.**
7. **Affiliation—the ability to live with others and have self-respect.**
8. **Other species—the ability to live with concern for animals, plans, and nature.**
9. **Play—the ability to enjoy recreational activities.**
10. **Control over one's environment—the ability to participate in politics and hold property.**

Nussbaum is not arguing that you need these *to be a person*, but that if someone has any of these, we probably should let them fulfill those capabilities as long as it doesn't interfere with the capabilities of others. From what I can tell, Adam, in every film and printed version of this story, has all of these capabilities to some degree or another. In some cases, as in Shelley's novel and in *I, Frankenstein,* he has them to a greater degree than some human beings. Well, what is a monster or a man to do when someone interferes with those capabilities? Wouldn't you fight against someone who tried to prevent you from fulfilling your capabilities—especially, say, *Life*? Is Adam really wrong to try to harm humanity? Hasn't humanity become an Other to him, by virtue of our trying to prevent him not just from flourishing, but from even existing?

There Is Rage in Me the Likes of Which Should Never Escape

We are speciesists. It seems to me that human beings have decided that the only things that should ever have rights are human beings. And then, we tend to restrict rights and kind treatment to the species we like. As a result, if something is too different from us, like Adam, we feel no concern when denying their capabilities. Certainly we feel that way about non-human animals. We torture them inside of factory farms that make Victor Frankenstein's corpse-riddled laboratory look like Santa's happy cottage. But that doesn't bother us. To quote another contemporary philosopher, Tom Regan:

> There are those who resist the idea that animals have inherent value. 'Only humans have such value,' they profess. How might this narrow view be defended? Shall we say that only humans have the requisite intelligence, or autonomy, or reason? But there are many, many humans who fail to meet these standards and yet are reasonably viewed as having value beyond their usefulness to others. Shall we claim that only humans belong to the right species, the species *Homo sapiens*? But this is blatant speciesism. (*The Case for Animal Rights*, University of California Press, 2004)

Really, if we think about it, the only reason why we think it's okay to kill non-human animals is because they aren't as smart as us and because they aren't strong enough to stop us. In other words, we've decided that they are inferior, and therefore not persons.

Now, I think the really interesting question is not whether or not we should treat Adam as a person but whether or not he should treat *us* as persons! Both the monster in Mary Shelley's *Frankenstein* and the one in *I, Frankenstein* are stronger than human beings. Shelley's monster is scarily fast, and he is *very* smart. He learns multiple languages, and he masters them; his prose is beautiful. So given our own logic, what reasons can we give Adam to be merciful? If being smarter and stronger is sufficient reason to subjugate others, then why should we not be subjugated? I bet we would appeal to criteria like Warren's and Nussbaum's. But aren't those the same criteria that Adam can meet?

Imagine that Adam corners you, Victor Frankenstein; he is towering and terrifying. His rage, emanating from his hulking body, seems to melt the snow around him. What possible reason could you give to him that he should not eliminate you, as well as all humans? Remember, Adam is not just denied personhood by Victor, despite his intellect, power, and capability; he learns about human evils through his studies of human history and Volney's *Ruin of Empires*. (Not to mention his rejection at the hands of cottagers *whom he was helping*). Despite all of his abilities, he was treated as one who was *dis*-abled. And what was the "disability"? Only the fact that he wasn't human enough.

Adam's hideous visage did nothing to reduce any of his physical or mental capabilities. Disability, it seems, has more to do with *who* we decide is unable rather than some supposedly objective criteria. Despite his physical and mental superiority, Adam laments,

> I was, besides, endued with a figure hideously deformed and loathsome; I was not even of the same nature as man. I was more agile than they, and could subsist upon coarser diet; I bore the extremes of heat and cold with less injury to my frame; my stature far exceeded theirs. When I looked around, I saw and heard of none like me. Was I then a monster, a blot upon the earth, from which all men fled, and whom all men disowned?

And, Victor's answer to Adam's question, *our* answer, is "yes." He is denied personhood. Like all those who we decide are too disabled, insufficiently human, insufficiently wealthy, insufficiently like us, he is cast out as the monstrous Other. And, tragically, unlike many of the Others we create, there was no one else like him, no one for whom he could be a person. Adam is an Other . . . even to himself. He cannot find hope in humanity or its history.

Adam despairs when studying humans through our literature. He is amazed by us, and abhorred:

> These wonderful narrations inspired me with strange feelings. Was man, indeed, at once so powerful, so virtuous, and magnificent, yet so vicious and base? He appeared at one time a mere scion of the evil principle and at another as all that can be conceived of noble and godlike.

Through our narratives he learns a great deal of what it means to be someone who we decide is insufficient or disabled. We choose those whom to ostracize, despite all of their other capabilities, because we create a category for entities who, *no matter what else there is to them*, they just aren't enough like us to count as part of the moral community. Adam weeps for the Indian other: "I heard of the discovery of the American hemisphere, and wept with Safie over the hapless fate of its original inhabitants."

He knows what fearful violence we will bring upon those who we can, and we will justify it by refusing to grant them personhood. I am not convinced that the creature's best reason for violence was the individual harm he suffered at Victor's hands, but instead the realization, given our history, that he will never be accepted, nor will any of his kin . . . all those who we decide are disabled, inferior, or foreign Others.

16
What Love Means to a Creature

MIRKO D. GARASIC

If you're a fan of *Frankenstein*, you can't have missed (and if you did you should try to catch it as soon as possible) Tim Burton's animated movie *Frankenweenie*. Genius that he is, Burton's rethink of the *Frankenstein* tale has a number of witty and perceptive elements (accompanied by some hilarious cameos such as the tomb of "Good-bye Kitty" addressing the popular brand).

One of the tributes that Burton skillfully pays to Mary Shelley's novel is his use of electricity and kites, with its obvious reference to Benjamin Franklin. But the electricity connection to *Frankenstein* is also very strong, in more than just the "animate the dead" kind of a way.

The connection between the two can be found in the subtitle of Mary Shelley's novel. Shelley seriously considered calling her novel "The Modern Prometheus" but instead that became the subtitle. And it's through that subtitle that we can discover what love means to a monster.

The Ancient Frankenstein

In the old Greek tale, Prometheus is the wisest of all the Titans. He brings mankind technical knowledge and enlightenment through the gift of fire, stolen from the gods.

Plato tells us that, after having created animals from earth and fire, the Greek gods asked Prometheus and Epimetheus to equip each of them with appropriate qualities. To avoid the extinction of any of the animals, Epimetheus gave quickness, strength, wings, and other powers to each species. However, not being very wise, he distributes those qualities carelessly and when he reaches humans, he has nothing left to give them. To make up for this, Prometheus decides to give humans fire and the technical arts, which he has to steal from the gods.

For this blasphemy, Zeus punishes him horribly: Prometheus is chained to a rock and every day an eagle tears out his liver and eats it. Every night his liver grows back and the cycle repeats. Because he is immortal, Prometheus is damned to suffer this dreadful punishment for all of eternity. Fortunately, he is eventually spared this suffering by Hercules.

Prometheus cared so much for humankind that he suffered horribly to help us. He loved humanity and would have liked to provide us with the political wisdom we needed, but unfortunately, this was out of his reach. And so human beings sadly remained unable to co-operate properly as a society. After some attempts to come together for safety in cities, humans returned to isolation because they were treating each other too badly to co-exist. Although the technical abilities to progress as a society were within their reach, the absence of the capacity to co-ordinate their actions made co-existence a hopeless dream, or so the myths suggest.

The Modern Prometheus

The parallel between Prometheus and Victor Frankenstein is clear in the painful consequences suffered by both and in their quests for technological advancement. Although moved by different goals, the Ancient Prometheus and the Modern one (Victor) link their names and their lives to the power of electricity—be it in the form of fire or that of electric current. Both create new life and both suffer, but Victor's sentence seems to be even worse than that of Prometheus due to the fact that he's not at peace with himself. Prometheus at least knew he had done the right thing.

Immediately after bringing the creature to life, Victor is disgusted with the result. His self-loathing increases significantly as time passes because, having already behaved wrongly, he further degrades his moral character by indulging in hate rather than love. Everyone dear to Victor dies, killed by the very creature he created but was never able nor willing to love for what it was.

Despite Prometheus's gift, humans were still too busy fighting each other to create a workable society. Moved by the incapacity of his creation to co-operate harmoniously, and fearing the extinction of humanity, Zeus eventually sent the god Hermes into the cities to confer justice and reverence upon people, so that humanity would prosper through the implementation of virtue. Hermes himself wasn't sure how such things should be given to human beings, should he follow the same system used to distribute the technical arts and favor only a few, or should he adopt a different method? So he asked Zeus:

> "Shall this [the distribution of the arts] be the manner in which I am to distribute justice and reverence among men, or shall I give them to all?" "To all," said Zeus; "I should like them all to have a share; for cities cannot exist, if a few only share in the virtues, as in the arts. And further, make a law by my order, that he who has no part in reverence and justice shall be put to death, for he is a plague of the state." (*Protagoras*, http://classics.mit.edu/Plato/protagoras.html)

Plato expands on Zeus's idea, and agrees that, while in the case of technical arts, Athenians—as well as humanity at large—are reluctant to hear the opinion of anyone but accredited experts in the field (be it a master chef or an architect), when discussing politics this attitude changes. When deliberating about political virtue, the very use of justice and wisdom *requires* the involvement of the community. He continues, explaining that Athenians or humans "think that every man ought to share in this sort of virtue, and that states could not exist if this were otherwise."

If we are to rise again from the political impasse of our time we must keep in mind this important message contained in *Frankenstein* through the re-use of the Promethean tale: *no matter how advanced our knowledge can become, nor how good our intentions are, scientific progress alone is not sufficient to guarantee a better society.* We need to find the just and *right* way of dealing with progress through the interaction with others.

Liquid Modernity

Zygmunt Bauman claims that, in this late modern era, we have moved away from a "heavy" and "solid" modernity (focused on hardware), to a "light" and "liquid" version of modernity (based instead on software).[1] In the "liquid modernity" described by Bauman, the individual is detached from some of the communal characteristics that make us a social animal. The different, the foreigner, the outsider (the "other" like Victor's creature) are all seen as a threat and, consequently, in our post-modern society we have lost trust in the community as well as the ability to rely on others to achieve greater goods. According to Bauman, society today exalts the affirmation of the individual, but only in theory. In practice, we are more alone than ever. Post-modernity has led us to become so individual-centered that we now resemble many different forms of being a Frankenstein.

Victor Frankenstein thinks that his own self-imposed isolation will bring him closer to humanity. We are now often in the same room as our loved ones, ignoring them while supposedly having improved our means of communication with the rest of the world via texts and social networking. What's even more striking when comparing our society with Shelley's novel, is the fact that *unlike* Victor (and so we may be even worse off) we are not putting our hands directly on the world we're trying to create.

Today if we need something fixed, we usually don't know how to fix it ourselves, so we call someone else to fix it. We don't really have to interact with the things, or people, surrounding us. We walk into the store, wave vaguely at a clerk who utters the same required words to every customer, and lurch, creature-like, towards the stuff we want, ignoring the others, and offering reflexive thanks to the cashier who has already moved on to the next "person" as we check out.

Bauman provides us with a new picture of what it means to be a human being in the Western post-modern world. Although we're surely more connected with the rest of the global community by technological means that were unthinkable until a few decades ago (Skype, Facebook, and the Internet in general), we have also given up on features that defined our interactions with other human beings as a way of expressing our individual preferences. One result is the dramatic fall in the birth rate. We aren't willing to dedicate as much time, effort, and connected-

---

[1] Zygmunt Bauman, *Liquid Modernity* (Polity, 2000).

ness as previous generations to another human being who jeopardizes our "freedom to be detached from all others."

This disconnectedness from others sooner or later catches up with us, and creates a deep discomfort produced by the awareness that, somewhere along the road, we have lost part of our identity. To fulfill our potential requires the interaction, the involvement with *the other*. To deny this is to deny what Victor's creature understood very well in a very instinctive manner.

Love and Hate

Prometheus's character is moved by two driving forces: the first one—most often stressed—is indeed his striving to gain technological and scientific knowledge. In itself, this might be a noble ambition, but it can easily turn into a search for power that blinds the initial goodwill. The resulting price paid by Prometheus (with his liver eaten by the eagle every day forever) and Victor Frankenstein (with his inability to stop his creature from destroying his life) represents the failure that we're bound to face if we are to follow our desire to overcome nature and change the order of things through science. This is a form of intellectual egoism: we love to prove to the world how smart we are for the sake of it, not out of actual necessity. But, there's a second force that is present in the original Prometheus story as well as in *Frankenstein*: love.

Due to our contemporary focus on "Frankenstein" as a synonym for "monster," we often forget that the emotion of love is central to Mary Shelley's novel[2] as it was for the original Greek myth. Prometheus ends up suffering eternal damnation specifically *because* he loves the humans he made out of clay. It's his concern with the unfairness of letting humans enter into the world without any of the appropriate qualities necessary to survive that pushes him to steal the secret of fire from the gods.

After rejection by his creator, which produced different forms of hate on both sides, the creature seeks love and asks

---

[2] According to a recent study that confronts two versions of the novel, it seems that the role of Mary Shelley's husband was much more substantial than that of a muse: this added "humanity" given to Frankenstein appears to be ascribed directly to Percy Shelley. See: *The Original Frankenstein*, by Mary Shelley with Percy Shelley, edited by Charles E. Robinson (Vintage, 2009).

Victor to create a female with whom he would finally have a chance for happiness, promising to leave and disappear forever. But Victor is incapable of doing this because he fears creating a "monstrous race" and—blinded by his hate for the creature—he destroys the unfinished female partner in front of the creature's eyes. This produces a second wave of hatred that will eventually end in the death of both.

This dualism between love and hate fits perfectly well with contemporary society. We use technology to achieve higher and faster results at work, but we do not seem to win any of that time back. On the contrary, we are constantly pushed towards accepting to lower our expectations of what we can be guaranteed as workers. Our flexibility is supposedly beneficial for the overall enterprise of the economy, but it does not help our human interaction.

We must not make the same mistake as Victor, and sacrifice all the beautiful things in our lives for the sake of destroying an external entity because it does not meet our standard of *right enough*. Firstly, we miss out on what we have (recall that if Victor didn't so stubbornly keep trying to kill the creature, he would not have lost *all* of his dear ones). In our case, we would be advised to consider a standard of "good enough": if we're obsessed with having more endlessly, we'll never be happy. A natural boundary for this excess has been historically represented by the community.

A parent, for example, might care more about preserving the environment once he or she has produced a child, because a better world is better for the child. The parent is now ready to enter a different phase of interpretation of the Promethean tale: giving up one's comfort and commodities for the sake of justice and love. Prometheus was ready to give up his own comfort and life for something not directly related to him, we too face such a challenge.

Good and Bad Science in *Frankenweenie*

In *Frankenweenie*, the dualism between love and hate present in *Frankenstein* is more neatly divided. The dimension of love is romantically represented by the tear that the young Victor drops on his dog (note the dog's exquisite self-referring name that links fire and electricity—Sparky!).

The counterbalancing emotion of hate (constantly present in Shelley's novel as well) is external to the main character, rather than *in* the young Victor: it is the surrounding society that is hate-filled. His frustrated and jealous classmates are obsessed with winning the first prize for the science project. The mayor is focused only on more power and incapable of loving his niece for what she is. And the community (including Victor's parents) are unwilling to accept the fact that Sparky might still be morally good although half-dead.

The one person capable of understanding the limits that we should impose to scientific research, is the very unconventional—and yet deeply committed—science teacher Mr. Rzykruski. Not surprisingly, given our natural tendency to exclude the unknown, he ends up being expelled from the school for providing the children with "too much knowledge." Before leaving the school, though, Rzykruski speaks with the young Victor, urging him to become a scientist, but not lightheartedly. Science is often thought to be related only to our rational side, but that's not so: we need to remain in contact with our emotions and our human nature in a more complete and loving sense.

Love is why the experiment with Sparky works while the others don't. In direct contrast with the original character of Shelley's novel, here the young Victor is moved by love, rather than by pride and arrogance. The way in which Burton portrays the boundaries of science deserves particular attention now, as we are enter a phase of human history where certain technological innovations could cause a permanent change, for better or worse. Genetic engineering, human cloning, and other science-fiction dreams are not far away, and we must guide our progress.

We don't have to fear science in itself, but science doesn't tell us the meaning of life. In the original novel, the creature gradually deprives Victor Frankenstein of his loved ones, and ultimately kills him. It is only then, when he is completely alone, that the creature realizes that killing his maker does not cure his alienation. His unhappiness, in fact, increases because his only real link with others—as well as his only hope to have someone like himself to love—has disappeared, leaving him alone.

Burton's *Frankenweenie* splits the themes of love and hate (and of good and bad science), through the parallel monsters created by the young Victor's classmates at the end of the movie. Unlike Sparky—who remains pretty much the same aside from some holes here and there and the flies buzzing around him—all those monsters are hybrid creatures that represent a deformed version of the initial animal meant to be rescued from death. In the case of the hybrids, the passion is present (all Victor's classmates want to win the first prize), but it is greed for power and fame, not love. And those are characteristics that—when taken to the extreme—represent a confronting attitude towards society. Being in constant competition with everyone is likely to leave you alone. Similarly, if the obsession to achieve personal glory becomes more important than ensuring a decent quality of life, things are likely to go very poorly indeed.

Love bonds are those that form communities, and lead us to experience happy lives together. Had Shelley's Victor been willing to love his creation, the story might have been a happier one, like *Frankenweenie*. And, we (despite our insistence that we're better off alone) *need* other people. And this is so, not just to produce the things we want and like, but—more important still—to give our lives meaning and purpose.

This is shown in the parallel love story of Victor and Elsa and their respective dogs, Sparky and Persephone. Even with this peripheral character, Burton is able to provide valuable links to both cinema (Persephone's post-electric shock hairstyle is a delicate reference to the film *Bride of Frankenstein*), and that ancient world to which Shelley constantly refers: the very name used is that of another forced lover in ancient Greek mythology—Persephone, the woman who was stolen by Hades to become the queen of the underworld, the kingdom of dead people (and dogs I guess!).

From Frankenstein with Love

In contrast to *Frankenstein*, *Frankenweenie* has a happy ending and finishes with the whole community of New Holland—including the formerly xenophobic mayor stripped of his prejudices through exposure to evidence—joining in the admirable effort of providing Victor with sufficient electricity to bring Sparky back to life for a second time. It's a very romantic ending that leaves us with some room for hope.

We do unfortunately live in a world full of homophobia, Islamophobia, racism, and sexism, but unlike Victor's creature, we can overcome prejudices from within society while he was excluded from even engaging in a discussion. So, if we care about a better world, we should consider Prometheus's dream and direct society toward a solid modernity rather than a liquid one. If we don't act quickly we might find ourselves, like Victor Frankenstein, and his unfortunate creation, alone and out of time.[3]

[3] I am particularly grateful to Aakash Singh Rathore and Daniel Halliday for their help and advice during the revision of the chapter. Agnes Lyu and Minh Dinh also deserve my gratitude for their support.

17
Getting Inside the Monster's Head

SPYROS PETROUNAKOS

As a work of literature or film, *Frankenstein* has been more about the famous monster than about its creator. Whenever the spotlight *has* fallen on the creator, Victor Frankenstein, it has often been as a cautionary tale of manic scientific ambition, curiosity, or the spooky attempt "to create a man after his own image," as Dr. Frankenstein says in James Whale's 1931 movie *Frankenstein*. Yet some of the story's adaptations have focused on the fascinating duality between the monster's external appearance and its personal, inner life.

That much makes sense, as duality is one of the main themes of the tale in Shelley's *Frankenstein*. One main duality is, on the one hand, between the inner lives of its two main characters, Victor Frankenstein and the monster, and, on the other, the outer events surrounding them. Itself a story within a story, *Frankenstein* switches between long stretches of introspection—the second "reality" within with minds of the characters—and the detailed descriptions of external places and people.

At the core of this narration is one of the most striking reversals that became a standard in writing and cinema, in many instances giving rise to a filmic fascination with the living dead, most recently with *I, Frankenstein*, the film adaptation of the graphic novel. This is the reversal from death to life represented by Victor Frankenstein's experiment, his single-minded pursuit of "bestowing animation upon lifeless matter," a phrase that appears more than once in Shelley's book. This experiment makes the work stand out within the theme of mad scientists creating life out of inanimate matter.

It also establishes it as a work that contains a variety of philosophical themes. The phrase itself, "bestowing animation on matter," comes very close to contemporary versions of the question, "How is the brain capable of consciousness?" In the words of one prominent philosopher, Colin McGinn, the problem of consciousness asks, "How can technicolor phenomenology arise from the soggy grey matter of brains?"[1] In other words how can our vivid personal experiences come from the sloppy grey mass of our brains?

The problem of consciousness, or of how we understand the mind, has also experienced various reversals, most notably in the work of philosopher Gilbert Ryle (1900–1976). The sort of reversal Ryle proposed brings to mind the visually stunning moment of the monster's creation in the 1910 film production of *Frankenstein* by J. Searle Dawley. This is a striking scene because the moment of creation, itself, is an act of directorial genius that reflects the theme of reverse creation from death to life: The monster appears to come into being from nothingness because the scene of the burning effigy is played backwards. In this example of striking inventiveness, given the fact that there were no special effects at the time it was shot, flames and smoke return to their point of origin to become the monster's flesh.

Parallel Lives

As a narrative, the book *Frankenstein* has at least one additional dimension compared to the movie. This is the dimension of the rich inner life of Victor. Frankenstein, which initially appears as passionate scientific ambition and then, almost halfway through the work, becomes a descent into a personal inferno of remorse. In both cases, the narrative that describes the external world in great natural detail runs parallel with the description of the turmoil within Dr. Frankenstein's psyche. Often, events in the natural environment surrounding the main character become a mere backdrop, as Victor Frankenstein ponders the monstrosity of his experiment, its consequences and, during a particular scene in the middle of Lake Geneva, suicide.

---

[1] Colin McGinn, *The Problem of Consciousness* (Basil Blackwell, 1991), p. 1.

The parallel descriptions of external reality and internal reality often converge onto the single point of Frankenstein's perspective. This is a work that celebrates the fullness of its characters' internal lives, which are described like internal universes that converge almost by accident. This idea of the mental as a world in itself belongs to the tradition that goes back to the work of René Descartes (1596–1650). According to Descartes's picture of the mind, our minds are distinct worlds that contain thoughts and feelings that can be fully observed only by us. Moreover, in the full version of Descartes's picture of the mind, we live our lives primarily from the inside out.

As a narrative, Frankenstein belongs to this Cartesian tradition of drawing attention to each person's own perception of the world. Its main character, Victor Frankenstein, conceives his project in the solitude of his own mind, which then becomes the stage of a personal nightmare of regret. In this sense, what leads him to an inspired experiment then becomes a prison he cannot escape from. The book's other characters, protagonists and narrators also strain under the weight of their own thoughts, scruples and disappointments. Telling stories and confessing their misdeeds appear to be their only pressure valves.

The Inward Gaze

The story's ebb and flow is a combination of real events and the moral minefield that results from the monster's creation. Once we go down the linear track of the story that leads to the monster's moment of creation, the narrative breaks up and proceeds along different paths. Victor Frankenstein is tormented but also appears to have plunged into a personal purgatory. His abhorrence and revulsion at his creation is transformed into a physical illness, a transitory madness, which lasts for months and nearly claims his life.

His well-being after his long recovery is shattered once again by the news of his brother's death, an event that brings about his departure to Geneva. There he catches sight of the monster for the first time in two years. But the sighting itself is a relatively minor incident compared to the moral labyrinth ahead of him. As if to make things worse, the moral dilemmas spring from a cascade of events that allows him little room to collect his own thoughts. His sense of loss and disorientation in that part of the story is reflected and described in terms of his thoughts trying, but failing, to catch up with a reality that is always ahead of him. Victor is guilty of having created a dangerous monster. But he is also given an opportunity to atone for this sin by becoming the savior of Justine who is falsely accused of a crime that, unbeknownst to everyone else, has been committed by his monster. But, though he knows the truth, he cannot set the record straight.

This is because the story of the creation of the monster is so outrageous that it is bound to lack credibility. He knows that no one will believe him and so what he says is bound to become the "ravings of a madman." Here, his only chance of release and atonement through a confession is lost. Victor is completely trapped in his inner world, which at this point has ceased to be believable to anyone else but himself. This is a form of double imprisonment: not only is he the only person who knows the truth; he is also in possession of a truth that he cannot communicate even if he tried.

But Victor Frankenstein's internal world is only one part of the story. From the second half of the book onwards we witness the internal life of the monster itself as it becomes humanized by daily observation of the De Lacey family in the cottage. Not unlike the ambitious Victor Frankenstein who's bent on revealing the secrets of nature, the monster is also driven to find "the cause of uneasiness" of the family it is observing and to "unravel" the "mystery" of how their language works. Reading these passages, we get a clear sense that the monster has been made in its creator's image. As we follow the internal dialogue of the monster's detailed observations of the family, we temporarily forget that its outward appearance could not be more different to its creator's. Yet these passages also inspire a sense of sympathy for the monster, its sincere attempts to come to grips with the world and to understand what makes humans tick.

On the Outside Looking In

Victor Frankenstein brings about moral change in the narrative in two ways: first, as the victim of circumstances and of his own single-minded pursuit of a project that goes terribly wrong. In a straightforward sense, as the creator of the monster himself, he's the prime mover of the story. But there's a second, equally interesting sense in which he brings about change. As a scientist with almost self-destructive ambition, he becomes a symbol of the search for a personal truth that puts moral considerations on the back burner.

In fact, from this perspective, the entire story is also an object lesson in the perils of this attitude: the monster is set loose, beyond its creator's control and initial calculation, to reap destruction. Its creator is unable to control it and, further, assumes little moral responsibility beyond acknowledging the ghastly nature of the beast he has set loose upon the world. After he recovers from his illness, Victor is relieved not to have to deal with the monster. It's only afterwards, when tragedy hits his own family, that the destructive nature of the beast begins to dawn on him. But even then, his moral sense and his internal dialogue detach themselves from his intention to act. We get the sense that he is swamped by his own thinking. Even when he considers suicide, he eventually reasons that he must stay alive to help his family find the real perpetrator of the crime.

The narrative's focus on the internal worlds of the characters is set during our initial meeting with Victor. The entire theme of the sections on his scientific ambitions is based on the idea of the two sides of reality and of genuine truths hiding behind the appearances of things. There, we find him drawing a distinction between the "outward substance of things" and the "inner spirit of nature," of entering "the citadel of knowledge," of "penetrating the secrets of nature." This sets out clearly the contrast between reality and its secrets, or between bodies and their inner mental lives, of two connected but also independent worlds that keep us guessing about what might lie on the other side.

The Private Life We Know Best

Descartes is known for his famous phrase "I think, therefore I am." This represents his response to an extreme form of skepticism, in which he doubts the existence of everything, including his own mind. The statement comes in the context of a thought experiment in which a malicious demon makes him doubt that the reality surrounding him is real. The thought experiment represents Descartes's way of reaching truth by a process of stepping back from the input of his senses, which he takes to be completely unreliable. His aim is to arrive at what he calls "clear and distinct" ideas. The process comes full circle in the realization that everything that the senses show us about the world can be doubted and that the only thing that cannot be doubted is that, right now, we're thinking.

But in contemporary philosophy of mind, Descartes's idea that the senses are an unreliable basis for knowledge is only part of his philosophical story. Another equally important idea attributed to him is the idea of an absolute distinction between mind and body. This in turn has led to what is often described as the Cartesian conception of the inner—the ability of each person to look into, or introspect, their inner life as a series of mental episodes, an internal theater available only to each person's internal gaze.

The main idea is that there is an inner private life that can be observed only by the person whose private life it is and only indirectly by other people. One result of this is that our inner life, in contrast to our access to the external world, becomes the field of absolute certainty. This works both ways: the more our thoughts, feelings and everything else in our mind set the standard of certainty, the greater our temptation to regard the external world as being full of things that might mislead us. The certainty with which we know *ourselves* ups the ante in another direction too because it means that others can know what goes on in us only indirectly, by trying to figure out the truth within us from our outward behavior.

A partition is set up between mind and world. The vividness of our personal world of thought and feeling often trumps the vividness of the external world around us. Descartes's idea of withdrawing from external reality to a single point inside the mind is very much alive in *Frankenstein*. It's at this single point, deep within the psyche, that Victor Frankenstein conceives his scientific experiment. It's also where he withdraws to when things take a turn for the worse.

One of the reasons for the persistence of Descartes's ideas through the ages is that they seem to make absolute sense of our daily experience. For example, it is in fact true that we can withdraw within our self in a way that might make us inaccessible to others and that thoughts and feelings are things that we may choose to reveal or conceal from others. Both these aspects of our inner lives support the Cartesian idea of the mind. It is also true that a great part of our everyday life is dedicated to trying, in one way or another, to make sense of other people.

It's equally true that we misread, misinterpret, misunderstand the thoughts and feelings of others, regardless of degree of familiarity. Here, if we accept the idea that what we're doing is trying to make sense, as if other people are enigmas, we are indirectly assuming that their thoughts and actions are hidden. And making sense from words and gestures is almost a daily task. To believe that in so doing we are trying to reach something within the person we are trying to interpret strengthens Descartes's conception.

It also seems true that whatever else we may doubt, the things we know most clearly are our own thoughts and feelings. We might even say that mind is indeed a world of its own by our mere everyday ability to sit still, immersed in thought or by the way our thoughts might hold us captive and make us temporarily unable to act. This is one of the reasons why Victor Frankenstein's struggle with his scruples and his bouts of temporary paralysis speak to us directly. His extreme predicament is eerily familiar to us, at least in the sort of intensity with which he experiences a type of imprisonment within his own self and his desire to find atonement and release. It's also why Descartes's thought experiment in which evil demons make him doubt every certainty also feels like familiar fiction in that it reminds us of the mind's ability to spin its own tales. But Descartes's experiment is also a direct reminder of Dr. Frankenstein himself in the opposite direction. The aim of the evil demon to make Descartes doubt everything that is certain is equally as outrageous as Dr. Frankenstein's project of putting life back into a corpse.

A Ghost within a Monster

The book's storyline takes another major plunge into the internal worlds of its characters when the monster tells its own story to its creator, Frankenstein. In describing his observation of the De Lacey family over a period of months, the monster also tells the story of its own gradual immersion in the ways of humans, and, most importantly, of how it came to understand human emotions and language. The description contains a detailed profile of the people the monster is observing, of their actions and interaction with each other and of their emotional states, which the monster gradually manages to decode.

This section establishes an ingenious symmetry between the Victor Frankenstein we have known "from within," as a man gripped by a scientific obsession, and the monster's own quest and insistence to understand its subjects. But here we see once again the emergence of the duality between the external and the internal realms, made particularly clear by the contrast between the monster's observation of the inhabitants of the cottage from a distance and its own internal dialogue, a sort of running commentary of its daily observations. Even more astonishingly, in a passage that also brings to mind the philosopher John Locke's dictum of ideas being either about objects in external reality or about what it calls "the internal operations of our minds," the monster describes in detail how it came to learn language.

The monster talks about the names that were given to the "familiar objects of discourse" such as fire, milk, and bread, and of the ideas "appropriated to each of these sounds." But then it also speaks of several other words, which, despite protracted observation, it could not yet understand how to apply: "good," "dearest," and "unhappy." What the monster cannot understand are terms that go beyond what is immediately obvious. But whether this should mean that they refer to hidden, or private events, is another matter.

The philosopher Gilbert Ryle was one of the most devastating critics of the Cartesian picture. He strongly opposed the idea that to understand these types of words we need to have direct access to the mental realm. The words that refer to our emotional life are not like objects in a room that we would need to see if we were learning the meanings of furniture-words. Ryle would be very happy with the passage that in Shelley's *Frankenstein* appears directly after the description of the monster's acquisition of language. In that passage, the monster says that it was able to respond directly to the joys and sorrows of the De Lacey family. It is this ability to respond directly to emotional states that is the basis for understanding words such as "unhappy." We understand other people's emotional states by observing their behavior and this is the basis for learning words that refer to emotions.

Turning the Head on Its Head

Ryle uses the metaphor of a walk for what allows us to understand language and the way words are connected to each other. According to Ryle, we learn language in the way that we reach a destination by walking—though we might not be able to describe the steps we took to get there. In contrast to Descartes, where everything seems to happen in the head, Ryle's idea is that to learn a language and how words are connected to each other we need to observe the "live force of things we actually say." Ryle turns the whole idea of how we learn a language on its head because he suggests that we learn a language not by learning what its words refer to but by exposing ourselves to it. It is a deep-end-of-the-pool method.

The idea is not immediately obvious and seems to go against our gut feeling that we learn the meaning of words by having things pointed out to us. Everyday practices and especially the way children learn seem to make Descartes's but not Ryle's ideas obvious. But coming to understand an approach like Ryle's is not a matter of delving in the depths of a particular theory. Rather, it's a matter of pointing to the things we actually do in the course of our daily lives—to the practices that we already engage in. Ryle's account draws our attention to these in an attempt to draw us away from the idea of private inner lives. He redirects our attention away from theoretical and technical complexities and towards what is already available in plain sight. The way he sees it, the Cartesian picture of an inner world of mental objects ignores the immediacy with which we respond to each other. When we react to people's feelings, for example, we do so immediately, without needing first to know what actually lies hidden in their heads.

What he proposes is a reversal of the way we think about the mental. To understand how we learn a language we should not look inwardly, but outwardly and draw connections between the different terms, much as we would understand how to play a game by understanding what each piece does and how it combines with the other pieces. Ryle attacks what he calls the "ghost in the machine," his way of describing the Cartesian mind as a place in which feelings occur secretly and privately.

The feeling that, despite its initial appeal, there is something wrong with Descartes's idea of a sharp distinction between the inner and outer realms becomes apparent if we consider our bodies. In a telling passage in Ryle's work *The Concept of Mind*, he describes how according to Descartes we should imagine our mind telling our legs, arms, and tongue what to do. But by drawing attention to the awkwardness of a distinct mind giving orders to a distinct body, Ryle shows that Descartes paints a picture of almost mechanical human movement that resembles Frankenstein's monster.

The (Inner) Lives of Others

If we now return to the passage where the monster describes how it teaches itself the meaning of words, we can read it in a different way. Initially there seems a temptation to assume that it can understand the language by seeing the objects the words are associated with. From this perspective, it seems to make sense that in observing the De Lacey family, the monster would understand a small group of words associated with everyday objects but not the words that refer to their emotions. This is so, we assume, because these other words point to something that is not available to the observer, to feelings or psychological states hidden within the people it is observing.

But if it's true that we learn only by associating words with things, the words others use to describe their feelings can never be understood because they point to things that we cannot see. Their faces and bodies, instead of directly expressing their thoughts and feelings, become shields that hide those very same thoughts and feelings. This is where we find a head-on collision between Descartes's and Ryle's views. On the one hand, we have the Cartesian view of an inner life that is fully visible only to us and only indirectly to others; and, on the other, the fact that in everyday life we do actually regard other people's feelings as being fully, and not indirectly or partially, visible in their behavior.

Ryle's contribution here is to remind us that visible behavior is our starting point when we make sense of other people and we begin to understand the words that refer to our emotions. We do not see others as mere bodies that express emotion only *after* we have managed to figure out what might be hiding within them. Unlike the monster who is merely a body before Frankenstein gives it life, we do not need direct access to what lies within to see other people's bodies as endowed with life. This is also the moral of the passages where the monster is observing the De Lacey family: What it sees from the very first moment are humans with emotional lives interacting with each other, as opposed to mere bodies that come alive only *after* the code of their inner thoughts and feelings has been cracked.

Here we also need to acknowledge the crucial role of the monster's appearance. Its role is not only to make the monster repulsive as an extra dose of drama. More than that, it uses the Cartesian idea of the body as something that shields the inner life of the mind and soul. In this sense, the monster's deformity makes full use of Descartes's idea of the body as an obstacle to the emotional life within. In this sense, the monster's body is made all the more terrifying because it is a body that doesn't wear its emotions on its face. In Victor Frankenstein's own terms, the true sense in which the monster's "dead matter" comes alive is not when the monster opens its yellow eyes, but when it begins behaving like a human being.

18
Come Back Dr. Frankenstein, All Is Forgiven

CAROLINE MOSSER

When we think of Frankenstein's creature, we often have the image of a big, monstrous villain. But, what Victor Frankenstein had in mind was far from this. In fact, he wanted to create a new race, a better race than human beings.

What went wrong? Why was Dr. Frankenstein's project bound to lead to disaster? A possible answer is that we're scared of what's different, especially when it challenges the superiority of the human species.

The assumption that Victor Frankenstein's project, the scientific enhancement of human body parts to make something that is more than human, was foredoomed to produce nothing but horror, may be mere prejudice—'humanistic' prejudice. We may now be ready to move beyond humanism to post-humanism or trans-humanism. We may be ready for a new Frankenstein.

While humanists tend to see the human body as the sacred location of human identity, post-humanists rely on a modernized understanding of the duality between body and identity. Post-human perspectives propose new definitions of humanity by integrating new types of bodies as they reject the traditional opposition between natural and artificial. This rejection leads to the creation of a combination of both—the "cyborg." The cyborg isn't necessarily a combination of human and machine, but may be the combination of human and "Other"—the "unnatural." What then is this Other "cyborg" thing, and should we let it become part of our "natural" human community?

We're all familiar with Mary Shelley's *Frankenstein: Or, the Modern Prometheus* and with its creature, who has haunted the popular imagination ever since the novel was published. This myth has created an association between attempts to enhance or create life through science and a certain lack of morality which leads to disastrous consequences. While sewing dead body parts together in order to create a new life seems unscientific now, the issues raised by this idea are relevant to new techniques like cloning and bodily augmentation.

Frankenstein is not merely a cautionary tale about science. It also provides critical insights into the values and rules that define our understanding of what it means to be human through the narration of the non-human, or "Other." In philosophy, the term "Other" refers to anybody who is not included in the dominant culture. In most cases, that culture is patriarchal, (governed by men) and relies on the idea of founding "fathers." The judgment of the fathers—whether represented by God or the biological father—is the absolute law. The creature's struggle with his own "father," Dr. Frankenstein, fits nicely into this representation of the Other and its attempt to break down the oppression of the father-culture.

The Creature's Desire to Be Human

In *Frankenstein*, the creature discovers himself and the workings of his society and environment. We witness the evolution of Frankenstein's creature, from his creation to his transformation into a socially aware being. The creature is like a child in its learning and its hurt feelings. Instead of a child growing into a man, we have an artificially created being trying to become a man—an evolution towards humanity in addition to adulthood.

The novel is not only educational but is also a warning about the need for education and about the responsibility of men towards their actions and creations of any kind. It echoes the usual concern for the role of childhood and education as primary elements in the construction of the adult character, an idea which led to a change in the perception of the child. According to the view which was still new when Mary Shelley wrote, society is not an escape from corrupted nature; it is what corrupts the child, who is innocent before he enters the social world. Frankenstein's creature is at first a model of the noble savage or innocent child, but only as long as he remains hidden away from society.

The very nature of the creature's thoughts are educational as he narrates his life experience from the day he was created to the moment when he is expressing his plea. Because he is attempting to convince Victor to see him as a good, human-like being, his narration focuses on his evolution from an innocent new-born to a reasonable adult. His story follows a path similar to human history. There is a parallel between the creature and humanity itself: in him we find the characteristic stages of human history or civilization.

Frankenstein's creature at first lives in nature, eating fruits and hiding in bushes or caves, a state which is similar to that of the first men, who were nomads. One of the first meaningful events of the creature's life is his discovery of fire, a discovery that is usually considered one of the first steps of humanity towards civilization.

Giving the Creature a Voice

Language learning is the next step towards a life that is more than mere survival; it parallels the political evolution from anarchy to a slave-master type of society and then to revolution. The creature's life shows human progress from a natural state to a symbolic representation of revolution; it is characterized by an identity quest and the fight for freedom. This intellectual and psychological growth is based on language.

Frankenstein's creature refers to language as a "godlike science." The creature knows that his ability to master language enables him to pretend to be human while he remains hidden. This is strongly suggested by the De Lacey episode: the blind De Lacey accepts the creature and treats him as a human being because he bases his judgment on what he *hears*. The creature's eloquence enables him to convince Victor Frankenstein to create a companion and to evoke empathy in Walton. Victor himself recognizes the discrepancy between his creature's language and body:

> His words had a strange effect upon me. I compassionated him, and sometimes felt a wish to console him, but when I looked upon him, when I saw the filthy mass that moved and talked, my heart sickened, and my feelings were altered to those of horror and hatred.

Language empowers the creature and his plea makes Frankenstein feel pity and almost consider him human until he looks at the creature's inhuman body. Mary Shelley implies that if Frankenstein's creature were not ugly, he would not be rejected. Language has often been seen as the primary characteristic that differentiates human beings from animals, a claim which is now impossible to make as our technology has proven that it is not the case.

But What Does It Mean to Be Human?

One of the first attempts to differentiate human beings from machines was made by Alan Turing, one of the pioneers in the field of artificial intelligence. He developed a test called the Turing Test. Turing argued that if a machine that we couldn't see could fool us *through language* that it was human, then we would have to treat it like a thinking thing.

If we believed it was a thinking thing and then changed our minds *just because we can now see it*, then the only reason we have is bias against machines. This test is especially interesting in our case because we can apply Frankenstein's creature's experience: the episode with the blind De Lacey ends with the creature being accepted as human while unseen. It has therefore passed the Turing Test. However, passing this test soon proves not to be enough; when the other members of the De Lacey family arrive and see the creature, they are terrified.

This physical element has grown more ambiguous as cloning techniques, cosmetic surgery, and robotics are in constant evolution, becoming more and more effective. The body can no longer be used to define or to identify individuals. Humanness is related to your sense of the self and to your ability to express yourself as a unique being. The expression of your sense of self is often considered dependent on recognition of your mortality. Humanness is identifiable by conversation with yourself about your own death. But this sense of mortality seems too similar to the survival instinct, which characterizes non-human animals as well as human beings.

Through this association with animals, the post-human creature (like Frankenstein) is also seen as a pre-human creature whose artificial nature is connected to the way we view animals. The relationship between pre-human and post-human is ambiguous, and it makes us reflect on human and animal instead of the difference between "natural" and "artificial." This distinction can be defined by the difference between mere "consciousness" and "being" as established by Robert Pepperell in *The Posthuman Condition* (Intellect, 1995). Consciousness is our thoughts at a single, specific moment. Being is built through the accumulation of thoughts leading to a certain consistency in the way we act in the world, and in turn, to an "ongoing sense of existence" (p. 100).

We think that most animals only live in the *now* while human beings act and think in terms of *time*—we think about the future and the past. Because of our peculiar relationship to time, human beings are able to develop identity and morality. These definitions also suggest that identity and humanness are not innate but constructed through time: they involve experience, repetition, and the influence of one's environment. This state of "being" is acquired, not inherited.

If empathy makes humans morally superior to other animals, then individual human beings can be classified according to their level of empathy—and how *human* they are. If so, how can we interpret creatures who do not show much empathy? This question is implicitly asked in *Frankenstein* by means of the opposition between Dr. Frankenstein's lack of empathy and the creature's empathy. Frankenstein's creature helps the De Laceys with their chores as much as he can, whereas Victor Frankenstein sacrifices anything or anybody standing in his way.

The challenge of accepting empathy as a defining characteristic of humanness is that it also undermines our own status as human because some of us do not show empathy. In *Skin Shows: Gothic Horror and the Technology of Monsters* (Duke University Press, 1995), Judith Halberstam reads the definition of the monster, here the creature, as a proof that the line between monster and human is not as clear as society claims it is. Our tendency to define the monster either in terms of human traits or as a representation of the non-human identifies the monster as an alien, as an Other. The monster becomes a mirror of ourselves as being in between humanness and monstrosity.

The presence of the monster reveals the monstrosity of our society as showed by the lack of efficiency during Justine's trial in *Frankenstein*. Justine is wrongly accused of the murder of Dr. Frankenstein's younger brother. Because society needs a culprit she will be held responsible. Dr. Frankenstein becomes monstrous because he refuses to tell the truth. Society becomes monstrous because it does not guarantee justice. The monster is therefore mirroring the society in which he lives, revealing what it wishes to keep hidden. The role of the monster, in Frankenstein *and* as a general cultural idea, is not then to define monstrosity or humanness, but to reveal how both are present in human beings.

Sociobiology and Frankenstein's Cyborg

In *Simians, Cyborgs, and Women* (Free Association, 1991), Donna Haraway proposes the cyborg as a concept that allows us to go beyond Western philosophy. This figure of the cyborg emerges through the association of biology and social sciences in sociobiology. The role of sociobiology in the theoretical construction of the cyborg is found in the idea that society and the body are constructed in the same way and are interdependent. In what Harraway calls "human engineering," social management is applied to the body: "Engineering meant rational placement and modification of human raw material—in the common interest of organism, family, culture, society, and industry" (p. 48).

Through the perspective of sociobiology, nature and the human body itself become "controlled machines" which are made of various cybernetic systems relying on communication to function properly. It is on the basis of this statement that she introduces the cyborg as a compound of both mechanical and organic parts. Because modern biology sees the human body as a machine, human beings are simultaneously represented as organisms and as machines, which, according to Harraway, makes us cyborgs.

Harraway's analysis is especially interesting because she alludes to Frankenstein's creature. Though she refuses to apply the creature's hope of being saved by his creator to her cyborg, her description of the cyborg fits Frankenstein's creature:

> Cyborgs are not reverent; they do not re-member the cosmos. They are . . . needy for connection . . . The main trouble with cyborgs, of course, is that they are the illegitimate offspring of militarism and patriarchal capitalism, not to mention state socialism. But illegitimate offspring are often exceedingly unfaithful to their origins. Their fathers, after all, are inessential. (p. 151)

Frankenstein's creature is aware that he does not fit into the Western representation of the cosmos. His only desire is to be connected with somebody and he is willing to leave human society if Frankenstein builds him a partner. In the end he rebels against his father, hence being unfaithful to his origins and rejecting patriarchy. Whether the creature is truly a cyborg or not, he shares with the cyborg the function of undermining a well-established Western ideology based on patriarchy and focused on European nations.

The Cyborg is "the Other;" it embodies all the ideas that do not belong to the West's traditional ideology of white male supremacy. Harraway's concept of the Cyborg is a good portrait of post-humanism. His very nature renders any analysis flawed because it cannot be defined. It represents the disappearance of boundaries between the Self and the Other, between the Self and its environment, between nature and culture. It embraces the idea of "every thing" and "every being" as interconnected.

According to Pepperell, the main characteristic of post-humanism is that it does not focus on the human being alone, but on the human being and its environment:

> Post-Humanism is about how we live, how we conduct our exploitation of the environment, animals, and each other. It is about what things we investigate, and what questions we ask and what assumptions underlie them. The most obvious manifestations of the end of humanism are those movements that resist the worst aspects of humanist thought: feminism—the movement against the domination of women; animal rights—the movement against human exploitation of animals; environmentalism—the movement against human exploitation of the earth; anti-slavery—the movement against human exploitation of other humans. The fact that all the movements exist suggests the gradual overturning of a hu*man*-centred world is well underway. (p.176)

Are We Ready for a New Frankenstein?

What kind of society would be willing to promote enhanced beings? Such a society would necessarily be open to new ideas and change and would be willing to go beyond the traditional representation of the body as sacred. An enhanced being would be superior to natural beings; therefore, such a society would be able to reconcile both enhanced and natural beings only by rejecting the core societal functions of dominance and power relationships. But the relationship to dominance underlies society's representation of the ideal individual, which in turn structures social relationships in terms of the opposition between the Self and the Other. Therefore, in order to truly embrace enhanced human beings, society must go beyond this dual (Self versus Other) representation of identity.

Going beyond the dual representation of identity as Self or Other is not an easy prospect because most of our values are divided into dual systems, each modeled on a system of representation which strictly opposes what is good to what is bad, denying any possibility of a middle ground. Because the representation of the Self versus Other is based on representations of the good versus bad and the dominator versus dominated, it lacks the middle ground necessary for societal tolerance of enhanced beings. As long as this middle ground cannot be found, any hope of enhancing the human body would be pointless because it would not be accepted by society as a whole. Such a middle ground has not yet been found. Because we have no middle ground, no allowance for "Others," we realize that any re-creation of life will always be treated as an "Other," outcast, hated, and oppressed. But, like the case of Frankenstein's creature, it is in humanity's best interest to find a place for that "Other," because if that new life is truly post-human it likely has the ability to do us great deal of good or a great deal of harm.

V

Dr. Frankenstein's Monster Assembly Kit

19
And We Thought *He* Was the Monster

MICHAEL MENDELSON

In the end, Baron Frankenstein stands by the door of his son's bedroom, inside a hallway that is inside of the house (Palace? Castle? We never get to see the outside, but we don't really need to) that is inside of a well-ordered village filled with people who seem to lead well-ordered lives.

Henry Frankenstein is inside the bedroom being taken care of by his fiancé, soon to be wedded after a slight interruption of an otherwise happy, pricey, and public wedding. Henry Frankenstein is, after all, the son of the Baron, and so he, his wife, and their son (everyone seems to hope it is a son), will occupy an important position in this well ordered village. No doubt there is a happy ending in the offing here.

True, there has been an intrusion into this well ordered and peaceful village, but the problem has been . . . well, let us say "disposed of," and all is right again. Order has been restored; everyone and everything seems to be back in its proper place. Soon the festivities surrounding the wedding will begin again, the wedding will take place, and the future will, no doubt, wind on in its well-ordered way: Henry will eventually become the Baron, and he will, it is hoped, have a son who will one day be the Baron, and he too will, it is hoped, have a son, and on and on it should go. A happy ending that should be the beginning of a reasonably happy future.

Baron Frankenstein, seeing his future daughter-in-law tending to his son, offers up a toast that sums all this up: "Here's to a son of The House of Frankenstein!" And so the movie ends. But, as we know, that isn't the way it begins.

It begins in a graveyard. Then, it shifts to an abandoned watchtower turned into a laboratory, and then comes the monster, and then comes the intrusion from outside the village that wreaks havoc on the inside of the village. But the source of the intrusion, the monster, meets his (its?) end in a burning windmill where the monster is destroyed by the flames.

Or is the monster destroyed? Surely, there's little room for doubt that the creature in the windmill is destroyed. But is that creature in the windmill really the monster? Henry and the villagers seem convinced that the horror is something that has come into the village from the outside. But maybe the horror is to be found inside the village. Maybe even the real *source* of that horror comes from the inside. But why do Henry and the villagers think that the creature is the monster?

To Be a Monster, Scene One

Well, he certainly *seems* to be a monster. To begin with, there's his appearance, which is almost but not quite human. There is the flat head, the stitched scars on his neck and hand, the protruding bolts on his neck, and the expression on his face. Unlike most faces we encounter, it does not have a wide variety of expressions. In fact there seem to be two main ones: an almost uncomprehending catatonic gaze, and the other one that is notably violent, even ferocious. True, we do see him smile—once. But even then, it's in a rather disturbing, unsettling context.

And then there are his gangly limbs which are in the right places but do not have quite the kind of proportions we would expect from a normal human being. This odd proportion is highlighted by the ill-fitting nature of his clothing. There is nothing to suggest that either Henry Frankenstein or his assistant Fritz are tailors, so we can only assume that these are the normal clothing of a normal human body, and it is obvious from a glance that they do not fit the way they ought to, and it is not just because the jacket is too small. The legs and the arms just don't match up the way we would expect them to.

And it is not surprising that the clothes don't fit quite right and that the arms and legs don't quite match up, because the body is not a normal body. It is an assemblage of body *parts*, collected from formerly dead bodies and pieced together by Henry and Fritz in the laboratory, which is itself a rather odd manner and place for a human to come into being, if in fact we still feel comfortable applying the word "human" here. To make all this a bit worse, as if it were not already bad enough, it is conspicuously pointed out that among these various collected body "parts" there is a "criminal brain," and *that* cannot be a good thing.

And this being is mute, incapable of uttering anything more than guttural sounds and growls. These noises reinforce our feeling that he is more than a little dangerous and a lot less than what we would want to call "human."

To Be a Monster, Scene Two

Even worse than the way he looks and sounds is what he *does*. He kills. Not just once, but three times, and he makes an unsuccessful but very determined attempt at a fourth. His first victim is Fritz, and while it is all done off-camera, the repeated screams make it clear that that it is done in a very painful and unpleasant sort of way. What we do eventually see is an eerily dark image of Fritz and Fritz's shadow, apparently hanging from some kind of hook. It is a haunting image that emphasizes the disagreeable and grisly nature of his death.

And then there's Dr. Waldman, who dies by having his esophagus crushed (and, perhaps, his neck broken?) by the creature's vise-like grip. Once again, not good. Worst of all is the third death. This is where we get that smile. He is playing with Maria, a welcoming young girl, throwing flowers into a lake and watching them float. Then the creature briefly smiles, picks her up, and throws her into the water, thus drowning her. Drowning a little girl is bad; smiling while you do it is *evil*.

As for that fourth attempt, although it is unsuccessful, it is not for lack of effort. The creature, having carried off Henry Frankenstein (his "father," insofar as he has one), tosses Henry's unconscious body from the top of a windmill. Henry hits a blade of the windmill, and then falls to the ground. That he survives is clearly not the intended outcome, and so we can add to the list of the creature's atrocities "attempted patricide." It is hard to rank such things, but attempting to kill one's creator-father cannot be a lot better than drowning a little girl. Dr. Waldman was indeed right when he exclaims early in the film, "It's a monster!"

Or so it *seems*.

A Short Intermission

James Whale, like a lot of horror film directors then and now, is engaged in a delicate and artful balancing act. He's attempting—quite successfully—to provide seventy minutes of entertainment (the standard length of a reel of film at that time) to an audience largely comprised of victims of the Great Depression, arguably the worst economic disaster in American history.

Seventy minutes of diversion and distraction to an audience that can well use it. And not just any old "diversion": it's "horror," a strange and interesting kind of diversion in it's own right, one that continues to attract and fascinate many of us. However, there is more than diversion and distraction going on. Whale is like many other of the great directors of early horror movies—F.W. Murnau (*Nosferatu*, 1922), Tod Browning (*Dracula*, 1931; *Freaks*, 1933), and Karl Freund (*The Mummy*, 1932; *Mad Love*, 1935), to cite a few. These directors knew that horror can entertain and distract in its own odd and fascinating way, but they knew that it could also do more. They knew that horror is a vehicle that can be used to make a point. For those who wanted it, the point was there. For those who were not interested, there was still the horror to keep them entertained.

Whale's *Frankenstein* (1931) is a prime example of this; one of the very best, I think. Here we have cinematic art in the service of philosophy, a movie that involves a "metaphysics" of sorts. And when I say "metaphysics," I mean it in the most straightforward sense: the attempt to uncover some "reality" that underlies "appearances": an attempt to uncover that which actually *is* the case in spite of how things might *seem* to us.

Film can be a very effective way to reveal the truth beneath the surface. After all, it is often said that a picture is worth a very large number of words (a thousand seems to be the standard figure). Upon close inspection, Whale's *Frankenstein* does exactly that, for here we have a compelling portrayal of the contrast between what *seems* to be the case and what actually *is* the case. And when all's said and done, what is the case is even *worse* than what seems to be the case.

Not Being Such a Monster After All, Scene One

And what *seems* to be the case? That he is a "monster," of course. Upon reflection, however, it's far from clear that the "appearances" support the "reality" of this conclusion. He, after all, did not choose the way he looks, and even if he did, it's not clear that the way he looks is enough to support the conclusion that he is some kind of "monster." A flat head, disproportionate limbs, ill-fitting clothing, odd facial expressions, bolts and scars—these are unusual, perhaps even unsettling at first glance, but they seem hardly enough to deserve the label of "*monster*." You might feel initial revulsion, but in the end, a bit of sympathy seems more appropriate.

And he did not choose the "criminal brain." *That* was the result of Fritz's clumsiness (and, perhaps as well, his lack of literacy?), and it is not quite obvious what conclusion is to be drawn from the fact that he has was given a "criminal brain." Then, as now, the notion of a "criminal brain" is a controversial one, and it appears deliberately ambiguous what Whale might have in mind by including this detail—a detail that's absent from the original novel which first appeared 1818, before the controversy emerged. There are going to be clues that highlight this ambiguity and suggest that, in spite of what we might think, the "criminal brain" doesn't explain as much as we might want to think it does.

Not Being Such a Monster After All, Scene Two

And those "clues" are directly related to the second reason he seems to be such a "monster": the things he does. That he kills. But why does he kill?

He kills Fritz, but Fritz is hardly an innocent victim of some "criminal brain." From the beginning, Fritz constantly torments him, most notably with fire, something the creature is clearly frightened by. And there's also the whip. Fritz likes to use the whip. The creature does not like it, not even a little. It does not require great insight for Henry Frankenstein to note that the creature "hated Fritz. Fritz tormented him so!" It's not a happy episode, but many have done more damage for less reason.

And Doctor Waldman, his second victim, having already uttered, "It's a monster!" later adds, "Shoot it!" There's little room for doubt that Dr. Waldman is the one who makes the first move, that he is the one who wants to kill the creature; Dr.

Waldman is the one who "picks the fight," so to speak. And so Dr. Waldman tries, and that is when the creature kills Dr. Waldman—the point at which Dr. Waldman is attempting to destroy our supposed monster by dissecting him alive.

Yes, Dr. Waldman did say he would try to do it "painlessly," and he does try a few injections. Maybe they are supposed to be lethal, but for whatever reason, they definitely are not. And, if you're the one who's going to be dissected, the prospect of injected painkillers is probably going to seem a rather minor point compared to the fact that someone is attempting to cut you into disposable pieces.

More complex and more interesting is the death of the young girl, the one time we get to see that smile. Here again, the context is important. He comes upon her at the side of a lake, and she's the one (and only) person that greets him without any sense that there is something "wrong" or "odd" about him. And so, she invites him to play, throwing flowers upon the lake, trying to make them float like "boats." And this is where we get the smile: a response to a brief interlude of acceptance by someone who wants to play, a serene and happy moment in the midst of seventy minutes that are otherwise confined to the range of the somber to the maniacal to the frenzied.

But soon the flowers are all gone, and the creature wants to continue the game. So, with a playful innocence that leads to a clearly unexpected and terrible result, he picks up the little girl, still smiling, and tosses her into the water, assuming she will float just as the flowers did. But he does not know that young girls don't float, and when he realizes this, he flees. We can clearly see that he is beside himself with horror. In fact, he seems even more horrified than those of us who have just viewed the terrible conclusion of this otherwise almost charming interlude.

And then there's Henry. It's no surprise that the creature should want to kill Henry Frankenstein. Henry is the one who brought him into this world. It's Henry who made *him* into the kind of creature that he is. It's Henry who abandons *him*, and finally, it's Henry who pursues *him*, leading a mob of townspeople, trying to kill *him*. And it is worth remembering that, from the very beginning, it's Henry Frankenstein who set in motion the events leading to this mess.

The Monster Revealed

And what exactly is this mess? To see that we need to look closer at the "reality" that underlies the "appearance" of what the film presents to us; we need to look deeper at the "metaphysics" of the film.

And no, the real monster is not Henry Frankenstein. Things are much more complicated than that, and the horror of it all is much deeper than that. Henry is surely part of the horror, but only just a part. And as for the creature, he now hardly seems to be such a monster after all. It is far worse: the creature now begins to seem something of a victim himself, regardless of whether he has a "criminal brain," if in fact there really *is* such a thing.

But there's more to the story here. It's not just that the creature himself is beginning to seem something of a victim. There is something deeper at work here. Now that we can see the creature in a more sympathetic light, the creature has become a point of contrast against which the reflective viewer can discern where the true monstrosity and horror is to be found. He is an example of what some philosophers like to call "alterity": true "Otherness," that which is so different that it cannot fit into any of the categories we use in our daily lives. These contrasts are present throughout the movie. There is, to begin with, his unusual and striking appearance. From the first time we see him in the laboratory to the final time we see him in the burning windmill, there is no getting around the fact that he (it?) looks so *different* from anything else we have seen before.

Then there's also the contrast between his environment on the "outside" and the "inside" of the village and the "inside" of the Frankenstein family's comfortable, somewhat plush dwelling. He comes from an unwelcoming landscape of gothic gray, an abandoned watchtower and a windswept, rain soaked rugged terrain. The village is a place of manmade order and comfort. This contrast is made even more conspicuous in the few minutes that see we him inside the village. Or, to be more precise, inside the Baron's dwelling, the inside of the inside, so to speak. He just doesn't fit there, even more than his clothes don't fit him.

And it's worth noting what he does *not* do when he is inside this very alien environment. He is clearly looking for Henry

Frankenstein, but he doesn't find him. What he does find is Henry's fiancé. But what he does *not* do is harm her. She screams in horror at his appearance, and he growls in return. But then she faints, and he retreats.

Yes, he retreats. This "monster" with that "criminal brain" does not kill her, and upon reflection, this should not surprise us. Unlike the young girl, Henry Frankenstein's fiancé does not welcome him, but she doesn't really pose any threat to him either. This brief encounter sharply highlights his "Otherness," and it also highlights the fact that we cannot regard him as simply engaged in some kind of relentless murderous rampage. That "rampage" is itself a plausible response to circumstances, circumstances which he did not choose, circumstances which he cannot control.

So what's *really* going on here? What's the point that's being made in these seventy minutes of images flickering upon the screen? The point: the monstrosity of it all, the horror of it all, is not to be found in this mute, odd looking creature that comes in from the outside. The monstrosity and horror is to be found on the "inside," where it has been all along, even before the creature was brought to life in that abandoned watchtower.

And to make matters worse, the monster is us. Worse even than that, we are also the creators of the monster.

Final Credits Where Credits Are Due

And so, we wonder, what does this mean and how can this be?

Because: he is as "Other" as "Otherness" can be while still being recognized as anything at all. But otherness is not a "property" like being "red" or "soft" or "crooked." Otherness is a "relation," like being "taller than" or "far from" or "on the other side of." A property can belong to one thing. To have a relation you need at least two. For something to be "other," it has to be "other than" something else, something in addition to itself.

And for us to be "who" or "what" we are, we need that relation of "otherness." In order for us to have an "identity," we need to have something—or someone or ones—with whom this identity can be contrasted. This is true at both the individual and the social level. My personality is unique to the extent that it is different from, or "other than," the personalities of other individuals. And socially, much of my identity is made up of the various groups and social institutions to which I belong, and these groups and institutions derive their identity through what sets them apart from (makes them "other than") different groups and institutions.

And thus, we constantly derive comfort from that which is like us, and in order to get this comfort, we must distinguish ourselves from what is not like us, what is "other than" us. And the more different something is, the more extreme the otherness, the more conscious we become of the distinction between us and that otherness. Indeed, if that otherness is extreme enough, it even becomes a threat to our identity, something that sets the stage for conflict as we attempt to maintain and defend our identity.

Yes, we derive comfort from our identity, but that comfort is more than a matter of simply belonging. It also requires exclusion in order that we can have the boundaries that our identity requires. In other words, if there is an "inside" where we belong, there has to be an "outside," where the monsters reside.

It can be something quite simple. To belong to a team or a club is to be different than those who are not members, and I often find comfort by belonging to that club or team because of the security it gives and the sense of unity with others who are also members. But sometimes it's not so simple. If that which is on the "outside" seems so different that it threatens the security and unity that our identity gives us, our comfort is threatened to the point where we must do what we can to protect ourselves from what is "outside." And so, that which is "different" becomes more than simply "different." In our minds, it easily becomes a "monster," something to be shunned and kept at a distance. And sometimes, we even want to destroy what we have come to call a "monster."

The creature seems to be a "monster" because he is so "other," so much different than from what we recognize as belonging on our side of the border that makes up our identity. And because he is so much "other," it is not surprising that he is met with such revulsion and resistance. And it is also not surprising that the cycle of violence and revenge emerges the way that it does.

We think the creature is a monster because we have little choice. He is a visual, graphic representation of one of the darkest aspects of what seems to be one of the most cherished parts of our individual and social lives: our identity and the comfort that it brings. But that comfort comes at a price, and that price is the often unreflective, almost instinctual and violent exclusion of that which would threaten that comfort.

Just as the creature has no name, we can't help but wonder how often we must do all this in a manner that we don't even recognize. Seventy minutes of diversion and distraction. And, for the reflective viewer, a somber question about just how much of the security of our well-ordered streets and well-ordered lives rest upon the nameless residents and remnants of burning windmills.

20
Adopting *Frankenstein*'s Creature

MIKE KUGLER

We in the West have a pretty insatiable appetite for stories of technical mastery gone very, very wrong. But it's hard now to imagine anyone vetoing the early attempts at medical treatment such as smallpox vaccinations or investigations into the cause and cure of cholera. We're far less comfortable, though, when discussing nuclear energy, genetically engineered food, or stem cell research.

Writers as diverse as John Ruskin, H.G. Wells, and Aldous Huxley suffered little doubt that the relentless technical enhancement of human power would eventually overwhelm our capacity for sympathy, generosity, and imagination. Even Sauron's ring "tech" in J.R.R. Tolkien's *The Lord of the Rings* suggests a twentieth-century anxiety over loss of personal integrity in the face of powerful technical mastery.

One of the inspirations for such stories, one of our great modern myths, Mary Shelley's *Frankenstein* (1818), is less about medical wonder and our horror at its unforeseen overthrow of our independence. It's more about the human creator's well-meaning but arrogant overreach, his sacrilegious procedures, and cruel abandonment of his new-born child to solitude, despair, and mass murder.

Such confusion has hounded Mary Shelley's tale since its publication in 1818. Decades later it was probably better known from its stage adaptations than the book itself. From Thomas Edison's movie version in 1910, through John Whale's classic of 1931 and Terence Fisher's *The Curse of Frankenstein* (1958), we follow one terrible misjudgment by Victor Frankenstein after another. His maniacal lust for power over natural life yields a horrible, mute Creature.

The fear of technology leaps out of the movie flea market of 1950s and 1960s sci-fi "B" movies, but also out of the far more imaginative and compelling *The Fly* (1986) or *The Prestige* (2006). They share an abiding distrust, if not terror, of some foreign irresistible power overthrowing our lives, getting "inside" us and "taking us over."

What technology, what medical intervention or technical transformation of my body threatens my independent, distinctively personal identity?

Much of this line of sci-fi and horror film-making came together in Ridley Scott's *Prometheus* (2012). Until the rest of this projected trilogy of films appears we can't know his exact claims. But building on the earlier *Alien* films (1979–1997) Scott links the human desire to create our own forms of life, for immortality, and finally to genetic engineering, signaled of course by the use of *Frankenstein*'s subtitle, "The Modern Prometheus."

By the movie's end, that unbelievable technical power is revealed graphically to be weaponized for genocide. The extraterrestrial "Engineers" who designed humans also engineer existing life to evolve rapidly into bio-weapons of mass annihilation. Like Dr. Frankenstein the "Engineers" cobble new species from existing ones; and they cannot control them. At first glance, it seems Shelley's Creature effortlessly becomes "the Monster," the living reminder of Dr. Frankenstein's violation of nature. But Shelley's horror was not of technology hijacking us at our most intimate, vulnerable moments. Shelley's terror was abandonment. This most powerful and enduring of modern myths, *Frankenstein* was Shelley's ambiguous understanding of human ego, creativity, and the technical augmentation of our power.

Shelley of course condemned Victor's failure to "revere" nature and his abandonment of his new child, the Creature. But she was far more sympathetic to him than later film-makers. Her story forces us into amazement at Victor's ability and audacity, but even further to sympathize with the Creature, and to hope we learn the proper lesson about risking frail *collective* human life for modern knowledge and glory. In Shelley's age of modern political and technical mastery of the world, the "revolutionary" scientist threatened the moral and spiritual integrity not so much of the individual, but of human community.

So what's worth rescuing from Shelley's story? Her book dramatizes how mutual love ignites our natural sympathies into moral character, and how a casual indifference towards love and family destroys that character, making community impossible. Shelley examined the political aftershocks of the French Revolution and Napoleon through the lenses of her father's and her husband's idealistic claims about human perfectibility. Challenging those top-down, authoritarian and quite male "Promethean" rebellions, Shelley narrated alternatively modern, face-to-face intimacies resembling a kind of communitarianism. She channeled her own frail home life into a stunning story of audacious idealistic rebellion and tragic solitude.

The Pale Student of Unhallowed Arts

The novel opens with a daredevil scientist and explorer, Walton, writing to his sister about his risky expedition to the North Pole. Finding a near-dead Dr. Frankenstein, Walton tends his injuries. The Swiss scientist recalls his happy privileged childhood, raised by loving parents in the intimacy of close friends. Frankenstein's tranquil youth in the sublime beauty of Geneva shockingly ends with the death of his young mother.

Grieving for her, Victor read furiously on the mystery of life. In college at Ingolstadt, at the time reputed among the most politically radical in Europe, he immediately sought the most advanced chemists and doctors. He soon began the solitary work of bursting through "the ideal bounds" of life and death. This obsessed and brilliant young medical student isolates the principle of life. Overcome with this revolutionary and divine knowledge, in a leap of imagination and arrogance Dr. Frankenstein prepares to build and resurrect the corpse he's built from organs robbed from graves, morgues, and even slaughterhouses.

Shelley's circumstances partly explain her endowing this young scientist with the confidence he could overcome human death and suffering. Her parents were two of the most notoriously radical thinkers of the age, the rationalist-utopian philosopher William Godwin and the educational theorist and feminist Mary Wollstonecraft. Ten days after Mary's birth in August 1797, Wollstonecraft died from infection. Haunted by her famous and absent mother, years later Mary often read at her mother's grave. Her generally content life with a father she adored and her older half-sister Fanny changed when her father remarried. Mary despised her demanding step-mother. Into the tense life of this teenager stepped the handsome, radical poet Percy Shelley. An admirer of Mary's father, Percy was soon pressing his love upon the lovely and brilliant Mary, even though he was already married.

In May of 1816 Mary, Percy, and Mary's step-sister Claire traveled to Lake Geneva to meet Lord Byron and Dr. Polidori. That June the famous ghost story contest inflamed Mary's imagination and the terrible daydream of "the pale student of unhallowed arts kneeling beside the thing he had put together" would ignite the novel published two years later.[1] Barely seventeen Mary had fallen in with the charismatic, talented and self-absorbed Percy Shelley. Her own father wouldn't speak to her. Percy's progressive ideas about marriage and family increased Mary's sense of vulnerability—he proposed to his wife Harriet to join him and Mary as "sister." The loss of her first child recalled her mother's death; Mary dreamed that her dead daughter was still alive. In October and December of 1816 Shelley's half-sister Fanny committed suicide and Percy Shelley's wife drowned herself.

The pall of loss hanging over her, by June Mary had begun the novel. Mary poured onto the page her reflections upon suffering, death and the promise of improved human life and society in a revolutionary age. What could the optimistic, and romanticized, moral and political preachments of her father and husband mean when faced with the kind of abandonment, loss, and sorrow Mary had endured? This broken-hearted teenaged prodigy challenged those "progressive" ideals by retelling an ancient myth on the origin and character of evil and death.

Doctor, Cure Yourself

Dr. Frankenstein did not seek to cure a particular illness or injury, but to re-invent humanity itself. Mary's husband and

---

[1] *Frankenstein: 1818 Text* (Oxford University Press, 1998), p. 196.

father as well as many others had celebrated the potential of human improvement. Audacious, "Promethean" men imagined perfected humans in societies of complete liberty and equality. Science promised human power over nature unmatched in any previous age. In the place of traditional sources of authority like nobles, kings, and the Church a new source of truth, the Natural world, would be revealed by science in the facts of human and social life or by art. Revolutions in America and France appeared to bring their hopes to life.

Mary Shelley was as aware of these ideas and their promise as any young person in Europe. The novel's prospect of "a new species" (p. 36) reproduced the "new man," "improved man," a "perfectible man" from Europe's most progressive and optimistic ideas in science and art. Her novel tested such hopes, a kind of "what if?" tale sparked by the promised advances of the human species in the modern age.

Dr. Frankenstein was not interested in slow, methodical scientific research. Like Mary Shelley he was part of a well-read intellectual aristocracy; he too was young when his mother died. His scientific training to end human suffering and eliminate death followed the noblest goals of reformers like her parents and her husband. Once Victor isolated the chemical and biological basis first of death, then of life, what could prevent him bringing that god-like knowledge to the immediate salvation of humanity?

Mary Shelley sympathized with Victor. Throughout the novel he inspires the love of fine people like the explorer Walton, his close friend Clerval, and his cousin and later wife Elizabeth, and others—people better than Victor himself. The young scientist clearly resembled Mary's husband. While she loved and admired Percy Shelley, his ethic of free love undermined any possibility that she and he would enjoy a stable and trusting family life.

Mary Shelley understood well the shroud under which childbearing women of that age lived. She had been raised without a mother by a distant father notorious for his written attacks on marriage and diminishment of the importance of family. Partly responsible for the breakup of Percy Shelley's first marriage, and suffering from the loss of her first infant daughter, Mary Shelley made healthy children, the stable family, and close friends the fragile foundation critical to a community's moral health. While Percy Shelley the charismatic reformer poet awed and inspired her, she had doubts about the idealism of a man who arrogantly imagined a perfectible humanity at the cost of family. Her Dr. Frankenstein sought reproduction of humans without women; he imagined and pursued this in total isolation from his family and friends. Victor was a graphic challenge to the ideas and character of a deeply loved but flawed husband.

Victor's arrogant, obsessive actions blossomed into aspirations to wield god-like powers, resurrecting the dead, and overcoming the ancient curse of sin and death. In Victor's dream of enjoying the worship of his new "species," Shelley recast her world's most widely known mythic story, the Christian tradition. In the Genesis account human rebellion against a good and just creator brought disease, painful childbirth, cruel work, and death. Why shouldn't Shelley's revolutionary scientist improve on the Creator's masterpiece, humanity?

Shelley begins to move from sympathetic explanation to Dr. Frankenstein's dangerous moral failings. To satisfy his revolutionary goals the young scientist abandoned his loving home for nearly three years. He violates corpses, not hesitating to use animal organs to build his "perfect" man. For nine months he conceived and constructed what he imagined to be the ideal human, designed as carefully as possible for beauty and physical perfection. While raised to have no terror of the supernatural Victor recognized that this work was destroying his mental health (pp. 33–39). Totally reclusive, unearthing bodies laid to rest under the sacrament of burial, conducting vivisections, and assembling rotting body parts by some hideous process, he was barely human by the time he completed the Creature. He conceived and carried out his disgusting and terrifying experiment forsaken in a moral desert of his own making.

Man Is but a Reed, but a Thinking Reed

How should we behave, caught between the power to realize our imagined greatness, and a future we put into motion we can neither predict nor control? Many romantic revolutionaries of Mary Shelley's age celebrated the rebellious individual against ancient tyrannical authority. Shelley shared the radical hopes of her father, mother, and husband for a truly free and equal society. But the legacy of the French Revolution and Napoleon left her far more suspicious of modern charismatic reformers, their utopian ideals, and the massive scale of revolutionary reform.

The Shelley of *Frankenstein* builds her ethics on the idealization of the "intimate circle" of like-minded family and friends. Children, as the Swiss political theorist Jean-Jacques Rousseau (1712–1778) and her mother Mary Wollstonecraft argued, should be raised by benevolent and permissive parents who would encourage the child's caring and sympathetic nature.

Victor's mixed motives—to serve the needs of humanity as a renowned, god-like creator—animated Shelley's criticism of the idealistic progressivism of her time. The Creature's story expresses Shelley's idealization of family and community. After the Creature's creator-father sought solitude to complete his blasphemous work, he abandoned his creation to solitude and despair.

No one with half a heart can fail to pity the Creature, so innocent and forlorn. Mary Shelley celebrates his natural brilliance and eloquence; he talks more like an artist and a philosopher than anyone else in the novel. The creature develops his benevolence and gregariousness without a single generous human gesture. Everyone rejects him. In a cottage he finds a family of political exiles, the De Laceys. They too are an "intimate circle" of family and close friends, a miniature community.

Despite his earnest work to earn their love they revolt at his hideousness and violently cast him away. Their rejection drives the creature to despair and hatred. Shelley thus explains violence and vengeance through unjust exclusion; while Dr. Frankenstein's sacrilegious evil was his own and nurtured in solitude, the Creature's evil matures through repeated exclusion from his natural and just claim upon human community. In this way she challenges her father's and husband's assertion of the individual over the intimate community. Finding and reading Milton's *Paradise Lost* the Creature decided he was a new Adam. Cast out from the "intimate circle" by the De Laceys, his last hope for a community crushed, he vows vengeance. Rejected and denied by Victor he becomes a Satanic rebel against his Creator and Father.

In her story Shelley tests the ideas of her father, husband and other radical reformers in a thought-experiment. Victor earns our revulsion for escaping the moral accountability an "intimate circle" of family and friends would have imposed upon his divine aspirations and grotesque work. Through the Creature's story Shelley asserts that affectionate company trains our innate sympathy into moral capacities. At the heart of her story Shelley challenged Victor's attempt to eliminate women and mothers from reproduction and child-raising. Frankenstein built his Creature alone, abandoned him upon realizing fully that he had created a living human, all of which violates the basic intimacy of motherhood and the home.

To a New World of Gods and Monsters!

One of my earliest reading memories is from an encyclopedia's condensed version of *Frankenstein*. All the classic shocking scenes are there: hubris, lightning, gruesome violation of bodies, the Creature's horrific crimes. But the scene that sticks is the grieving, heart-crushed Creature scooping up his creator's body and leaping from the window of Walton's cabin onto the polar ice, disappearing into a white desert. The sublime thrill and sadness from that terrifying scene is as vivid now as it was forty years ago.

With some notable exceptions like Whale's *The Bride of Frankenstein* (1935) and Kenneth Branagh's *Mary Shelley's Frankenstein* (1994), popular revisions of the *Frankenstein* story have typically abandoned Shelley's complex combination of idealistic and revolutionary convictions. Other works closer in spirit to Shelley's novel are comic books like *Bernie Wrightson's Frankenstein* (Dark Horse, 2011), Kevin Grevioux's noir detective revision, *I, Frankenstein* (Darkstorm Studios, 2013), and Nick Dear's play, *Frankenstein* (Faber and Faber, 2011). But in most modern versions of the tale the insanely obsessive scientist, working in fevered solitude, lives on, and the Creature rarely inspires pity; most often he's just a nearly unstoppable monster. Shelley's anxiety over solitude among the debris of the modern, extended family seems forgotten.

Today's Frankenstein myth probes our fear that the technical powers will overcome us, get inside, changing or corrupting our distinctive personhood into something unrecognizable or beyond our ability to manage. While such issues seem philosophically intriguing they say more of us than Shelley. Her terror was solitude, isolation; she made the lonely, even ugly, loving person the horrible counterpart of a loving circle of like-minded family and friends. Shelley used ugliness as a modernized "mark of Cain," explaining the community's rejection of the pitiable individual. The Creature's hideousness and exclusion strongly contrasts an earlier incident where an outsider is warmly invited to join an extended family, when Victor's father brings his beautiful and gentle cousin Elizabeth to live with them (pp. 19–21).

For centuries the Christian church had taught that evil and suffering were consequences of human rebellion against God's sovereignty. A range of writers in the Enlightenment and French Revolution promised the human power to minimize human suffering. Shelley took this "enlightened," revolutionary impulse to press the boundary between human and divine. Her reckless scientist vows to eliminate human suffering and natural death. He can realize that arrogant ambition only in a grotesque parody of creation and the Christian resurrection.

The Creature's astonishing capacity to become in near complete isolation empathetic, gentle, and articulate points to Shelley's highest hopes for a small, face-to-face community of equal citizens, suggesting a new kind of human being. But love denied becomes an agony, and the Creature turns to revenge. Shelley sympathized with but did not defend the revolutionary violence of Europe's common people and the poor. The cycle of retribution and violence between the Creature and his father Victor is primal. Despite Dr. Frankenstein's clumsy imitation of human beauty, his new-born Creature like the first Adam remains innocent. Unlike the first Adam the Creature falls into sin and violent rebellion against his creator as the victim of injustice, brutally driven from community after community. The novel then is in tension with itself, pulling between Shelley's distrust of unrealistically optimistic human power expressed in technical intervention, and with her hopes for the modern liberation of human potential.

Shelley was nineteen when she wrote *Frankenstein*. Her unsettled life echoed back the tremendous anxiety of revolutionary transformation across Europe. Fearing solitude in an age promising the transformation of human nature and society, she borrowed the most enduring and powerful myth in European culture, recasting its biblical symbols for a new age of audacious, charismatic revolutionaries. She answers her Promethean age with a story about love, its power, and the failure to reward it.

What if Victor had adopted the Creature and raised him in his home? The novel's repeated images of adoption and family life suggest a subtle manner of pushing the reader to this question. The redemptive hope of the novel whispers at every moment the Creature expresses his solitude and despair. Our ability to sympathize with the Creature implies his power as an icon of our own isolation, even desperation. Shelley's moving account of innocence betrayed and abused asserts that despite the horrifying circumstances of his "conception" the Creature is like us. If his flesh is "wrong" he is nonetheless human.

21
Why Science Is Horrific

JEFF EWING

Science can be very dangerous, especially when it plays God. Mary Shelley's *Frankenstein* is just one of many horror stories that show us how dangerous it can be to play that game.

Frankenstein, and many of the horror movies and novels that follow in its large, lumbering footsteps, depict the scary potential uses of science and technology. A similar concern about the out-of-control and terrible consequences of science has been voiced by various thinkers and writers.

The philosophies of Marxism and Ecofeminism have been exceptionally critical of using science and technology to play God. They argue that it can cause the mistreatment of workers, women, indigenous and nonwhite peoples, and even of nature itself. The "scientist as a god" perspective, they argue, treats those groups as if they are merely things to be used for power and profit.

Penetrating Nature's Recesses

In Mary Shelley's *Frankenstein*, the product of unrestrained science and technology (and Victor Frankenstein's hubris) literally runs amok. From an early age, Victor Frankenstein has, in his own words, always "been imbued with a fervent longing to penetrate the secrets of nature." Frankenstein is specifically concerned with the "elixir of life," allowing him to grant mankind power over disease and death, as he ponders "what glory would attend the discovery, if I could banish disease from the human frame and render man invulnerable to any but a violent death!"

Frankenstein is instructed in modern natural philosophy, rejecting older alchemical practices, but 'natural philosophy' (the older term for 'science') disappoints him. He expresses "contempt for the uses of modern natural philosophy. . . It was very different, when the masters of the science sought immortality and power; such views, although futile, were grand."

Victor's waning excitement with science is rekindled by his instructor, M. Waldman. Waldman describes the "modern masters" of science and natural philosophy, who

> penetrate into the recesses of nature, and show how she works in her hiding-places. They ascend into the heavens; they have discovered how the blood circulates, and the nature of the air we breathe. They have acquired new and almost unlimited powers; they can command the thunders of heaven, mimic the earthquake, and even mock the invisible world with its own shadows.

Victor's mind becomes again "filled with one thought, one conception, one purpose. . . I will pioneer a new way, explore unknown powers, and unfold to the world the deepest mysteries of creation." Frankenstein's pursuit of scientific progress and knowledge is explicitly derived from his desire to know the innermost secrets of the natural world, and his desire to bend nature to his will—absolutely and completely.

Ecofeminism and the Critique of Science

Ecofeminism begins with the insight that, particularly in Western civilization, the oppression of women, nonwhite, and indigenous peoples, and nonhuman nature have historically been interconnected in theory and practice. Maria Mies and Vandana Shiva explain that modern civilization is structured with the world organized into dichotomies, where one "half" is subordinated to the other—"nature is subordinated to man; woman to man; consumption to production; and the local to the global, and so on."[1]

All of these populations have long been subsumed as "nature" by colonizing white European and American men. Social practices in Western civilization have been oriented

[1] Maria Mies and Vandana Shiva, *Ecofeminism* (Fernwood, 1993), p. 5.

towards the instrumental use (the use only for personal gain) of these groups; they are treated as raw material for the pursuit of power and profit. This mistreatment is called "Othering" because those groups are treated as an "Other," an outsider to be conquered, subdued, and enslaved to the will of the powerful.

Ecofeminist theorists argue that this Othering impacts the development of science and technology. Val Plumwood shows how those groups have been treated as mere objects to be used by science after the Enlightenment. In this approach to science, science and technology have been developed to extract the secrets of the world, which is treated as a mechanical external world without mystery or value in and of itself. Carolyn Merchant highlights how this mechanistic treatment of the world reordered reality "around two fundamental constituents of human experience—order and power."[2] In other words, systems of domination and science have both been unified around the "Othering" of dominated groups. The dominated are now seen by science and the powerful as passive objects, treated as part of the "raw materials" of nature.

Frankenstein's Penetration of Nature's Recesses

Victor Frankenstein is inspired to practice science and perform his experiment from a desire to *master* and triumph over nature and natural processes. He desires power over the most natural and untouchable processes—life and death themselves—and his relation to nature in this scientific endeavor is marked by no reverence. To Victor,

> The world was to me a secret which I desired to divine . . . curiosity, earnest research to learn the hidden laws of nature, gladness akin to rapture, as they were unfolded to me, are among the earliest sensations I can remember.

Victor is enraptured by the thought of learning nature's hidden laws through the scientific method, and is so above all other considerations. Similarly, Merchant argues that the

---

[2] Carolyn Merchant, *The Death of Nature: Women, Ecology, and the Scientific Revolution* (Harper and Row, 1980), p. 216.

scientific method is now focused on attaining power over the natural world, and the rejection of "unpredictable animistic sources of change" in favor of mechanistic order—*both* of which are found in Victor Frankenstein! We see this in Victor's rejection of earlier alchemists in favor of rationalistic, mechanistic natural philosophy, and his attribution of any frightening or supernatural elements regarding darkness or death to mere superstition. Victor has an order-structured orientation towards the natural world, which he uses to gain knowledge of the natural world, and through that knowledge, power over it.

Victor's method is a pure example of the science Plumwood criticizes, where the "knower" is superior to nature and free from its limits, and knowledge is "forced or tricked from a mindless and passive nature by a superior exclusively active and rational human mind." We see this in the language Victor and his natural philosophy mentors use to describe their method and domination over nature. M. Waldman, the more kind of Frankenstein's mentors, describes how natural philosophers "penetrate into the recesses of nature, and show how she works in her hiding-places," describing the study of nature as the "penetration" into nature's "recesses"—suggesting force (and perhaps even rape), by *taking* knowledge from it. This perfectly illustrates Plumwood's critique of the scientific orientation, where "male knowers are seen as wringing from a nature pictured as a debased and passive female slave tortured to yield up her secrets.

Nature is referred to as "she" and "her," directly interpreted as female, passive, and overcome by an active and rational human mind. Victor elsewhere explains, in his description of the evolution of his desire to understand nature, that "I have described myself as always having been imbued with a fervent longing to penetrate the secrets of nature," echoing the language of his mentor, with his desire for knowledge itself conceived as a "fervent longing" for this penetration.

The scientific worldview portrayed in *Frankenstein* perfectly illustrates the orientation towards nature as a female and passive Other, to be "penetrated" by a superior rational man. Both Frankenstein's violation of the laws of nature in the creation of his monster, and the consequences he unleashes yet cannot control, reflect Plumwood's insight that this orientation to nature has been the cause of our ecological crises. Science under these conditions becomes a Frankensteinian monster, out of control, and threatening the very lives of those it touches.

The Marxist Critique

Marxian theory begins with acknowledgement of the ultimate dependence of humanity (alongside all other species on the planet) on successful relationships with nature for their survival and successful reproduction. For humanity, this is their relationship with nonhuman nature, with which they must interact to meet their needs, which is accomplished through labor (this process referred to as "production") with the aid of various "tools."

The development of these tools and technologies creates to a large degree the potential for the successful meeting of needs—without the adequate tools, the rest of nature cannot be transformed for human purposes. Similarly, control over those tools and the "resources" of nature (the "means of production") gives those in control of them (through ownership) an ability to coerce labor from those without access to resources and the means of production. Those with ownership over the "means of production" become the ruling class, while those forced to work on unequal terms and to unequal benefit become the "working classes," and the specific forms these classes take vary by economic system, types of ownership, and the level of technology—and thus by the capacity for production to meet qualitatively and quantitatively different needs.

As the owners of the "means of production" gradually monopolize wealth, technology in production, and resources, technological development becomes over time largely biased towards profitable technologies, ignoring many of the other potential results of those technologies, and neglecting many potential lines of technological development that would be useful or beneficial but not profitable.

In the *Economic and Philosophic Manuscripts of 1844*, Marx argues that "natural science has invaded and transformed human life all the more *practically* through the medium of industry," and predicts that "natural science will lose its abstractly material—or rather, its idealistic—tendency, and will become the basis of *human* science" when society stops focusing on profit and focuses instead on people.

In *The German Ideology*, written jointly by Marx and his friend Friedrich Engels, Marx highlights how capitalism "made natural science subservient to capital and took from the division of labour the last semblance of its natural character." Technological and scientific developments, to Marx and Engels, are necessary to enable a classless future, but capitalism in so many ways inhibits their capacity to do so through its power over 1. what gets researched; 2. the approach and analysis of that research (biases in its interpretation and what it omits and); 3. what gets translated from research on paper to actual produced goods in life; 4. how those goods are distributed; and 5. how those distributed goods are used.

Das Monstrum: Marx Versus Victor

Victor Frankenstein's atomistic and mechanistic approach to nature is critiqued by Engels, just as we have seen it critiqued by ecofeminist thinkers. The relation of humanity to nonhuman nature is not treated holistically, and neither is it conceived in terms of a *relationship*—instead, nature is treated as an object that humanity is above and acts upon. Partway through the novel Victor escapes his troubles into nature without the intent to dissect it. In this brief moment, Victor notes, "my health and spirits had long been restored, and they gained additional strength from the salubrious air I breathed, the natural incidents of our progress."

Victor was taught "to love the aspect of nature," whereas his earlier scientific non-relation to nature "had cramped and narrowed me" from "a selfish pursuit." Victor recognizes his approach to nature, related to his approach to science, was the cause of his troubles and dysfunction, and it took a true *relation* to nature to recover.

Victor does not hire someone whose work he benefits from (indeed, there is no "Igor" in *Frankenstein*—his first "assistant" comes with the 1931 film *Frankenstein*, but in that film the name is Fritz, and is not Igor until two films later, in the *Son of Frankenstein*, 1939)—so the instrumental use of workers is not so present. While Frankenstein *does* treat nature as a mere "thing," as "raw material" in the same way capitalists do—nature is merely the means to Frankenstein's ends, and as a consequence, Frankenstein studies natural elements "in their death, not in their life," and his resulting scientific and technological creation literally surpasses in power his ability to control it.

A key insight of Marx and Engels in regards to the development of science and technology is that while the development of scientific knowledge and technology to a degree is necessary for a maximally emancipated, well-off, egalitarian life, we need not treat technology as an end in itself. Marx and Engels advocate a science that treats nonhuman nature and people as more than objects to be controlled, and which can meaningfully contribute to human life.

Towards his own end, Victor claims "in a fit of enthusiastic madness I created a rational creature and was bound towards him to assure . . . his happiness and well-being," but denies the creature a companion because "my duties towards the beings of my own species had greater claims to my attention." Victor shows both defensiveness—he recognizes his creation was 'madness' and admits responsibility, but argues that he ought not to repeat the experiment for the protection of humanity.

Victor's pursuit of science results in the *opposite* of a contribution towards human life—it resulted in its detriment. Among Victor's final cautions to Captain Walton were to "seek happiness in tranquility and avoid ambition, even if it be only the apparently innocent one of distinguishing yourself in science and discoveries." Victor is so ashamed of the products of his science for humanity at the end of his days that he cautions others to avoid *science itself* to avoid those negative consequences.

The other side of this is the recognition that the treatment of nonhuman nature as having merely instrumental value, subjugated by the pursuit of other values such as power or profit, is doomed to have harmful and out of control consequences in the long term—as we have seen with Frankenstein and his monster. What we can hypothesize is an indirect, nearly parallel relation between the actions of Victor Frankenstein and the laws of capitalism. Both relate to nonhuman nature as an instrumental thing to be dominated in the pursuit of an external standard—power for Frankenstein (for despite his claims to humanistic goals, he consistently highlights the desire for knowledge and power over nature as his true motivation), and profit for capitalists.

The necessary consequence is the destruction of or harm to those affected—in Dr. Frankenstein's case, anyone he's ever loved, and in the case of capitalism, most non-capitalists of all species within its territories (including, for example, many workers, their dependents, nonhuman nature, those who can't work).

A Marxist-Ecofeminism Without Supernatural Horrors?

Victor Frankenstein's approach to science involves the instrumental use of nature—its degradation to the status of a passive "object" with instrumental value, to be "penetrated" by the literal man of science in the pursuit of knowledge and power. Ecofeminist theorists criticize both this orientation to nonhuman nature (an orientation frequently extending to dominant relations to women, nonwhite, and indigenous peoples) and this approach to science and technology. Marx and Engels also criticize the impact of class society—particularly capitalism—on science and technology.

The impact of capitalism on the development of science and technology has resulted in advances, but advances biased towards profitability, which affects science's orientation, development, and purpose. This misdirection of science promotes the instrumental use of nonhuman nature (just as under capitalism nonhuman nature, nonwhite and indigenous peoples, workers of all genders, and women outside formal economic production are all treated as without value excepting their profitable uses).

Both Marxian theory and ecofeminist thought, then, criticize when science and technology are oriented towards profit and power. *Frankenstein* creates a perfect metaphor for the consequences of such biases—the products so easily spiral out of control, destroying themselves and everything they touch.

Science and technology need to be freed from the imperatives of power and profit in order to prevent the accidental creation of innumerable kinds of Frankenstein's monsters, wildly spiraling out of control. Marxist and ecofeminist thinkers would further agree that the only way to have scientific and technological developments that are independent of power and profit would be through a radical change!

They agree that we need to replace the social relations and structures that treat workers, women, indigenous and non-white peoples, and nonhuman nature as having merely *instrumental value*—as objects that can be used and abused, exploited as resources rather than as valuable beings with agency of their own. We can only avoid the scientific and technological creation of so many Frankenstein's monsters when we overcome systems of oppression where some classes, genders, races, sexualities, nations, and species are privileged over others.

22
The Human and the Monstrous

Cynthia D. Coe

Most movie and TV versions of Mary Shelley's novel *Frankenstein* make a monstrous misrepresentation of the Creature: they portray him as incapable of normal human speech or thought, driven by primitive and irrational desires, and almost robotic in his movement. The Creature is depicted as clearly *inhuman*.

These portrayals directly contradict how he is described in the novel. In terms of physical appearance, the Creature is much bigger than normal human stature and hideously ugly, but in other ways he displays very human characteristics. He moves agilely, speaks eloquently, formulates arguments, reflects on his condition, makes moral judgments, experiences fear and joy and grief, and has complex and sometimes contradictory motivations.

When we exaggerate the difference between the Creature and human beings, we miss a central emphasis of the novel: the way that the Creature challenges our understanding of human nature, and the line between the human and the non-human.

A second common mistake in popular references to *Frankenstein* is also illuminating. In *The Onion Book of Known Knowledge*, the entry for Frankenstein reads: "You are probably looking for Frankenstein's *monster*, you idiot."[1] "Frankenstein" was the last name of the Creature's creator, *not* the name of the Creature. (But in correcting what I am here identifying as the

[1] *The Onion Book of Known Knowledge: A Definitive Encyclopaedia of Existing Information in 27 Excruciating Volumes* (Little, Brown, 2012), p. 79.

second mistake, calling the Creature by Victor Frankenstein's name, the editors commit the first mistake, representing the Creature as a monster.)

In the novel, the Creature has no name, reflecting his abandonment by Victor and general alienation from human society, but in most popular renditions, he has been called Frankenstein, as if, at long last, he had been adopted. This second error, calling the Creature "Frankenstein," works in the opposite direction from our first error of making the Creature seem totally inhuman. Which is it—is the Creature completely inhuman or confusable with Victor Frankenstein himself?

The novel itself is more ambiguous about the relationship between the Creature and his Creator. *Frankenstein* is a meditation on the line between the human and the inhuman, and the ways in which that boundary seems clear, but really isn't. The worry that preoccupies Victor is that he has created a demon rather than a human being, but in fact his horrified reaction to the Creature stems from his suspicion that his creation blurs the boundary between the human and the inhuman. Victor is terrified of those creatures who stand on that line, and so are many of us. The Creature calls into question our own humanity, or our familiarity to ourselves.

Creature Versus Monster

Mary Shelley goes out of her way to make Frankenstein and his Creature resemble each other, to the point of putting the same words in their mouths. In response to the execution of an innocent servant convicted of killing the Creature's first victim (William, Victor's young brother), Victor says, "*I bore a hell within me*, which nothing could extinguish."[2] When the Creature finally reveals himself to the De Lacey family, and they run screaming from him, he cries out:

> I, like the arch fiend, *bore a hell within me*; and, finding myself unsympathized with, wished to tear up the trees, spread havoc and destruction around me, and then to have sat down and enjoyed the ruin. (p. 111, my emphasis)

---

[2] *Frankenstein: Or, The Modern Prometheus* (Oxford University Press, 1993), p. 68, my emphasis.

Both of these statements refer back to John Milton's representation of Satan's despair in *Paradise Lost* (1667). Shelley plays with the idea that human beings resemble both gods and demons. We are creators and destroyers, but we're also finite and fallible, in terms of our knowledge and moral judgments. Despite or because of this doubling between himself and the Creature, Victor refuses to acknowledge the Creature as a "fellow creature," or as a being to whom he could ever have moral obligations.

Immediately after the creation, when the Creature wakes Victor up in his bed, he reports: "I beheld the wretch—the miserable monster whom I had created. He held up the curtain of the bed; and his eyes, if eyes they may be called, were fixed on me. His jaws opened, and he muttered some inarticulate sounds, while a grin wrinkled his cheeks. He might have spoken, but I did not hear" (p. 40). And he will continue not to hear.

Victor immediately calls the Creature a "monster," and for the remainder of his narrative consistently uses the terms "demon" and "fiend" to describe him. But the term "monster" is in itself interesting, deriving as it does from the Latin term for "showing," as in "demonstration." Initially, the word meant (neutrally) a sign, or (more negatively) an omen. Somewhere in the tangled history of the language, however, a slide was made by which the omen of something bad became the bad thing itself.

The monster, the tangible sign of something evil, is assumed to be itself evil, without much attention paid to what the sign refers to, as if there were nothing except the monster to worry about. In Victor's case, this functions psychologically as a way to protect himself from the complexity of his responsibility. If he can convince himself (and, eventually, others) that the Creature is entirely evil, he need not ask about the origins of that evil, or how he might be morally implicated in the Creature's actions.

He reduces the problem to the issue of eliminating the Creature from his life: first by literally running out of the room, then by attempting to kill him, then by agreeing to make a companion creature so that the Creature will go live in the wilderness, and finally by attempting to pursue and kill him again. Victor tries to fit the Creature into familiar narratives by representing him as an object, an animal, and a monster. In this way, he's able to maintain his own self-understanding as a mostly innocent victim and a heroic, even divinely authorized, defender of humanity. He entirely avoids the idea that the Creature is a sign, although admittedly an ominous sign, of the possibilities of human nature in general and within himself in particular.

The Uncanny

When we think about reproduction, we tend to worry that what is reproduced will not be a living or faithful copy of the original. You might have this frustration with a worn-out copier, but this is also the anxiety that drives us to worry about what children are learning, who our heroes and models are, whether a piece of currency is a forgery, or whether someone actually knows what they're talking about or just mouthing some idea they don't understand.

The danger that Victor faces is the opposite of this problem. He doesn't produce a dead copy of a human being, but instead produces something that doesn't really look human and yet has the intellectual, emotional, and sensory capacities of human beings. The Creature breaks the boundary between the human and the inhuman, and shows us the weakness of that boundary, as he himself recognizes:

> Cursed creator! Why did you form a monster so hideous that even you turned from me in disgust? God in pity made man beautiful and alluring, after his own image; but my form is a filthy type of yours, *more horrid from its very resemblance.* (p. 105, my emphasis)

An alien who looks like an alien is not that worrisome; we just kill it. An alien who looks like or acts like a human being is a much more difficult problem for us to deal with. Somehow we're implicated in the similarity, as if we too might not be fully human. In the same way, a foreigner who looks like a native citizen presents a threat that a readily identifiable foreigner does not. This may be part of why anti-Semitism has a particularly violent edge to it. Unlike someone of African or Asian origin, Jews in Europe were not recognizable as foreigners (although Nazi anthropologists tried to establish visual guidelines) but are rather understood as "parasites."

The genocide of the Jewish people in Europe was the attempt to kill off an internal enemy, understood not just as a threat living within a community, but a set of characteristics that were projected out onto one segment of a culture, which was thereby demonized. As Vincent Pecora puts it, anti-Semitism positions Jews as "the embodiment of the non-West within the West, the internal difference that the West simultaneously most wishes to disavow and can never manage to disavow fully."[3]

Victor's quest deeply parallels hatred of, and attempts to eradicate, an *internal* divide. Converting the Creature into the monster, the fiend, or the demon is Victor's attempt to repudiate what he doesn't want to acknowledge about himself. Popular representations of the Creature have largely perpetuated this fantasy, without calling attention to its psychological significance—what it tells us about an all-too-human tendency to refuse to recognize how our anxieties express more about us than they do about the object of that anxiety, and the moral implications of that refusal. In various national histories (including in the United States), successive waves of racism and nativism have imaginatively created a pure, law-abiding, and virtuous "citizen" in opposition to a entirely external, and criminal *enemy*. But, in constructing that boundary, cultures fail to recognize how these characterizations cover over a messier reality, and its moral complexity.

The horror of the Creature is that he is neither entirely human nor entirely inhuman, nor is he easily categorized as merely an animal or a demon or a thing. This ambiguity provokes what Sigmund Freud calls the "uncanny"—the *unheimlich*. Freud is fascinated by the fact that two German words that appear to be clear opposites in their grammatical structure, *heimlich* (homely) and *unheimlich* (unhomely), share the connotation of something concealed, obscure, and secret. Freud suggests that we often experience the uncanny when we are not sure whether something is alive or dead (as in *Scooby Doo* cartoons, when the eyes in a portrait suddenly move, or when we walk into a dimly lit room and see a clown doll in the

---

[3] Vincent P. Pecora, "Habermas, Enlightenment, and Antisemitism," in *Probing the Limits of Representation: Nazism and the "Final Solution,"* edited by Saul Friedländer (Harvard University Press, 1992), p. 167.

corner), but the similarity between the Creature and us also provokes this sensation.

Freud concludes that we experience the uncanny when we encounter something that has been repressed: some emotionally charged idea that cannot be consciously recognized. He puts a psychoanalytic spin on Friedrich Schelling's definition of the uncanny as "something which ought to have remained hidden but has come to light."[4] In other words, the uncanny is that which is both familiar and unfamiliar, that which belongs to us but which we attempt to repudiate.

In Victor Frankenstein's case, he grapples with his monster as the sign of his own possibilities and moral failures. The Creature is Victor's own evil, projected out onto an external figure, in order to avoid acknowledging that responsibility. He ends up with an imaginary self-conception, one that is morally simpler than reality, and this self-deception helps to bring about very real brutality.

Moral Failures

Victor takes almost no responsibility for the Creature's violence, despite the frequent descriptions of his mental anguish, and he refers to himself as "guiltless." He first presents his scientific aspirations as attempts to overcome the power of death, but through the course of the novel we see him indirectly bringing about the death of most of his family, his closest friend, and his newly-wed wife. Instead of coming to terms with this disconnect between his intent and the consequences of his actions, Victor treats the Creature as a responsible being (a demon, a monster) who has committed murder, rather than random killing. He has created a being whom he treats as morally responsible, without recognizing the Creature as a person, in many ways like himself. After hearing of his brother William's murder, he comes upon the Creature on the outskirts of Geneva and leaps to the conclusion (rightly, as we later find out) that the Creature is responsible for this murder.

A being who can be held accountable for his or her actions is a being with freewill, and a being with freewill is normally

---

[4] Sigmund Freud, "The Uncanny," in *The Complete Psychological Works of Sigmund Freud* (Hogarth, 1955), p. 241.

treated as a being who is "morally considerable"—not a rock or a ballpoint pen or an insect, to be (as the situation demands) used or thrown away or squashed with a shoe. We tend to treat a free being as worthy of respect, in a way that mere things and even most animals are not, to us. But Victor both attributes freewill to the Creature and denies him personhood, even when the Creature very reasonably argues for the obligations that creators have to their creations: "I am thy creature, and I will be even mild and docile to my natural lord and king, if thou wilt also perform thy part, the which thou owest me" (p. 77).

Shelley allows us to observe Victor rationalizing a contradictory view of the Creature, as a demon (with a free but malignant will) and an unfree animal (whose malignancy is instinctual or otherwise inevitable). Just before he dies, he admits that he had obligations to the Creature, but that those obligations were trumped by the need to protect humanity in general. He cites the "malignancy" of the Creature as justification for his own refusal to create a companion and his attempts to kill him.

Shelley suggests throughout the novel that failures of empathy—the ability to recognize in another being someone like yourself—are moral failures, and they create the tragedy of the novel. The bonds of family and community are humanizing bonds, for the most part. Victor speaks lovingly of his early life with his family, a kind of paradise before the fall. It is by observing (not even directly interacting with) the De Lacey family that the Creature first takes on recognizably human traits, learns language, and indeed comes to love and care for this family.

But the Creature is denied love and empathy, even from the De Lacey family, and so when he first speaks with Victor, he demands a companion creature, so that he doesn't have to be alone and unloved. When Victor destroys the unfinished companion, the Creature goes about making Victor into a creature in his own image—alone—by killing Clerval and then Elizabeth. Victor's family is almost entirely dead, he is without friends, and, by pursuing the Creature into the Artic wasteland, he leaves normal human community.

Yet the Creature's relationship to Victor is much more complex than pure hatred. When he speaks to Walton at the end, he seems to feel real sorrow for all the suffering he has inflicted on Victor, and weirdly mourns his passing. Throughout the novel, which in her 1831 introduction she calls her "hideous progeny" (p. 197), Shelley presents the Creature as a sympathetic character, in stark contrast to how Victor treats him. This is not to imply that the Creature is an innocent victim. We can interpret him as morally responsible for the violence that he commits, but also trace how that violence arises out of his circumstances. He's neither simply a monster nor simply a victim; and in this way we see how unclear our comfortable moral distinctions really are. If a monster can also be a victim, precisely because he was treated as a monster, and his victim far from innocent, our simple categories of good and evil cannot be maintained.

How *Frankenstein* Addresses Us

In his preface to *Frankenstein*, Percy Bysshe Shelley explains that he (writing as the author) has chosen a supernatural narrative in which to display "the truth of the elementary principles of human nature" (p. 3). Given Victor's errors we should not repeat his attempt to treat the Creature as a monster; nor should we pretend that Victor himself is only an inhuman monster. Victor demonstrates the possibilities within human nature, at least in Mary Shelley's eyes. He may be, in Harold Bloom's phrase, a "moral idiot," but this is a form of self-protective idiocy that is familiar to all of us.

Frankenstein is commonly read as a warning about mad scientists, or about technology outrunning our capacity to understand its consequences, and it can function in that way. But there is a deeper concern: that of "moral madness"—our self-deceptive tendency to project evil onto others, and the evil and brutality that we engage in as supposedly excused by that projection. We have to be suspicious of, for instance, political narratives of victimization, often used to justify revenge or harsh control of various kinds. Casting immigrants as criminals, or critics of Westernization or globalization as barbaric, sets up a story in which there can be no complex responsibility, or tenuous boundaries between insiders and outsiders, those who are part of the community or threats to it. And then we have to ask what exactly is being protected, and at what cost.

In writing *Frankenstein*, Mary Shelley warns us about our own monstrosities, which we may refuse to recognize but which stubbornly and uncannily declare themselves.[5]

[5] My philosophical interest in *Frankenstein* originated in an interdisciplinary first-year seminar called "Technology and the Human Condition" at Monmouth College, and was furthered by my preparing for lectures on Mary Shelley's novel in the William O. Douglas Honors College at Central Washington University. I owe thanks to a great many students and colleagues for wonderful discussions about this uncanny book.

23
The Monster that Therefore I Am

JESSIE DERN

On a dark and stormy night in November, after years of stressful, toilsome, and obsessive work, the moment that Victor Frankenstein has been waiting for is finally within reach: he is about to unlock the secret to life itself. However, he unleashes more than just the spark of life—on this night Frankenstein's actions give his name infamy.

When the dull-yellow eyes of his creature open, Frankenstein remarks that "the beauty of the dream vanished, as breathless horror and disgust filled my heart."[1] In a blinding flash of both electricity and creativity—Frankenstein's creation instantly transforms from blessed masterpiece to damned monstrosity.

Frankenstein condemns his creature as a monster before it even moves, acts, or speaks. What does he see in his creation to bring on this reproach? What really makes a monster? It is perhaps more than just ironic that the name Frankenstein gets associated with the monster more than it does with the man. Could Frankenstein the man be just as much a monster as his creation?

In her novel, Mary Shelley is inviting us to think about who has the power to create names and labels that judge and denounce others. Who gets to decide who's a monster? This question puts the center of our focus squarely upon Frankenstein himself, who projects his fear and anxiety about his own powers and their untold consequences onto his creation. From the moment the monster makes its first gestures, facial expres-

[1] *Frankenstein* (Dover, 1994), p. 35.

sions, and inarticulate sounds, Frankenstein is never able to really see or understand the monster except through the lenses of his own guilt-ridden glasses.

We will see that he who calls someone a monster may be a monster himself. Who better to help us see this than someone who is a *monstrous* philosopher and a philosopher of monstrosities? Twentieth-century French philosopher Jacques Derrida writes artistic and argumentative "Franken-texts" that challenge the way in which traditional philosophy has depended on banishing the strange, the foreign, the mutant, and the abnormal from the altar of truth and knowledge. Derrida says that labels are riddled with the motivations and judgments that the labeler has about him or herself in relationship to the "monster," and the labeler fails to realize that the power he has to judge begins to resemble the negative traits that he accuses of the other. And what is a monster to do about all this? Derrida suggests that challenging a label really becomes a journey of self-exploration, something which Frankenstein's monster never gets the chance to take.

A Monster Is Made

The labeling of "monsters" abounds in Shelley's novel. Justine, the housemaid and friend wrongly convicted of the murder of Frankenstein's younger brother says that "ever since I was condemned, my confessor has besieged me; he threatened and menaced, until I almost began to think that I was the monster that he said I was" (p. 58). Elizabeth, Frankenstein's future wife, distraught that the innocent Justine could be seen as guilty says that "men appear to me as monsters thirsting for each other's blood" (p. 63). Even the monster himself, after being rejected by all of society, accepts the status that has been given to him by the others: "I became fully convinced that I was in reality the monster that I am" (p. 80).

If Justine isn't really a monster, even though she almost let someone convince her of that, then Shelley wants us to think that Frankenstein's creature—*the* monster—is perhaps other than as Victor Frankenstein represents him. We have only his account to go on, the word of a man who is the epitome of the "mad scientist." For years, Frankenstein had been in restless pursuit of what he called the hidden laws of nature—the very essence of life—a power so god-like that he said he wanted to use it to "banish disease from the human frame and render man invulnerable to anything but a violent death" (p. 22). In order to do this, he lost sight of everything else: his family, his schooling, his friends, his health, his sanity. He began to feel invincible, where even the lines of life and death could be redrawn by him alone.

It turns out that what he devoted his life and energy to, and what he put care in creating, was really an ugly, animated mess of discolored dead flesh from corpses that from now on will be the stuff of nightmares. Can the monster be a monster simply because it is hideous? Frankenstein seems to think so. Does he have any real reason to fear the monster at this point, since so far it is only guilty of being alive and hasn't actually done anything yet? If not, then what's really going through Frankenstein's head at this moment?

Frankenstein can never see his creature as anything other than an ugly mistake, though he has mistaken the creature's ugliness for the self-hatred he is feeling about his own actions. Once alive, this *thing*, this not-even-human being, has become the manifestation of Frankenstein's pride, his foolishness, his immoderation, and own fears of failing in what was supposed to be his moment of glory. Frankenstein rejects his creation as a wretch—a despicable and contemptuous enemy—and unleashes it onto the world because Frankenstein never felt as if he should be responsible for it and is repelled by the sight of it.

Here's how Frankenstein describes their first encounter:

> By the dim and yellow light of the moon, as it forced its way through the window shutters, I beheld the wretch—the miserable monster whom I had created. He held up the curtain of the bed; and his eyes, if eyes they may be called, were fixed on me. His jaws opened, and he muttered some inarticulate sounds, while a grin wrinkled his cheeks. He might have spoken, but I did not hear; one hand was stretched out, seemingly to detain me, but I escaped, and rushed downstairs. (pp. 35–36)

Has the creature really done anything to deserve this reception? Frankenstein's response is to avoid, rather than to confront. These don't seem like the actions of a man who just moments before was confident enough to admit he was forming a new species, the scientific results of which would help to create eternal life for all of humanity. Perhaps later on when the monster comes back to destroy Frankenstein's life then it deserves his disdain and hatred, but the creature doesn't go from beautiful to ugly to enemy to the source of life's destruction just by coming to life, even if its life represents those possibilities.

Victor Frankenstein, the Monster

Nearly every film adaptation of Frankenstein portrays the monster as a larger than life destructive force—everything Frankenstein imagines him to be!—while Frankenstein is a joyful, self-congratulatory, eccentric scientist who revels in his god-like ability and newfound responsibility as a creator, boasting to the curious on-lookers who have come to witness such a momentous event. These movie depictions are an idealized version of good and evil, and don't help us see Victor Frankenstein for who he really is: a monster in his own right.

How does it really play out in Shelley's novel? Victor has kept himself in isolation to hide his secrets, and on the night of the monster's creation he has a nervous breakdown, vowing never to tell anyone of what transpired. His creature becomes the source of his own personal obsession and torment as well as the outlet for his hatred and rage. Once we hear from the creature himself about what he has gone through over the years and what he needs from Frankenstein—the only one who is able to bestow such a request—we can see Frankenstein's true, *monstrous* colors: he can't see how his actions have led to the monster's actions, and he thinks more of killing his creation rather than helping him.

Frankenstein is more worried about how he appears to others than the consequences of rejecting the monster. When his closest friend Henry Clerval suddenly arrives and comes to his aid on the night of monster's creation, Frankenstein could not even tell him about what happened for fear that he would be perceived as insane. Later when he heard that Justine was being sentenced to death for his brother's murder, which he knew was done by the hands of the monster, he would rather let her die than step forward. As time goes on, and as his situation with the monster becomes more and more unbelievable,

Frankenstein even thinks it would better to let others think of *him* as the murderer of his friend Clerval rather than the monster, who had killed Clerval in a fit of rage over Frankenstein failing to keep the promise he made with the monster to make him a companion.

Now you might think that nothing Frankenstein has done is nearly as bad as what the monster does in retaliation, but think of it this way: no one was harmed on the night of his creation, and the monster did not hurt anyone until he sought out Frankenstein's family specifically to hurt Frankenstein. This should lead us to think about what Frankenstein has done to deserve such a reaction. If violence breeds violence, Frankenstein's actions toward the monster must be truly wretched.

Now ask yourself this question: would you be inclined to like someone that you already considered to be a monster? Frankenstein's condemnation of his creature from the minute he was alive puts a shadow over all of their interactions. When the first word that Frankenstein says to his creature is "Devil!", you know it is not going to be an impartial conversation. Once he realizes that his suspicion that the monster killed his brother is correct, Frankenstein further assumes that his creation is an inherently violent being "who delights in carnage and misery" (p. 50) because he cannot understand how his rejection and the rejections of other humans have driven the monster to react, to vent his anger and frustration at humanity, and even get revenge for what he has considered unfair.

Yet, wouldn't you be amazed if you ran into your creation years later and he could make fires and shelter, and speak and reason with you in your own common language? When the monster first speaks to Frankenstein, he says:

> I expected this reception. . . . All men hate the wretched; how then, must I be hated, who am miserable beyond all living things! Yet you, my creator, detest and spurn me, thy creature, to whom thou are bound by the ties only dissoluble by the annihilation of one of us. You propose to kill me. How dare you sport thus with life? Do your duty towards me, and I will do mine towards you and the rest of mankind. If you will comply with my conditions, I will leave them and you at peace; but if you refuse, I will glut the maw of death, until it be satiated with the blood of your remaining friends. (p. 68)

The monster is smart enough to point out Frankenstein's own hypocrisy: how is it that the person so set on creating life, is now set out to destroy it? Frankenstein is the only one who can fulfill the monster's desire for a companion and for friendship by creating a female like him so that they can live out their days alone and in peace away from humans. The monster says: "I ought to be thy Adam, but I am rather the fallen angel, whom thou drivest from joy for no misdeed" (p. 69). While this may not be true at the time he said it (for he already had killed Frankenstein's brother), it was true the night of his creation. Frankenstein lets his emotions trump the monster's pleadings because he sees what the monster says as a demand and as a threat. Frankenstein feels the victim of the whole situation because he cannot see how his repeated rejections of the monster have caused him to be this way. It is here that Frankenstein becomes himself a monster, since he decides that regardless if he is the only one who can help the monster, the monster is not entitled to friendship, companionship and sympathy from anyone.

Derrida's Encounters with The Other

How do you become a monster? Even those humans we have called "monsters" across history didn't start out that way. Much like monsters, Jacques Derrida writes about rogues and animals, which he says are labels that are infused with the labeler's perspective about him or herself in relationship to these "monsters." He says that those who label the *Other* as a monster which is foreign, strange and misunderstood are trying to point out that that which is other to them represents a threat. The Other may be perceived as a threat to my reality and way of life, even to the general order of things in the world like a sense of right and wrong. However, those who label something or someone as Other may cause that thing to remain foreign, stranger, and misunderstood often *because* of this label. Derrida says that this label is always created in a negative or pejorative sense, and the one creating it is using a twisted logic that says more about him or her than it does about the Other.

In *Rogues*, Derrida says that a rogue—an outlier to a group and someone who goes against traditional norms, thus someone who is seen by the group as hostile to it, and perhaps even seen as a scoundrel and delinquent—is always being called a rogue by those who deem themselves to be respectable and representative of the moral order. Those who think they are in the right because they are in the majority have a power and strength in numbers and in traditions and habits, giving themselves a sense of authority to judge someone outside of their group.

When Frankenstein feels that the monster is making a threat in order to get what he wants, he says: "no torture shall ever extort a consent from me. You may render me the most miserable of men, but you shall never make me base in my own eyes" (p. 104). This means that Frankenstein wants to be seen, even in the eyes of the monster, as an authority that has the power to judge but is immune from judgments from the outside, judgments that he would think are off-base precisely because they come from the outside.

Derrida says that often those who call out the other as a rogue or monster are trying to hang on to and secure good and moral ideas they hold about themselves by juxtaposing themselves with the other who can then been seen as bad or immoral as a consequence. Frankenstein wants to be seen as a good human being who is entitled to a happy family life and loving wife that waits for him, but he's trying to reassure himself of this by saying bad things about his creature.

Being called a rogue by someone else is almost never considered to be a good thing. Derrida says "it is never a neutral attribute . . . it causes a normative, indeed performative, evaluation, a disdainful or threatening insult, an appellation that initiates an inquiry and prepares a prosecution before the law. It is an appellation that looks already like a virtual interpellation."[2] What Derrida is saying here is that the person who calls out the other as a rogue is making a judgment that goes beyond calling someone "wrong"; it shows hatred and ill-intent.

When Frankenstein calls his creature a monster from the moment it awakens, this is a condemnation that goes beyond a feeling that the creature is not natural or a threat to humanity in general—he's saying that he hates what is outside because to him it's a threat that challenges him personally. This means

[2] Jacques Derrida, *Rogues: Two Essays on Reason* (Stanford University Press, 2005), p. 64.

that we often define ourselves through a negation of the Other so that we can see ourselves in a positive light. Those that condemn the Other through a label are always acting out of a certain agenda and out of a power structure that elevates themselves while lowering the Other in the process. Victor Frankenstein has created a system of judgment where the monster can never be "good."

In another text by Derrida, *The Animal that Therefore I Am*, he says that it is a human tendency to name the Other, like how humans often distinguish themselves from animals. What's interesting is that the term "animal" or "animals" isn't really a name at all! It's a generalization that says those who are not humans are animals—where "animals" could mean hundreds of different species, or even refer to someone who has acted "inhuman." Animals never call themselves that! As Derrida says, the one who says "animal" is, in fact, human. He says "animal" is a word that "humans have given themselves the right and authority to give to the living other,"[3] and they have done this in and through language, thus in the very way that is denied to those who are being labeled. In calling his creature a monster, Frankenstein is trying to identify himself precisely as human—as having language, reason, morals, values—and in the process makes the creature inferior because it doesn't yet have those things.

There remains one final twist. Derrida says that those who vilify are simultaneously creating an enemy for themselves, and in turn become an enemy to someone who already feels threatened. This power to name and destroy the reputation of others is not the work of a higher moral power, it is a rogue power—a monstrous power—and seems to be a mirror of the thing being said about the other. Frankenstein is a monster because he projected all his fears and anxieties about life onto the monster so that he could feel better about himself, a monster who was seen as his nemesis even before he had done anything wrong. While we could say that Frankenstein saw the monster as a greater threat to all, he could never acknowledge that the monster was only a threat to everyone *after* everyone's actions—and his own—toward the monster had provoked him.

---

[3] Jacques Derrida, *The Animal that Therefore I Am* (Fordham University Press, 2008), p. 23.

What's a Monster to Do?

Whoever fights monsters should see to it that in the process he does not become a monster.

—Friedrich Nietzsche, *Beyond Good and Evil*, #146

In the end the monster lives up to his name by killing Frankenstein's brother, his best friend Clerval, his wife Elizabeth, and Frankenstein himself dies in the pursuit of his monster across the continent. Did the monster necessarily have to be a monster? In *Romeo and Juliet*, Juliet doesn't care what family Romeo comes from and says: "What's in a name? That which we call a rose by any other name would smell as sweet." So what if Frankenstein's monster had a name, like Adam, or Victor Junior? Would he still be a monster? Why doesn't the monster just give himself a name? The reality of it is that the monster just doesn't have that kind of freedom—he can't recognize his own freedom—a freedom that is different from Frankenstein's power to name his creation a monster. The monster has bought into all of the horrible things said to him by humans and can't see any other way of being.

We've been focusing so much on the idea that Frankenstein created a monster of his creature and at the same time he became a monster himself, but we haven't thought that in Frankenstein becoming a monster, the monster himself has become somewhat human. In the end, the monster cannot really respond to what Frankenstein has done because the loneliness and despair he has felt because of the actions of everyone toward him overshadows his desire to strike out on his own. The monster, backed into a corner, is left with nothing else to do except to react violently to people's disdain and judgment. We might wonder if there's any way for the monster to escape these problems, and another way for the monster to live.

If the monster wants to live his own life, he doesn't necessarily need a name—especially if he lives on his own—but he does need a sense of self. Everyone has to have an answer to this question of "Who Am I?" from time to time, if only to know what we really want, feel, and value. When the monster realizes that he is interested in friendship, companionship, literature, and questions of truth and knowledge, he simultaneously feels that he is not even entitled to think about these things because he is not a part of the human world. It's no coincidence that what is at stake in the question of who is a monster is really a question of what is friendship. How can we befriend a monster?

In his books, Derrida takes up being a "monster" for a different reason. He sees the *monstrous*—the foreign, the strange, the different—as important because it's a means of thinking another way, of reaching for something beyond the traditionally human, and as a way to challenge and critique those ideas and categories that keep the Other from being a part. Derrida ends up saying things like "the rogue that *I* am" and "the animal that therefore *I* am," and at first we might think he's just showing the same kind of defeat that the monster is. But what if he is trying to say just the opposite?

What if Derrida is trying is trying to be more playful, and is trying to come up with something that the rogues and monsters can do? No one has given the monster a name because they do not want to truly recognize him as a somebody and not a something, and as potentially a good being and not merely a violent force of destruction. The only way for the monster to realize that he could have a name is to challenge his label.

In Shelley's novel, the monster may never be able to recover any independence of his own because his vengeful actions against Frankenstein and his family may have in fact solidified his status as a monster. The monster was not capable of seeing things any other way than through the eyes of revenge, because he was never shown anything but fear and violence from others. During the time before he killed Frankenstein's brother, he could have challenged his label, and decided he did not want to be a part of Frankenstein's rejection.

Yet by the time Frankenstein hears the monster's eloquent voice, his hopes and his humanity, it's already too late.

VI

You Can Learn from My Mistakes

24
If We Could All Be Dr. Frankensteins . . .

JOHN V. KARAVITIS

Beginning with Mary Shelley's work, which was conceived in a dream one rainy summer night in 1816, there have been countless book and movie adaptations of the Frankenstein legend. At the kernel of this legend is a medical doctor, many times depicted as a mad scientist, whose illicit medical experiments lead to the discovery of the secret of life. By the end of the story, however, the scientist ends up paying the ultimate price for daring to learn this secret.

A prolific American suspense novelist, Dean Koontz has joined the long list of authors who have tried their hand at reinterpreting or extending the Frankenstein legend. Koontz's efforts span a series of five novels, with a storyline that has its origins in a slightly modified version of the Shelley tale. Here, Dr. Frankenstein's first act of creation failed, with the original monster rebelling against its creator, killing his wife, and fleeing to America. Dr. Frankenstein then turned his efforts and advanced knowledge of medical science and biology to extending his own lifespan and modifying his body.

In Koontz's alternate world sequel, Dr. Frankenstein now goes by the name Victor Helios, a brilliant scientist and the owner of a biotechnology company in New Orleans. Helios/Frankenstein now applies his advanced knowledge of the medical sciences, specifically genetic engineering, to creating a "New Race" of humanity devoid of moral frailties and physical limitations.

Biomedical enhancements and genetic engineering are now a major focus of medical research. Cloning, gene therapy, smart drugs, and bionics all provide examples of the continued advances in medical science that may one day offer decay and disease-free immortality. The advanced medical knowledge that Koontz's Dr. Frankenstein has taken for granted over the last two centuries could become readily available within our lifetime. And conquering disease and disability, even death, may not be the end of the story. Medical science could overcome all fundamental physical and mental limitations making people "more than human," or "posthuman."

But what would it mean to live in a posthuman world, a world where biomedical enhancements are the norm? Could the world of Koontz's Dr. Frankenstein provide any insights into the consequences of these advances in medical science? Contemporary philosophers are struggling to find a way to deal with the issues raised by these ideas. In a posthuman world, there is no guarantee that human nature as we know it will still exist. Morality is defined by behavior, and behavior flows from an organism's nature. So, in a posthuman world, the role of morality becomes uncertain. The extreme situation described in Koontz's Frankenstein novels, applied to our world, could lead to a world without morality.

Which Way to Dr. Frankenstein's Castle?

Contemporary philosophers, pondering the issues raised by advances in medical science, generally fall into one of two camps. In one camp are those contemporary philosophers labeled "bioconservatives." Bioconservatives question the wisdom of applying the knowledge of genetic engineering to human beings. Some even argue that such research should not be pursued in the first place. These philosophers fear that the unintended consequences resulting from these new biomedical technologies may prove harmful to society, and I think Mary Shelley would have agreed with them.

In the other camp are the "bioprogressives," philosophers who appear to be more accepting of, and perhaps even too eager to embrace, the coming possibilities inherent in the advances of medical science. Given the speed with which medical science is advancing, the promise of deliverance from disease, disability, and even death does seem very close at hand. Koontz's Dr. Frankenstein already possesses knowledge of medical science that today can only be dreamed of, and the consequences of using this knowledge should concern us.

How eager should we be to embrace the limitless possibilities of such advanced medical knowledge given that, at every turn, Koontz's Dr. Frankenstein uses it to create soulless and amoral beings, inhuman replacements for humanity? Who's right, the bioconservatives or the bioprogressives?

Dr. Frankenstein Vows to Break Nature's Grasp

Harvard University professor Michael J. Sandel may be the best example of a bioconservative philosopher. Sandel explores the moral questions raised by advances in medical science, and warns against the hubris these technologies engender.[1] He makes a distinction between medical science used to care for and heal people and medical science used to "improve."

Sandel focuses on a handful of examples where the application of medical science and genetic engineering is raising serious ethical questions—the use of performance-enhancing drugs in sports, the off-label use of FDA-approved drugs and technologies, the creation of designer children through genetic engineering, and eugenics.

The most prominent example today of biomedical enhancements lies in the field of sports. Performance-enhancing drugs are banned from use in sporting events because they're seen as conveying an unfair advantage to those who use them (imagine trying to play football against one of Dr. Frankenstein's monstrous creations). Although the use of training programs, diet, special clothing, and other approved technologies, along with the result of the "genetic lottery" that gives the lucky few a natural ability that the many lack, are all perceived as legitimate forms of enhancement, there is a moral outcry when performance-enhancing drugs are used.

Legitimate forms of enhancement require hard work, consistent effort, the sacrifice of time, and the exercise of free will. The moral issue here is that illegitimate forms of enhancement

---

[1] *The Case against Perfection: Ethics in the Age of Genetic Enhancement* (Belknap, 2007).

provide sought-after benefits without requiring any effort. Koontz's Dr. Frankenstein has no moral qualms whatsoever about applying his vast medical knowledge to enhancing his own body to eliminate all of his physical frailties. The bodies of the "New Race" are also physically superior to those of normal humans, and they acquire these superior bodies with no effort.

FDA-approved drugs prescribed for "off-label" use raise further moral questions regarding biomedical enhancements. That is, once a drug has been approved by the FDA to treat or cure an illness or disorder, doctors are free to prescribe such drugs for any other physical or mental ailment or condition. One example of this is the use of human growth hormone. Once used to treat dwarfism, it's now also used by professional athletes (for its effect on promoting rapid healing), older people (who seek to forestall the effects of aging), and growing children (who fall into the "less than average" height range). In the academic arena, college students have begun to use drugs like Ritalin, which are approved by the FDA for attention deficit hyperactivity disorder, in order to allow them to study for longer periods of time.

We may wonder if there could be any moral issues in the off-label use of FDA-approved drugs. However, we find the same problem here that we do with performance-enhancing drugs in sports. Here, the benefits of studying are obtained without the same level of internally-motivated hard work and effort, without the same expression of human agency and free will. Who earns the "A" grade in a class? Is it the student, or his medicine cabinet?

For Koontz's Dr. Frankenstein, these moral questions are irrelevant. As with performance-enhancing drugs in sports, all that matters is going beyond nature to achieve one's goal, regardless of the cost or the consequences.

By Playing God, Dr. Frankenstein Destroys Human Nature

Whether society should aspire to using biomedical enhancements at all becomes the ultimate question. Sandel sees biomedical enhancements and genetic engineering that go beyond medical care as eroding human agency and freewill. Sandel worries that people may be so focused on the fruits of biomedical enhancements and genetic engineering that they will ignore the risk that such changes will result in the re-making of human nature to something other than what it now is.

Sports provide an excellent example of this risk. Even though athletic skill is, in part, dependent upon a genetic lottery ("if you want to win at the Olympics, choose your parents wisely," the saying goes), nevertheless, success in sports requires years of diligent and willful practice and sacrifice. Indeed, one of the main points of sports is to exalt the virtues of sportsmanship and goal-oriented hard work.

Success in sports celebrates and rewards diligent practice and effort undertaken over years. Another example of the remaking of human nature lies in genetic engineering which will allow parents to dictate the physical and mental characteristics of their children. As Sandel puts it, the use of medical science beyond simply restoring health constitutes "a Promethean aspiration to remake nature." (Recall that the complete title of Mary Shelley's novel is *Frankenstein: Or, the Modern Prometheus.*) For Sandel, the threat here is not the specter of eugenics, that perfect human beings will be created, but rather that these choices represent an attitude of willfulness against human nature.

For Sandel, the only enhancements which would be morally acceptable would be those applied to capabilities which could generally improve the quality of life. Other than this single exception, Sandel's position is clear: biomedical enhancements that go beyond medical care are morally *wrong*. Taken to the extreme, Sandel's examples seem to suggest that, in a posthuman world, human nature may be so radically altered that morality may cease to exist. With everyone having access to the biomedical enhancement technologies of Dr. Frankenstein, would anyone still be considered "human?"

In the first book of Koontz's Frankenstein series, *Prodigal Son*, Dr. Helios muses about "the power of the human will to bend nature to its desires. . . . All that mattered was the triumph of the will."[2] We seem to be following the same path as Dr. Frankenstein, bending nature to our will. Hubris indeed.

---

[2] Dean Koontz and Kevin J. Anderson, *Prodigal Son* (Bantam, 2005).

Dr. Frankenstein Re-writes the Book of Life

A more assertive and permissive approach to the issues surrounding biomedical enhancements has been taken by philosopher of bioethics Allen E. Buchanan. Buchanan argues that biomedical enhancements are not fraught with the dangers that more conservative philosophers would have us believe.[3] Rather, biomedical enhancements and genetic engineering should be looked at from a rational vantage point. Evolution has done, in its own blind, haphazard, meandering way, what medical science is now allowing us to do (at least with lab animals). Although there are indeed risks and benefits to any endeavor related to biomedical enhancements and genetic engineering, in Buchanan's opinion, the benefits would far outweigh the manageable and controllable risks.

Buchanan sees a number of areas where advances in these technologies could benefit humanity. The body could be made more efficient, allowing for the extraction of more nutrients from any food source. Increasing the body's capacity for thermal regulation would allow for greater adaptability in response to severe changes in climatic conditions. The immune system could be strengthened so that the fear of cancer, pandemics, and plagues would recede into the distant past. Moral behavior could possibly be enhanced, leading to more altruism. Buchanan sees only benefits from advances in these technologies, and he discounts the possibility of any real danger.

One of Buchanan's arguments that supports this positive attitude is that an organism is not a "seamless web." By this he means that modifications in one area of an organism's genetic makeup need not result in negative effects in other areas. Unfortunately, Buchanan's position appears to ignore discoveries in genetics which demonstrate that even small differences in an organism's genes can result in large and unexpected changes in its overall nature. This eagerness to embrace advances in medical science seems to take us down the road traveled by Dr. Frankenstein. Consider the following examples:

---

[3] *Better than Human: The Promise and Perils of Enhancing Ourselves* (Oxford University Press, 2011).

- Chimpanzees and human beings share, by one estimate, 98.7 percent of the same DNA,[4] and yet, there is clearly a world of difference in both the physical and mental characteristics between the two species. Chimpanzees and their close cousins, the bonobo chimps, are even closer to each other genetically, yet their comparative social and sexual behaviors are astoundingly different. Bonobo chimps are known for their hypersexual behavior (it occurs constantly and indiscriminately, and may involve all age groups intermingling, adults as well as juveniles), whereas chimpanzees exhibit higher levels of aggression. Small differences in their genetic makeup have produced significant differences in their natures. Differences in their natures result in differences in behavior, and it is actual and expected behavior that defines morality. The morality of the bonobo chimps, for example, certainly does not reflect our morality. Neither does the morality of the creations of Koontz's Dr. Frankenstein. The members of the "New Race," created to replace humanity, lacked free will and empathy. Instead, blind obedience and an indifference to committing murder defined their morality.

- Dogs and wolves are considered to be members of the same species, but are different subspecies: dogs are members of *Canis lupus familiaris*, whereas wolves are members of *Canis lupus lupus*. Dogs and wolves diverged around 11,000 years ago, probably due to the fact that the ancestors of dogs that scavenged around early human settlements were able to digest starchy food in addition to meat. Dogs exhibit juvenile characteristics in adulthood: they bark, are relatively tame, sociable, and trainable. Wolves rarely bark in adulthood, and they are independent and difficult to handle. As dogs and wolves can interbreed and produce viable offspring, they are by definition members of the same species. However, their behaviors are vastly different. Small differences in their genetic makeup have produced great differences in their natures. Here again we see that differences in natures result in differences in behavior.

---

[4] Ann Gibbons, "Bonobos Join Chimps as Closest Human Relatives," *Sciencemag* (13th June 2012).

- In 1959, a Russian scientist, Dmitri K. Belyaev, wanted to see if behavior is determined by biology. He took wild silver foxes, and over successive generations of breeding, found that selecting for a single characteristic—tameness—resulted in many unexpected physical and behavioral changes. After forty generations of breeding ever more tame silver foxes (the only criterion that ensured selection for breeding was how aggressive the animal became in the presence of a human being), the animals were indeed made quite tame. However, the structure of their heads changed; their fur lost its natural luster; and the animals no longer had a musky odor. Most surprisingly, the animals behaved like puppies in the presence of their caretakers. In other words, like dogs, these adult silver foxes exhibited juvenile characteristics in adulthood. Thus, a change in one single characteristic of the nature of the silver foxes resulted in what has to be considered, for all intents and purposes, at least a different subspecies. Using only techniques of animal husbandry, and nothing more complicated than wire cages in a barn, Belyaev changed the nature of his silver foxes in just a few dozen generations. The selection of a single behavioral characteristic, tameness in the presence of human beings, resulted in many distinct physical and behavioral changes. Although Buchanan's position is motivated by the benefits that he sees accruing from biomedical enhancements and genetic engineering, this example alone should caution us strongly against blindly following the path of Koontz's Dr. Frankenstein.

Have We Arrived at Dr. Frankenstein's Castle?

Who could possibly refuse the benefits that would result from these medical technologies, especially the chance to defeat disease and death? However, the peril of unintended consequences from biomedical enhancements and genetic engineering must give us pause, regardless of how enthusiastic we may be about the chance to defeat disease and death. Given the examples shown above, an organism's genes are in fact more like a "seamless web," and one which cannot be modified with impunity.

Suppose that genetic engineering could be used to enhance intelligence at conception. Parents would demand that their offspring have the advantages that accrue from superior intelligence. But what would be the unintended consequences of intentionally raising future generations' intelligence by such an extraordinary amount? Would our descendants be living in a world of philosopher-kings, or would they all be carbon-copies of Koontz's Dr. Frankenstein? This Dr. Frankenstein is a megalomaniacal genius with no moral qualms about killing innocent people or even destroying all life on Earth. In which of these two worlds would one find a human morality?

Given the examples above, we can see that changing genetics can change behavior, and thus the moral landscape. By changing our own genetics, we run the risk of changing the very basis by which we define morality. Could we find ourselves creating descendants who truly believe that murder would not be immoral? Koontz's imagining of Dr. Frankenstein points to exactly that. Could we ever truly ensure that any changes in our genetic makeup would not destroy our human nature?

A theme that runs throughout Koontz's novels is Dr. Frankenstein's belief that he never makes mistakes in creating new life forms, regardless of the fact that this narcissistic view is repeatedly disproven. In the first three novels, the members of the "New Race" created to replace humanity are constantly turning away from their programming, falling prey to mental breakdowns, and on occasion suffering from bizarre physical metamorphoses. In the fourth and fifth novels, the Communitarians fall victim to obsessive-compulsive disorder, whereas the Builders' bodies undergo chaotic and unpredictable changes. Yet Koontz's Dr. Frankenstein never accepts that he may have erred. "He knew that his genetic formulations and flesh-matrix designs were brilliant and without fault."[5]

Behold! The Monster! *IT IS US*!

Johann Konrad Dippel (1673–1734) was a wandering student of theology and alchemy who is believed to have been the basis for Mary Shelley's Dr. Frankenstein. Born in Castle Frankenstein, overlooking the Odenwald in Germany, he was

5 Dean Koontz, *Dead and Alive* (Bantam, 2009).

condemned for his unorthodox religious views. He spent years attempting to create the *elixir vitae* that would confer everlasting life. Thus, the ideas of manipulating nature and cheating death are not new. What is new is that we now have a clearer understanding of the natural world through modern science. Today, fantastic advances in medical science, perhaps even the immortality that eluded the real Dr. Frankenstein, are now distinct possibilities.

What will these advances in medical science mean for us? With different people choosing different biomedical enhancements, will there be common points of reference that people can use to relate to one another? Can human nature, and thus morality, have any meaning in the world of Dr. Frankenstein?

Bioconservative philosophers like Michael Sandel see biomedical enhancements as potentially destructive of human nature. Yet destructive or not, they are here to stay, and will become even more incredible in the years to come. They will also become pervasive, as the cost of providing these enhancements can only fall.

Bioprogressive philosophers desire the fruits of advances in medical science, but they have perhaps not sufficiently thought through to the potential problems that might arise. Allen Buchanan argues that biomedical enhancements and genetic engineering promise more benefits than risks, and that there is no viable argument that absolutely proscribes their use. However, as was noted above, an organism is more of a "seamless web" than Buchanan and others may want to accept. Small differences in an organism's genes can result in large changes in physical characteristics and behaviors. The examples noted earlier show that unintended consequences can indeed occur with changes in an organism's genes. Who would want to gamble with our human nature, only to lose it completely, as did Koontz's Dr. Frankenstein?

Surveying the current state of philosophy regarding biomedical enhancements, we find ourselves in a curious position. The great philosophers all spoke about the importance of human nature and its connection to morality. Contemporary philosophers are divided on whether biomedical enhancements and genetic engineering would have either no effect on, or merely enhance—or perhaps even destroy—human nature.

The role of morality in a world where everyone could be like Dr. Frankenstein is uncertain. Taken to the extreme, the posthuman world of Dr. Frankenstein has the potential to be quite bleak. Until now, people have been unable to change their "human" nature. We are born with our physical limitations and our moral frailties, and live constantly with the specter of death hanging over us. As human beings, we all share the same nature. No man is an island, but, if we were all Dr. Frankenstein, with easy access to biomedical enhancements and a chance at immortality, all that one might find on the map of morality would be islands.

In the final book of Dean Koontz's Frankenstein series, *The Dead Town*, one of the replacement humans muses about the difference between its kind and the soft, messy, troublesome humans that they will soon completely destroy. "Efficiency equaled morality; inefficiency was the only sin their kind could commit."[6] Thus, the world that Koontz's Dr. Frankenstein is attempting to create, a world without illness, or physical or mental imperfection, messy emotions, even death, would be a world devoid of human morality. There would be no common ground, no shared rules of behavior or clear expectations, for like creatures to act upon.

The great philosophers, unencumbered by our dazzling scientific advances, knew human nature all too well. Intoxicated by our intellectual successes, and driven by our unquenchable curiosity, we are rushing headlong in order to change ourselves and that which makes us human—perhaps even destroy it in the process. Perhaps we shouldn't be so eager.

---

[6] Dean Koontz, *The Dead Town* (Bantam, 2011).

25
Why It's Wrong to Make Monsters—or Babies

JOE SLATER

When Dr. Frankenstein created the monster, he did something *wrong*.

Most of us accept this. Perhaps you think he was wrong because he was playing God, or because he was playing with body parts of the deceased. Perhaps you think he was acting too recklessly or that his real crime was abandoning the creature, leaving it to find its own way in a dangerous and hostile world.

I will give you another reason why he was wrong to do it. This argument, however, applies not only to creating monsters in a laboratory, but also conceiving of children naturally.

On the original cover matter of *Frankenstein: Or, the Modern Prometheus*, Shelley quoted Milton's *Paradise Lost*, with the following:

> Did I request thee, Maker from my clay
> To mould me man? Did I solicit thee
> From darkness to promote me?

This highlights an important parallel between the positions of every human being ever to have existed, and that of the monster. Nobody asked to be born—or made. Why then is it okay to make someone go through that?

What Is Anti-Natalism?

Anti-natalism, generally speaking, is the view that human beings should stop having children. A wider scope of anti-natalism, which I will consider here, claims that we should stop creating offspring, including monsters.

There are several types of anti-natalist argument. One holds that human beings are bad for the planet, environmentally speaking, so the best thing for Earth would be if there were no humans. The Voluntary Human Extinction Movement follows an argument of this variety. You can argue for anti-natalism in lots of ways. You might just think children are bad, so people shouldn't have children (but that argument is unlikely to convince anyone!).

Anti-natalism has received some serious attention in philosophical circles recently as a result of a 2006 book by David Benatar called *Better Never to Have Been: The Harm of Coming into Existence*. In his book Benatar makes a strong claim that coming into existence is always a serious harm and that, as the title suggests, it would better if no one had to endure it. Benatar provides an extended and sophisticated series of arguments. In this chapter I'll provide a short, simple argument for anti-natalism. Though I won't appeal to any of Benatar's specific arguments, much of what follows is informed by his book.

Because of the annoyance of constantly referring to a creation like that of Frankenstein as "the creature," "the monster" or something of the like, I will refer to it as 'Adam,' as in the graphic novel adaptation, *I, Frankenstein,* and will refer to lab creations of that sort by the plural 'Adams'.

A Sentient, Autonomous Monster

Sentience and autonomy are two important concepts when acting in ways that affect others. "Sentience" is the quality philosophers often cite when considering whether something counts as a moral agent. If a being is sentient, there is something it is *like* to be that thing. It makes sense to ask of sentient things "what was that like for them?" but the question seems misplaced, silly (or like some poetic device) when applied to a non-sentient thing. We can sensibly ask what it is like for Boris Karloff to have bolts in his neck, but if someone were to ask what it is like *for the bolts* to be inside his neck it seems as if something has gone wrong. Sentience seems to be a requirement for pain or pleasure.

In practical ethics, sentience is seen as very important. If a being is sentient, this seems to give us some reason to respect its interests, as it has interests to be respected. Peter Singer is an advocate of animal rights, who suggests that the equal consideration of interests is the fundamental basis of equality. It seems as if it would be wrong to kick a dog (or a Frankenstein-esque dog-like creature) if it will feel pain as a result. If a character is sentient, they should be considered when they are affected by a decision.

As well, as being susceptible to physical pleasure or pain, people (and monsters) can be harmed in other ways. They can be disappointed, scared, bored, or depressed. They can have plans, dreams, and hopes, and be harmed by these not coming into fruition. Not all sentient beings will be able to do this. In our communities we associate with people who can, and we follow certain rules that make our existing together easier or more pleasant. A being who's able to analyze situations and give himself rules to follow in accordance with them is not only sentient, but also *autonomous*. How autonomy is best defined is controversial, but for present purposes, let us say someone who is able to consider options, evaluate them reasonably, and freely choose among them is autonomous.

Adam is certainly sentient; he describes the pain of being shot in the shoulder. He is also autonomous. We know this because of the reasons he provides for his actions. He tells of how he weighed up his options after human society shunned him and why he decided to do various things. Creatures that are autonomous are different to those that are merely sentient in that we hold them responsible for their actions, and we would also treat them differently.

A Simple Argument

The argument I will provide has only two premises, and a conclusion which follows from them.

1. The Harm Premise: In normal circumstances, it is wrong to knowingly inflict harm, or do something with the knowledge that it will impose harm, upon an autonomous being without their permission.

2. Inevitability Premise: All autonomous beings *do* suffer harm (harms, really), and we know this.
3. Conclusion: Creating autonomous beings is wrong.

The second premise, that sentient lives *just do* involve harms, I take to be a fairly obvious one. Everyone does experience sadness, injury, or ill-health. Unless we suffer a premature death, we will suffer the ageing process. Most people are likely to witness friends or family members suffer or die, and will therefore suffer vicariously. Anyone who reaches an age at which they are appropriately self-aware inevitably suffers harms in their lives.

Any life can be seen as continuing degrees of harm, until ended by death. As Adam said in Shelley's *Frankenstein*, "I learned that there was but one means to overcome the sensation of pain, and that was death—a state which I feared yet did not understand." Anyone considering parenthood, or attempting to construct an autonomous life-form in a laboratory, knows this if they think about it. We might think that the good things in a person's life outweigh the harms, but all that matters for this argument is that there are harms in every autonomous life. That's all I'll say about this for now, as I think what I have labeled the Harm Premise is both more controversial and interesting.

Now, let us consider the Harm Premise. It does seem completely plausible that, in normal circumstances, it's wrong to cause someone harm without consent. The "in normal circumstances" clause is there to escape some obvious exceptions. In some emergency situations, like if you have been attacked, it wouldn't be wrong to use reasonable force to defend yourself. Similarly, if someone is about to be hit by a train, you would be completely justified in pushing them out of the way even though the fall might hurt them.

In most cases the Harm Premise will seem correct because, in general, harming someone is wrong anyway, but there are circumstances when it might be necessary. If someone has a disease, they may require a painful surgery, but if it saves the person's life we usually think it's better if they go through with it, than get killed by their ailment. Even in cases like that, however, when it seems clear that the other person would benefit overall, if there is to be any harm, you should get the person's permission first. That's why we have consent forms.

So, after a brief look, the argument looks okay. You shouldn't cause anyone harm without their permission. If you conceive a child or create an autonomous monster, you will condemn them to a great deal of harm (and you can't get their permission). So, you shouldn't conceive a child or create an autonomous monster.

When responding to an argument with an apparently problematic conclusion, like that proposed above, there are three main responses that philosophers could venture upon. First, we might question the reasoning we've gone through to take us from the premises to the conclusion. An argument is valid if its premises entail the conclusion. If something has gone wrong in the reasoning, it is *invalid*.

Another possibility is that we could challenge one of the premises. Even if an argument is *valid,* it might not be *sound.* An argument is sound if the reasoning is fine and all the premises are true. If one of the premises is dubious, the argument is compromised. Alternatively, we could question whether the conclusion is actually as bad as it first appears. We might "bite the bullet" and just try to explain why that conclusion strikes us as so off-putting, but still accept that it is likely to be true.

Non-identity of Monsters?

The most likely problem in the reasoning from the premises to the anti-natal conclusion relates to the "non-identity problem." This is a major problem when considering the ethics of future people'.[1] If a person doesn't exist, how is it possible to wrong them?

Normally when a harm is caused, a subject of the harm is identifiable. If you attack someone with a pitchfork, the person or creature attacked is harmed. When that person hasn't been born, or made, that person doesn't exist yet. You certainly can't attack a non-existent person with a pitchfork. So we might say that the Harm Premise is true, but the claim that it is wrong to inflict harm upon an autonomous being would be restricted to autonomous beings that *actually* and *currently* exist.

[1] The non-identity problem was introduced by Derek Parfit in his 1987 book, *Reasons and Persons.*

Considering this train of thought might make us think that we could accept both premises and still deny the conclusion that it is wrong to create life. Yet despite this argument, ordinary reasoning suggests that persons who don't exist *can* be harmed, and that it is wrong to do so.

Consider the following situation: Dr. Frankenstein has constructed a body and is ready to infuse it with life, but he realizes at the last minute that the brain is damaged. He could turn on his machine and activate the body, but the resulting Adam would be seriously mentally impaired. Alternatively, he could build or dig up a new brain. The creature that came to exist, we may imagine, would be completely different and perhaps not at all mentally impaired, and have a higher quality of life.

In this example, we might say that he should wait and build the non-impaired creation. We could even suggest that if Frankenstein were to activate the first body, with its defects, that that creation would live in constant and intense pain. In this case, it certainly seems wrong to bring *that* creature into life.

However we respond to the non-identity problem, it seems that we must, somehow come to the conclusion that acts can wrong people of the future. The mere suggestion that we can't identify a specific existing person harmed doesn't seem to escape the anti-natalist conclusion. Perhaps there is a solution here. Maybe it lies in thinking about how and why our obligations to actual people differ from our obligations to future people. This is something that might be interesting to think about, but for the sake of continuing the discussion, I will assume that the argument is valid.

Aside: Non-autonomous Monsters?

Strictly speaking, you might argue that the conclusion of this argument isn't really anti-natalist. It rules out the building of autonomous monsters, or having autonomous offspring, but doesn't say anything about sentient but not autonomous monsters or offspring. You might create Franken-fish—fish created by a similar method to that used by Frankenstein—for example. Similarly, you might have children that you do not intend to reach a level of mental development sufficient to count as autonomous.

While breeding Franken-fish seems fairly innocuous, deliberately creating human beings never to become autonomous seems horrific. However, it is not ruled out by the conclusion. That is mainly because the scope here is autonomous beings, and as such is not exhaustive. The argument's conclusion says that breeding autonomous life is wrong, but that doesn't mean breeding any non-autonomous life is permissible.

The Harm Premise is Wrong . . . ?

The second response that we might have to this argument is questioning the premises themselves. If an argument is valid and the premises are true, the argument is classified as *sound*, which means that the conclusion must be true. If it is merely valid, it means one (or more) of the premises could be false, so the conclusion doesn't definitely follow. With only two premises, we're fairly limited in what we might question! As I've suggested before I find the Inevitability Premise fairly obvious (but I promise I will reconsider it before the end). Why then, should we accept the Harm Premise?

Instead of the Harm Premise given above, you might think we could have a much simpler premise, like "It is wrong to cause harm." As suggested in the surgery case, the train case or the self-defense case mentioned above, we need something a bit more sophisticated because sometimes causing some harm, in the end, is the right thing to do. We can find causing some harm a source of entertainment. Consider contact sports, like ice hockey or American football. Often people will be harmed while participating, but it would seem mistaken to say it's wrong to play.

Perhaps then a premise of the sort "It is wrong to cause harm, unless it is for a greater good." This would explain what is right to do in the surgery case, the train case and the self-defense case. Something like this, if followed by everyone, would also guarantee that all harms only happened for a "greater good," which sounds nice. If we reject the Harm Premise in favor of something like this, we can then say that it's okay to have babies or build monsters because it's for the best in the long run.

If the Harm Premise Is Wrong, Why Does It Seem So Right?

One problem with accepting that's it's okay to harm for a "greater good" is that it's unlikely that everyone would agree on a "greater good," so disagreements would certainly ensue. It's also very difficult to know what consequences an action will have, so although you might think you're hurting someone for a greater good, you might be mistaken.

In *The Bride of Frankenstein*, once the monster makes friends with the blind hermit, he seems content to learn and enjoy the company of his new friend. It would probably have been for the best if he was left there out of trouble and learning. When the townspeople enter, however, they think the best thing to do is to drive the monster out, which leads to the hovel being burnt to the ground.

This objection to the "it is wrong to cause harm unless it is for a greater good" premise is an objection to the ability to *apply* the premise, not to the premise itself. You might think that the premise is right, but that it is, in practice really difficult to tell what the "greater good" is. Against this, we might ask about people who knowingly do things that are bad for themselves. Consider a smoker, or fairly heavy drinker. Let's say that they're not addicted (or depressed, incapable, or anything that would compromise their ability to make autonomous decisions), that they accept that in the long run they are causing themselves harm, and yet continue anyway. They do it in private, so no one else is harmed by their smoking or bothered by their drinking. If you took their cigarettes or alcohol away, let's say for the sake of this argument (we might not think it's true in real life) that they would have a better life. Is it okay to take away their possessions (broadly construed, harming them) for their own good? If you don't think so, the only reason why seems to be that as autonomous agents should be allowed to do such things, in accordance with the Harm Premise.

If that example didn't persuade you, imagine Dr. Frankenstein has a friend who will soon die without a new kidney. He remembers that he put two perfectly good kidneys into Adam, both of which would be perfectly suitable. Realizing that Adam might not want to donate them, he tranquilizes him, steals a kidney and gives it to his friend. Both of them go on to live full lives. Presumably this was for a greater good, but is stealing organs without permission acceptable behavior? We could quickly amend the suggested premise to need a greater good *for the person harmed*, but then we still have cases where someone could have life-improving surgery, but chooses not to. It still seems wrong for a surgeon to perform unsolicited surgery. The Harm Premise again seems to be a much more reasonable notion.

One explanation for why we might think this is offered by John Stuart Mill (1806–1873). In *On Liberty*, he suggests that the foundation of a free state should be that everyone—all autonomous beings—should be able to do whatever they want, just so long as it doesn't hurt anyone else. As an autonomous individual, you have the right to make mistakes, to do stupid things with your life: people themselves should be able to choose what they want to do with their lives. This is why consent is important when doing something that's likely to involve harm to others, even if it's for the best.

This is supported by common criticisms against authorities. Governments are often criticized for "butting in," trying to control peoples' lives. If a person or group of people are partaking in an unusual activity, you might say "leave them alone; they're not hurting anyone." We think they have the right to act as weirdly as they like, even if we think they'd be better off if they stopped.

The Harm Premise gets a lot of intuitive support from our practices, as well as our view of rights. It seems to be for the very reasons that we would accept the Harm Premise that we have a dislike for overly paternalistic or controlling government policies. I accept that we might think that something is wrong with the Harm Premise, but rejecting it seems to require coming up with new answers for a lot of important questions about how people should live together and the rights to one's own life.

Why Do We Resist So Much?

The final option, when faced with an argument like this, is to "bite the bullet," to accept the weird conclusion. Here, that means accepting that it's wrong to have children or build Adams. By any standards, that's a pretty big bullet to bite!

The twentieth-century philosopher G.E. Moore rejected a skeptical argument in a way that became known as a "Moorean shift.' An argument that called knowledge into doubt concluded that you can't know anything about the exterior world, even simple things like knowing that you have hands. Without responding to the actual argument, Moore claimed that he *did* know that he had hands, so the argument was wrong. That it is permissible to have children doesn't sound like such an immediate fact as having hands, so this response doesn't seem available, but it does seem persuasive. In a situation where we're faced with such a counterintuitive conclusion, the very least we can do is explain *why* we find it so counterintuitive.

David Benatar suggests that one reason for this might be our pro-natal bias and provides several examples of this.[2] It makes sense that we would have an inherent pro-natal bias. Every person alive today is the descendant of generations of procreators. If a person was to have an anti-natal genetic predisposition, they would presumably be less likely to produce offspring, and this disposition would be winnowed out of the gene pool. This explanation doesn't apply to what Dr. Frankenstein does, which might provide one reason why it seems convincing to us that he is wrong in creating life the way he does, whereas doing so the "normal" way seems acceptable. Our pro-natal genetic bias makes us think it's okay to have kids, but we still think it's weird or creepy to build Adam.

There is obviously something very *natural* about having children and that point can't be suggested for anything Dr. Frankenstein creates. There isn't any reason to think, however, that because something is natural, it is also good. Pain, suffering, and disease all came about naturally, but we don't generally think of these as good. We might think that it's in *our* nature to reproduce, but saying this is only to admit that we naturally possess a pro-natal bias. Such a bias might still lead us to act wrongly.

As well as having a genetic pro-natal bias, we might also be seen as having a pro-life bias. Clearly self-preservation is required so that people can reproduce, so a disposition to stay alive, even if that might not be the best thing for you to do, is

---

[2] *Better Never to Have Been,* p. 9.

more likely to result in procreation. David Benatar suggests that people have an "unduly rosy picture" of how good their lives are, so though many people might believe that their lives have been good, that the benefits of life have outweighed the harms they've suffered, they are often mistaken (p. 59).

Benatar argues that this confuses people into mistakenly thinking their lives are good, while actually every life is a harm. That's a very strong claim, which you might enjoy thinking about, but my argument doesn't need anything that strong. This sort of "unduly rosy" view of our own lives could provide more explanation as to why we think creating other autonomous beings—human or monstrous—is permissible.

Our pro-natal bias isn't just genetic. There is a social expectation in many cultures that we will, and perhaps should, get married and have children. People who don't have children are often seen as weird. Once again, opting to rear life in a different way, whether it's like Dr. Frankenstein by creating your own monsters or like someone who instead rears lots of cats, is seen as weird. Doesn't it seem odd that choosing not to have children is financially beneficial, allows a person to spend more of their leisure time doing whatever they want and doesn't cause any gross physical inconveniences like pregnancy, yet it is perceived as the weird choice?

There are also government policies which exhibit pro-natal biases. A state would obviously struggle in the long term if no one was reproducing. Before too long there would be fewer people in the workforce, having to support an elderly population. To prevent that, governments with low birth-rates are likely to introduce extra benefits for couples having additional children. That there is a pro-natal bias at work genetically, socially and institutionally goes some way to explaining why we might be so reluctant to accept an anti-natal conclusion.

The Remaining Options and the Shocking Conclusion

Our options are to find a problem with the reasoning, reject the Harm Premise or accept anti-natalism. One alternative is to see if we can work around the Inevitability Premise. All autonomous human beings—unless genetically altered or perhaps under a permanent drug induced bliss—*will* experience some harm. What about autonomous monsters? If Dr. Frankenstein was to tinker in such a way with Adam's brain, such that he cannot experience harms, Adam would be exempt from the argument.

Whether it is *actually* possible that a being could exist in such a way that they couldn't be harmed might be questioned though. It's perfectly coherent that a person might experience no *physical* pain. The condition known as CIPA (Congenital insensitivity to pain with anhidrosis) makes a person unable to perceive pain, along with any other nerve-related sensations, but they may certainly still be harmed. They have goals and dreams like anyone else, and the prevention of succeeding in those goals would still count as harms. As not only physical pain, but also the hindering of one's interests can count as harms, it is difficult to see how a person could be immune to harm.

Perhaps we could imagine an Adam who experiences no pleasure or pain, has no interests, no hopes and no dreams. Let's call him Robotic Adam. Alternatively, let's imagine that Dr. Frankenstein has worked on a special brain to be perfectly satisfied by everything that happens, named Super Adam. Every moment in Super Adam's life is perfect. Perhaps he has hopes and dreams, but they are all so minimal (or lucky) that they are all satisfied, and because of his constitution, he never gets tired of this, never bored of the bliss, and never valuing any moment less than the last. I don't know if Super Adam is at all possible, but something of this sort would escape the Inevitability Premise.

So now I've explained why having kids is wrong. So don't do it! No monsters either, unless you can build Super-Adams! I'm kidding . . . kinda, but it is something to think about. You probably want to reject the Harm Premise of the argument, but why? If you think it just *feels* wrong, you might be just as mistaken as Dr. Frankenstein. At the time, he *felt* he was doing the right thing too. It does make you wonder, are we really doing the right thing when we have children . . . or monsters?[3]

---

[3] Special thanks to Yu-Ting Su for introducing me to anti-natalism and offering suggestions for further reading.

26
Why Bad Things Happen to Good Monsters

TRIP MCCROSSIN

How, if there is already so much evil in the world, could Victor Frankenstein introduce still *more*? Reading Mary Shelley's *Frankenstein*, we can't help but wonder about this, about the nature of "good and evil" generally, and also, more specifically, about the "problem of evil."

The problem of evil is usually posed as a question: "Why do bad things happen to good people, and good things to bad?" It began its life as a theological problem, as far back as the Old Testament's Book of Job, and in various places since, including the monster's favorite book, Milton's *Paradise Lost*, where Job's problem is generalized to all, as the problem of how, if God is all-knowing, all-powerful, and all-loving, and yet there *is* so much evil in the world, we may "justify the ways of God to Man."

The problem is also a secular one. How, as the secular version goes, can we make reasonable sense of a world replete with seemingly unreasonable suffering? Whatever other problems he may have, the monster surely has this one—as do *we*.

When Will the Monster Die?

Shelley ends her story with a sad and troubling image. The monster has discovered his creator, recently dead as a result of their long struggle, and, bemoaning the tragedy, speaks movingly of his own death by suicide and the possibility of an afterlife, at which point, as Shelley concludes her manuscript, he springs from the cabin window "onto an ice-raft" and "pushing himself off" is "carried away by the waves" as we lose "sight of him in the darkness & distance."

Left with so tantalizingly open-ended an image, we naturally strain to see what's become of him. Where has he gone? His talk of suicide was a promise, yes? Might he change his mind? If so, to what end, and if he's "not even of the same nature as man," for how long? Depending on our answers, we are more or less distant, more or less at risk, more or less anxious.

As Shelley's story has taken root in popular culture over the years, through a long series of adaptations and interpretations, from James Whale's 1931 classic, *Frankenstein,* to the most recent entry, Stuart Beattie's *I, Frankenstein*, the question of the monster's survival and temperament has been a persistent theme.

In the three classic movie sequels to *Frankenstein*, for example, the monster appears continually able to survive attempts on his life: the burning of the castle in the original, the destruction of the laboratory at the end of *Bride of Frankenstein*, being thrust into a pit of molten sulfur at the end of *Son of Frankenstein*, only to be found entombed, but alive in *The Ghost of Frankenstein*, at the end of which he seems finally to die, engulfed by fire, but have we not witnessed him suffer a similar fate already? We can't help wondering about the monster's survival, but also about his temperament. Would such attempts be called for, we wonder, if he were not so threatening, but would he be so threatening if were not so poorly treated?

More recently, in the Dean Koontz *Frankenstein* series of novels, from 2004 to 2011, the monster not only survives, but does so clear into our era, and not only this, but has also retrieved his original benevolence, helping to save humanity from his creator, who has also survived, but with his original scientific outlook having taken on newly disturbing dimensions. More recently still, in 2013, we not only have *I, Frankenstein*, but also Andrew Weiner's movie *The Frankenstein Theory*. The latter is based on the idea that Shelley's novel is a "fictionalization of one of the most incredible true events in human history," that the monster again survives into our era, living still within the Arctic Circle, and that a distant relative of his original creator, Professor Jonathan Venkenheim, recently disgraced for his theory, has set out in search of him, in fulfillment of life-long personal ambition and in pursuit of professional redemption.

While the expedition is ultimately endangered by the monster, Venkenheim is persistently reassuring, that they can and should "appeal to its humanity," that the monster "is capable of reason . . . not some mindless animal . . . reacts violently to fear and to anger . . . is something that has been searching for companionship its entire life ... has been rejected over and over again . . . is intelligent . . . will respond to a sympathetic hand." The appeal goes tragically unheeded, however, leading to a grisly monster's-bride twist in the end.

I, Frankenstein, on the other hand, based on a graphic novel by the same name by Kevin Grevioux, has the monster also surviving into our era, but, more interestingly, in the spirit of Koontz's narrative, also retrieving his original benevolence, even while haunted by a recurring nineteenth-century nightmare.

> Things force their way into my mind uninvited to disturb the peace in my soul. It's always the same. "I'm being *born again*. One moment I'm standing in front of my father . . . The next, I'm running for my life. Then I *strike*. And become . . . *undone*. I become the *beast*. The *monster*. The *abomination*. And my rage will not be denied . . . Then I wake. The dream again. But it wasn't a dream. It was *true*. It was a long time ago, but it happened. That monster is dead. I can't go back. I won't.

He can't and won't, that is, dedicated as he is to protecting humanity, this time not from his creator, but from legions of long dormant monsters: "There is a *war* coming. A war mentioned only in hushed whispers and the shadows of time. A time when the sons of God and the daughters of men produced *monsters* upon earth. When the *flood* came they were defeated, but they were not undone. They would rise again to finish what they started and end the time of man on earth."[1] The monster, once again his original benevolent self, is all that stands now, it seems, between humanity and oblivion.

Depending on the monster's survival and temperament, then, we are more or less distant, more or less at risk, more or less anxious, and maybe also more or less hopeful.

---

[1] Kevin Grevioux, *I, Frankenstein* <http://ifrankenstein.thecomicseries.com/comics/first>, this passage and the preceding one from pages 1, 22–24.

If Victor Is the Modern Prometheus, Is His Monster a Modern Job?

The parable of Job has never wanted for fans. The very best that humanity has to offer, even by God's standards, Job sees his happiness turned suddenly to the worst possible suffering and misery, which, unbeknownst to him, God and Satan have cavalierly agreed to in order to test his faith. Job ultimately does keep the faith, and for this he is redeemed and rewarded. Hence the parable: however comforting it may be to know what we understand we cannot, most importantly the reasons why we suffer, if we resist the hubris of the attempt, while remaining faithful that such reasons exist, but are not for us to know, then our suffering will end, eventually, and we will be, as Job was, redeemed and rewarded.

The parable enjoyed renewed resonance in the seventeenth and eighteenth centuries, with a variety of translations, paraphrases, and interpretations by a variety of poets, theologians, and philosophers. The problem of evil was certainly in the public eye, then, and so likely part of Shelley's general mindset, in the form of these various engagements with the parable of Job, including the monster's favorite book, *Paradise Lost*, and the century-long controversy that began with the publication in 1697 of Pierre Bayle's widely read and debated *Historical and Critical Dictionary*.

Bayle argued that in spite of the Enlightenment's faith in the power of human reason, understanding God's apparent inaction in the face of the overall misery of the human condition is a task that human reason is simply and literally unable to accomplish. He was untroubled by such a deflation of reason, leading naturally he thought to a corresponding inflation of faith, but for others, his assault on reason was insufferable, first and foremost to the so-called "Optimists" who flourished in early decades of the eighteenth century.

Running together "natural evils," such as earthquakes and illnesses, and the "moral evils" we also suffer, as a result of our intentional cruelty toward one another, Optimists exonerate God and render the world perfectly reasonable by simply denying the existence of innocent sufferers, and rendering natural and moral evils alike simply the wages of sin. Everything is, according to Optimism, as it ought to be in this, "the best of all possible worlds." This all came to a crashing end, as Susan Neiman vividly describes, on the morning of November 1st, 1755. The cataclysmic earthquake that struck Lisbon that day, and the inferno and tidal wave that followed, killed tens of thousands of its citizens, and with them the Optimists' response to the problem of evil. The scope of the suffering simply overwhelmed any hope the Optimists had of reasonably equating what we suffer with what we deserve and what's ultimately good for us. From the death of Optimism emerges a more conflicted sort of choice, for Shelley and for us, between the competing perspectives offered us by Jean-Jacques Rousseau and François-Marie Arouet de Voltaire.

Their very public rivalry, around how best to respond to the tragedy of the Lisbon earthquake, and to the problem of evil more generally, is a signal event, Neiman contends, in the advent of "Modernity." Being modern may mean different things to different people, but at its core it means at least a firm distinction finally between moral and physical evil, and the transformation of the problem of evil from a theological problem into a secular one as well.

So, is the monster cut from Job's mold, and is he a modern Job to boot? That Shelley likely had the parable of Job in mind general speaking, does not, in and of itself, make the monster properly Job-like, but if at the same time we listen to him, it's difficult not to hear in his cries and pleadings echoes of Job's own. He is repeatedly and unreasonably mistreated, in each case with a "howl of devilish despair," first by the De Laceys, whom he has cherished, then by the rustic, whose child he has just saved, and finally by his creator, with whom he had not long ago been "content to reason," even while knowing full well that he was the author, passively or actively, of his suffering.

In other ways, though, the monster appears just as distinctly unlike Job. His general lament, "This was then the reward of my benevolence!," goes ultimately unrequited, even his creator denying him any reasonable comfort, and in the end he loses his faith in the reasonableness of his creator's actions, and of humanity in general, and moves from sufferer to punisher. How is it that he begins life in the spirit of Job, and yet in his struggle with Victor seems to stray so far from it? A clue may be that in his favorite book, *Paradise Lost*, he reads of God and creation, Satan and the rebel angels, Adam and Eve in the Garden of

Eden, its forbidden tree of knowledge of good and evil, succumbing to temptation and being expelled, and so on and so forth, and reads it all as "a true history," which "moved every feeling of wonder and awe," but *not*, it seems, as *his* history.

The monster's problem of evil is a secular one, of justifying not "the Ways of God to Man," but "the Ways of . . . Man" *to monsters*, given that the former appear to be the considerably more monstrous of the two. In this, if he's a Job, he's a modern Job, in that *his* problem of evil is a *secular* problem, and as such it is also *ours*.

What's a Modern Job to Do?

Rousseau insisted perhaps most fundamentally, as Shelley was aware from her studies, that we are not naturally corrupt, but rather by our own design. "*All* is good leaving the hands of the author of things," he famously tells us at the outset of *Émile*, "but degenerates in human hands," in the spirit of the monster's description of himself, as he begins to tell his story to his maker, "I was benevolent and good; misery made me a fiend."

Our salvation is in our own hands, he insisted, by means of a quest for self-knowledge, first to confirm our basic goodness, to devise then a useful history of the accumulated causes of our corruption, not unlike what the monster finds most striking in Volney's *Ruins of Empire*, and finally a better way to educate ourselves for, and organize ourselves into society. Rousseau believed absolutely that we *could*, and *should* do this, and that we *would* remake ourselves in the process, leaving behind finally our generally alienated state, and happily regaining our former benevolence.

However appealingly Rousseau's hopeful perspective may have seemed, though, still we may find it, as Voltaire found it, to be ultimately inadequate in the face of persistently unreasonable suffering. As Neiman has argued, two competing traditions of response emerge in the wake of Lisbon, one beginning with Rousseau and insisting, as above, that "morality demands that we make evil intelligible," the other with Voltaire and insisting that "morality demands that we don't." Perhaps we are better off, as Shelley might have thought, as the monster might have too, and as we might still, to follow Voltaire's famous character, Candide, in declaring that in the face of ever cleverer theories and ever persistent evil, the best we can do is to shrug and, in isolation from society, and with limited companionship, more narrowly "tend to our garden."

The monster had learned from Volney the sad history of humanity, after all, and turned away "with disgust and loathing." Had the sort of quest for self-knowledge that Rousseau had envisioned been taken up, however, and yielded the will to correct the corruption revealed, and a program with which to do so, then perhaps he could have entered society more safely than what he experienced in attempting to join the De Lacey family. Ironically, it had been taken up. The monster may perhaps be forgiven for being hopeful, that is, in that he would also remember from Volney, along with "details of vice and bloodshed," a vision reflecting, with some reservation, the hopeful revolutionary spirit of the times.

In the novel's closing moments, in response to Walton's moral outrage, the monster defends in equally moral terms his remorse over the death of his creator, and in general the misery he has wrought. In the process, he lays out his plan for his own extinction, seemingly promissory, though in reality perhaps it is only a longing. He bids farewell to his recently deceased maker, in the more generous mindset now afforded him, "if yet, in some mode unknown to me, thou hast not yet ceased to think and feel, thou desirest not my life for my own misery," but rather so that "I might not cause greater wretchedness" to greater numbers. Once this is done, he has left only to take comfort that "soon [... my] spirit will sleep in peace; or if it thinks, it will not surely think thus," and to bid to Walton his final farewell.

The monster's final plea is equal parts sadness, disbelief, and self-loathing in response to the loss of his former uncorrupted benevolence, which, taken together, form the basis for his passionate rejection of Walton's accusations of hypocrisy in mourning his maker's death. At the center of all of this is the monster's admission that his preferred benevolence could not withstand, it seems, the tortures of the problem of evil at its most fundamental. Worse even than bad things happening to good people, that is, are good things happening to bad. The monster "pitied" Victor, he admits, and "his pity amounted to horror," and he "abhorred" himself as a result, and when he discovers that Victor, who had caused him such misery and despair, "dared to hope for happiness," then what could he feel but "impotent envy and bitter indignation."

Key here is that he *felt* these things, was *filled* with such malevolence, but seems no longer so, having acquired a new sort of self-awareness. As we lose "sight of him in the darkness and distance," we can't help but wonder how long he will survive, and to what end. As we wonder this, remembering his struggle with the problem of evil, and the apparent change in temperament that appears to result in the end, we cannot help but wonder whether the right sort of self-knowledge is indeed the answer, for the monster and for us, and that it can eventually be had, even while we may always be at risk from the Victors of the world.

27
Good and Ugly

WILLIAM RODRIGUEZ

> My heart was fashioned to be susceptible of love and sympathy, and when wrenched by misery to vice and hatred, it did not endure the violence of the change without torture such as you cannot even imagine.

We may not want to admit it, but we all know that we often make our decisions, our *ethical* decisions, based on beauty and ugliness. What we find attractive tends to be "right" and what we find repulsive, like Frankenstein's monster, is "wrong."

Even though ethical reflection seems to be a rational activity, many ethical decisions are made based on purely instinctual and irrational motives. Kenneth Branagh's 1994 *Mary Shelley's Frankenstein* disrupts our ways of determining moral goodness and moral ugliness: in Branagh's movie it's Victor Frankenstein who's morally decrepit and the "ugly" monster who excels at morality—he is a moral *virtuoso* until humanity fills him with hate.

Are Beauty and Morality Related?

Plato (427–347 B.C.E.) was one of the first philosophers to examine the meaning and value of art. Plato believed all art was a *mimesis* (an imitation) of all forms. He established a connection between aesthetics and moral evaluation.[1] For Plato,

[1] *Republic*, III, line 402d.

beauty serves the purpose of taking us from physical beauty to the beauty of the mind.

Plato believe that art, drama, and music play important roles in the formation of character. Art influences behavior as strongly as culture and environment, and artistic representations provide positive or negative models of character and conduct. We can still see this way of thinking not just in *Frankenstein* but in every movie or novel that employs ugliness or deformity as a kind of visual stand-in for evil.

Colin McGinn, a philosopher at Rutgers University, developed a theory of morality that examines the connection between evaluations of beauty and assumptions about right and wrong. For the sake of argument, McGinn suggests there are two species of human beings. "G-beings" are people who are sympathetic to the joys of others and empathic with the suffering of others.[2] These are people whom we might consider to be of good character.

The second species of people, called "E-beings," exhibit the opposite characteristics. These people not only take pleasure in the suffering of others, they also feel pleasure in causing suffering in others. In fact, the more pain E-beings can inflict on others, the more pleasure they receive. McGinn concludes that E-beings will be likely to become moral degenerates or evil persons, while G-beings will be likely to become moral exemplars or virtuous persons.

The Aesthetic Theory of Virtue (ATV) asserts that virtue is connected with beauty of the soul, while vice is connected with the ugliness of the soul. A virtuous character excites and heightens our sense of beauty. A deprived or evil soul is expressed in unsightly and horrific terms. While this beauty and ugliness is not physical, we can see the connection made by ATV between beauty and goodness as well as between ugliness and evil. McGinn points out that in our stories a virtuous person, a person of good character, reflects attractive qualities and an exemplary character. In contrast, an unattractive person, like Frankenstein's monster, is usually depicted in negative terms, lacking moral goodness (pp. 92–122).

---

[2] Colin McGinn, *Ethics, Evil and Fiction* (Oxford University Press, 2007), pp. 61–64.

But we should not forget that discussions of beauty are related to questions of personal, subjective taste. Our judgment of beauty is then projected into determinations of right and wrong. This is very worrisome! But, before we elaborate this concern, I need to make a distinction between aesthetic value and aesthetic judgment. Aesthetic value relates to our ability to discriminate values of beauty at a sensory level. These appraisals or "valuations" are dependent on sensations that give rise to feelings of pleasure or disgust. Aesthetic judgments, though, usually go beyond purely sensory discrimination. These judgments involve factors that may be culturally conditioned (desirability) or psychologically conditioned (subconscious behavior). We know that many of our aesthetic judgments include social judgments. Food, for example, that appears enticing and attractive to people of one culture is often described as "disgusting" by people of another culture. (Consider our reactions to the idea of eating bugs.) Our disgusts often have no rational foundation!

Our Monstrous Fascination with Monsters

Our story begins during a storm at the North Pole, when Captain Walton (Aidan Quinn) on an Arctic expedition, encounters a fatigued and emotional Dr. Victor Frankenstein (Kenneth Branagh). Dr. Frankenstein recounts a tragic and horrifying account which serves as a cautionary tale against unbridled scientific enthusiasm while at the same time toying with conventions of beauty. Dr. Frankenstein has been pursuing a monstrous creature of his own making. The monster has killed everyone he loved and destroyed everything he worked for. This is significant since the monster is presented as the embodiment of evil. Yet McGinn reminds us that:

> The monster has always been with us. Misshapen, deformed, hideous, terrifying—the monster prowls and lurks, bent on doing us unprecedented damage. He is strong, agile, determined . . . He belongs where we fear to tread . . . He needs us . . . We dread him . . . He is always with us . . . (p. 144)

Even though monsters are considered evil and moral imperfection personified, they are also a projection of our weakness and innermost fears. We're not merely the victims of their rampage and destruction, the monster is a representation of our capacity for virtuous deeds and exceptional evil. Human beings can be exceptionally responsible moral agents and exceptionally detestable moral degenerates. In other words, we can be lovely heroic exemplars of virtue or ugly monstrous exemplars of vice at any given moment.

According to McGinn, science shows us that under the skin we are all like the creature: "Just as the creature is composed of other people's bodies, so we are probably partly composed of matter that was once part of each other's bodies" (p. 151). McGinn's true fact of biology may appear repulsive to many. We're also uncomfortable in our skin. We suffer from body issues, we see ourselves as physically imperfect, and may even see ourselves as deformed "freaks." Finally, we have problems adapting to our familial roles. As children we struggle with the fear of abandonment, and in many cases, (like the creature) we must find our way alone in this cruel and harsh world. This tarrying realization leads us to the conclusion that our closest relations, those that gave us life, can also be the perpetrators of monstrously evil acts.

If we fear monsters, this leads to an obvious question: Why are we so fascinated by them? Mary Shelley's novel *Frankenstein* establishes that the Creature strikes a deep interest and concern in us because it represents the alien or the other. This distinction between us and it can be understood in terms of our fear of the stranger or outsider. The fear of uncertainty, including death, at the hands of the foreigner is quite common for humans. The fear of the other becomes perverse when the creature represents unfortunate marginalized people due to their physical divergence from a culturally accepted norm. The Frankenstein's monster, stitched together from the body parts of criminals, outcasts, and victims of a cholera pandemic is the ultimate projection of the fear of the monstrous other. If the creature is us, be it the result of our moral depravity or diseased deformity, we see ourselves in him because in him we see our own nature (p. 149).

The Good and Virtuous Frankenstein Family

A series of flashbacks take us to Victor's formative years in Branagh's movie version of *Frankenstein*. We're treated to a serene initial scene of a doting mother and a loving son. This mother-son relationship is cut short by her death while giving birth. Three years later at her gravesite, Victor pledges himself to defeat death. This series of flashbacks offer interesting insights into dynamic of the Frankenstein family. One can only conclude that this attractive and virtuous family harbors deep, ugly, and depraved secrets. This conclusion seems to have been intentional by the filmmaker.

Branagh's version of the Frankenstein story is probably closer to the source than other adaptations. But, what distinguishes this movie version from others is the fact that Branagh set out to examine the complexity of human relationships. As Branagh put it, this is more than a monster story; this is a movie that touches upon sensitive topics of human interaction.[3] At the heart of this film we find the tortured interactions between father and son, mother and son, husband and wife, father and child. By creating an intricate web of relationships, the film precariously skirts taboos of incest, the Oedipus Complex, paternal neglect, and emotional abuse. These underlying themes challenge the convention that the handsome and attractive Frankenstein family is an example of virtue or moral goodness.

We cannot deny that Caroline Frankenstein was a loving mother, but something about her does not feel right. We're treated to a scene where a young adult Victor is hard at work studying. His mother however attempts to seduce him from his work. We cannot help but feel discomfort over this playful exchange between mother and son. The scene gives a strange feeling that begs for a closer examination of this relationship. Victor's hysteria at the moment of his mother's death, and his pledge to defeat death, led me to the conclusion that unresolved issues between Caroline and Victor exist.

Even though an incestuous relationship between Victor and his mother is implied, the incestuous relationship between Victor and his "sister" Elizabeth is explicitly embraced by the movie. Elizabeth was orphaned and adopted by the Frankenstein family when Victor was young. Over time Elizabeth and Victor fell in love and pledged to marry each other. Victor in fact refers

---

[3] *Interview Magazine* <www.interviewmagazine.com/film/kenneth-branagh>.

to her as his "lover/sister/wife." At their wedding night, as they are about to consummate the marriage, Victor declares: "brother, sister no more; husband and wife."

These early scenes of young Victor center on the relationship to his mother and the absence of his father. It appears that young Victor's interest in making a name for himself stems from a need to distinguish himself from his father and gain his admiration. The apparent tension between father and son is made worse by the death of Victor's mother. We're treated to the horrific sight of her lifeless, blood stained corpse entangled in the obstetrics table stirrups. It seems as if the incestuous mother-son relationship is castigated by the father in an attempt to circumvent the completion of Victor's oedipal designs to replace him and take control of the family legacy. Branagh's *Frankenstein* seems to hint at an untoward relationship between the Baron and his servant Ms. Moritz. There are a couple of exchanged glances between the two that seem to intimate familiarity.

Finally, there seems to be a mother-daughter conflict between Ms. Moritz and her daughter Justine. In the novel, Mary Shelley insinuates an untoward relationship between Justine and the Baron after the death of Ms. Moritz. Shelley seems to create an inverted version of Victor in the person of Justine. While the Baron ignores and is neglectful of his son, he showers her with attention and affection.

The pattern of paternal neglect continued with Victor's paternal neglect of the Creature, and the emotional abuse Victor burdens it/him with. Immediately after Frankenstein creates the Creature he concludes that the creature is flawed: "evil stitched to evil, stitched to evil." After the revulsion of realizing what he had created, Victor wrestles with the creature and restrains it. We're not sure whether the creature was the aggressor, but Frankenstein is convinced of the creature's evil and assumes it has been killed.

The creature awakens, frees itself, and flees. Frankenstein is nursed back to health by his classmate Henry Clerval (Tom Hulce) and discovers that the cholera epidemic has killed a significant number of people, possibly even the Creature. Frankenstein seems to relish the thought that his creation has died of exposure to the elements. Frankenstein seems to take pleasure in the abandonment and neglect of his creation.

We're surprised to learn that the first two words spoken by the creature are friend and father. This is significant since the Creature is seeking a surrogate affectionate relationship outside of Victor. When the Creature has the opportunity to confront his neglectful father, he asks: "You gave me these emotions and didn't teach me to use them." Throughout the narrative, as the Creature exacts his revenge on Frankenstein, we see continual attempts at reconciliation. This infantile attempt to reconcile with the negligent father, not unlike Victor's attempts with the Baron, culminates in two heart-wrenching scenes at the end of the movie.

Dr. Frankenstein expires in Captain Walton's cabin after recounting his trials and tribulations. After a fruitless attempt at capturing the Creature, the captain and crew are surprised to find him weeping over the dead body of his father. "Why do you weep?" asked the captain. The creature responded in an expression of outward anguish: "He was my father." The movie concludes with the creature choosing to accompany the funeral pyre of his dead father, as it melts into the cold waters of the North Pole.

Monstrous Pursuits

Victor Frankenstein goes on to pursue medical studies at Ingolstadt, where he is mentored by the disgraced Professor Waldman (John Cleese). Frankenstein continues Waldman's work and creates a being out of the body parts of deceased corpses. Frankenstein believes that "we can design a life that is better than us." The creature's birthing scene mirrors the scene of his mother's death and younger brother's birth quite neatly.

Branagh's laboratory goes beyond Mary Shelley's description of a "workshop of filthy creation." In the words of Branagh, the attempt was to "make as many explicitly sexual birth images as possible." Although, Shelley leaves it to the reader's imagination, Branagh presents a laboratory where a "huge phallic tube shoots eels at an enormous womblike sarcophagus." Disillusioned and embittered at the treatment suffered at the hands of society, the Creature follows his creator with the intention of seeking revenge.

The Creature confronts Frankenstein by asking: "What kind of people is it in which I am comprised? Good people? Bad people?" Frankenstein replies carelessly that they are materials and nothing more. At this point the Creature seems to have a simple twofold agenda: to question Frankenstein regarding his motives and to ask for a companion. The Creature insightfully asked: "Do I have a soul?" This is more than a philosophical question. The creature wants to get to the heart of what it means to be human. The question also has profound ethical significance since it intends to establish moral status of the creature.

CREATURE: Did you ever consider the consequences of your actions? You gave me life but then you left me to die. Who am I?

FRANKENSTEIN: I don't know.

CREATURE: And you think I am evil?

FRANKENSTEIN: What can I do?

This line of questioning seems to confirm that based on his ugly physical appearance and the lack of a soul, the Creature is morally deficient. In fact it is the opposite. The Creature is innocent and the victim of the conventional moral understanding. The Creature is in essence turning convention upside down by establishing that morality is not based on superficial categories of aesthetics. It is at this point that Frankenstein's actions, place in doubt the aesthetic theory of virtue attributing moral beauty to the good doctor. We are drawn to the conclusion that the created being is more human than the en-souled creator. In addition the Creature is clearly asserting his humanity, dignity and moral worth.

The Creature continues to assert his humanity by requesting a companion. He informs the doctor that a creature like himself will not hate him. "For the sympathy of one living being, I will make peace with all." The Creature further humanizes himself most eloquently by reflecting on his ability to love and hate. "I have love in me the likes of which you can scarcely imagine, the rage the likes of which you will not believe. If I cannot satisfy the one, I will indulge the other." The morality of the Creature is innate and implicit and not dependent on his ugliness. The immorality of the Creature is in effect the product of outside forces that shape his moral worldview.

Finally, the Creature's request for a mate is an attempt to create an alternate moral community not based on the superficialities of beauty.

Will the Real Monster Please Stand Up?

Feeling the sting of his father's rejection, and the pain of his father's unwarranted abuse, the Creature seeks refuge in the city only to be victimized by the villagers. Not deterred, the Creature sets out to find human kindness and community with an almost childlike innocence. The Creature comes across a poor peasant family that is struggling to secure provisions for the winter. The Creature emotionally bonds with the family and through an act of compassion harvests the produce that has been impacted in the hardened soil. The family, puzzled by their benefactor and good fortune, attribute the act to a "Good Spirit of the Woods." Here the filmmakers are challenging the aesthetic theory of virtue by attributing moral goodness to the ugly creature as well as a "Spirit."

In an interesting twist of fate, the Creature comes to the defense of the family daughter and blind old grandfather at the hands of an abusive landlord. Grateful, the old man brings him into the cottage, acknowledges his humanity and courteously asks him why he is hidden in the shadows, and why does he not have friends? The Creature answers that he hides from the fear of people and makes an interesting contrast between himself (who is ugly) and his father (who is beautiful). The conclusion, in the mind of the Creature seems to be that Frankenstein has abandoned him because he is ugly.

When the head of the Creature's surrogate family discovers him in the hut, he beats him, chases him outside and the family moves away. Heartbroken, the Creature returns to the empty hut and burns it to the ground. This is the final betrayal. The Creature, who only sought to be loved, has found nothing but pain and rejection. From this point on he has lost hope in the goodness of human beings. His final determination is to have Frankenstein create for him a companion and to seek out an existence in seclusion from human beings.

Kenneth Branagh's retelling of the Frankenstein story makes it clear, that monsters are made and not born. The Creature's first encounter with a human being results in his rejection by his father. His first encounter with society is met with hostility and violence. Even though he is gentle and kind, he is unjustly treated. Even though he is morally responsible and seeks to help and protect those in need, he is rejected and abused. Even though his first word is friend, he is treated as the other, a stranger to be feared. The Creature, a moral virtuoso, is led to bitterness, anger, rage, revenge and murder. The Creature turns the aesthetic theory of virtue upside down: the attractive Doctor Frankenstein is the moral degenerate, while the ugly Creature with-no-given-name is the moral virtuoso.

The Creature Within

The horrifying conclusion we are forced to is that the Creature fascinates us because we see so much of ourselves in him in disguised form (p. 168). The Creature has forced this truth into our consciousness through brutally physical means. Truth be told, we're all closer to Frankenstein's Creature than we are to Frankenstein's idealized family. On another level we are one step removed from the good doctor. As human beings we are capable of great moral depravity regardless of our physical attractiveness or physical unattractiveness. We fear the monster because the monster is us. We don't fear the doctor because he is what we idealize. In the final analysis we are the creator and the creature.

The greatest strength of the movie lies in its portrayal of good and evil. Branagh's Frankenstein is attractive yet shallow, maybe even morally deficient, while De Niro's creature is innocent and kind in spite of his repulsive outward appearance. It's here that we uncover the monster that lies within each and every one of us. In both forms the monster confronts us. It is also at this point that our conventional portrayals of good and evil fall short. Ultimately it's easier to accept that evil is unattractive and out there, than to accept that evil may be attractive and lurking inside of us.

The Mad Creators

Elena Casetta is a Research Fellow at the Center for Philosophy of Science of the University of Lisbon and a member of LabOnt (University of Turin). Although scientists agree that nothing like Frankenstein's creature can actually exist, she believes that there's room for hope.

Danilo Chaib wrote his PhD on conductorless orchestras at the Equality Studies with the School of Social Justice, University College Dublin. It all began in 1987, when he discovered that orchestral conductors are in fact, monsters created by Victor Frankenstein's great-grandson, Dr. Stein. He wrote a song about it, called "Dr. Stein." However, a guy from a German band called "Helloween" stole it and it became one of the biggest heavy metal hits. Danilo teaches at the Escola de Musica de Brasilia in Brazil.

Cynthia D. Coe is Associate Professor of Philosophy and Director of the Women's and Gender Studies Program at Central Washington University. Her respect for Kenneth Branagh was dented but not destroyed by his lousy and grotesque version of Frankenstein—nobody needs to see that much placental fluid.

Jessie Dern is Abby Normal in her own right, Jessie has "mastered" the philosophical art of bestowing life on ideas, creating many frankentexts over her years at Villanova University. She now trains her students to make their own monsters.

Jeff Ewing is a graduate student in Sociology at the University of Oregon. In honor of the work of Victor Frankenstein, he hopes to do a dissertation stitched together from pieces of existing works—a little *Das Kapital*, a dash *of Crime and Punishment*, a paragraph from *The Art of War*, some recipes from *Mastering the Art of French Cooking*, and three pages from the phone book.

John R. Fitzpatrick is a lecturer in philosophy at the University of Tennessee, Chattanooga. He received a PhD in Philosophy from the main branch of the University of Tennessee in Knoxville in 2001. He is the author of *John Stuart Mill's Political Philosophy: Balancing Freedom and the Collective Good* (2006), and *Starting with Mill* (2010). He is a contributor to several popular philosophy books which does not necessarily make him a virtuous individual but does indicate that he is far less alienated than Victor Frankenstein.

Jai Galliott dabbles in philosophy at Macquarie University in Sydney, Australia, and is an associate of a killer lab, the Consortium on Emerging Technologies, Military Operations, and National Security. His research concerns the ethical, moral, and legal consequences of using all things deadly, whether made of steel or flesh and bone.

Mirko D. Garasic joined the Centre for Human Bioethics in 2011, as an Erasmus Mundus Fellow, and remains affiliated with the Center for Ethics and Global Politics, LUISS University in Rome. He has published a number of works on human enhancement, biopolitics, circumcision, enforced medical treatment, hunger strikes, and infanticide. He has decided to give all of that up so that he can write about *Frankenstein*.

Michael Hauskeller is an Associate Professor in Philosophy at the University of Exeter. He read natural philosophy at the University of Darmstadt, which is only three miles from Frankenstein Castle where, in 1673, his fifth great-grandfather, the alchemist Johann Christoph Dippel, was born, rumored to have been the model for Shelley's Victor Frankenstein.

Keith Hess is a PhD Candidate in Philosophy at the University of California, Santa Barbara. He spends his days studying, lounging on the beach, and re-animating dead tissue.

Dale Jacquette is Senior Professorial Chair in Logic and Theoretical Philosophy at the University of Bern, Switzerland. He is author or editor of thirty-three books and has published more than 350 essays in philosophical journals and books, especially in logic, analytic metaphysics, and selected figures in the history of philosophy. "What have I done?", he is often heard desperately to exclaim in the middle of the night. If he could return in time to a cobwebbed eighteenth-century experimental laboratory, he would ex-Hume the still warm corpses of some late great philosophical minds of the

European Enlightenment, and replace the no longer functioning components of his own overwrought central nervous system with galvanically recharged dead smart guy brain plasm.

John V. Karavitis CPA, MBA, has reviewed many books in the popular culture and philosophy genre from the solitude of his isolated ivory tower located somewhere in the Chicagoland area. Now, John is on the other side of the fence, and has given life ("It's ALIVE! It's A-LIVE!") for the first time to a chapter of his own. If you listen closely, you can hear the footsteps of the town's philosophers approaching, all bearing torches, quite eager to let John know just how much they appreciate his reviews.

Christopher Ketcham is Visiting Assistant Professor at The University of Houston Downtown School of Business, specializing in risk management. After several abortive attempts, he has been unable to create a viable succession plan for the Victor Frankenstein and Sons family business even though the franchise value of the family name remains strong.

Skyler King is currently studying English and Philosophy at the University of Missouri-Kansas City. He has written chapters for various books on popular culture and philosophy. After studying Frankenstein for a few years, he discovered a secret formula that transforms knowledge into an accessible liquid form and he plans to plead with the White House to drink this Vial of Ultimate Knowledge.

Daniel Kokotz is a doctoral candidate at the Ruhr-University Bochum in Germany. While he is working on the philosophical problems of anti-aging enhancement by day, he spends his nights patrolling the local cemetery to prevent the bodies from being stolen by eager scientists. Unfortunately, in spite of his efforts, some have gone missing lately.

Mike Kugler has a PhD from the University of Chicago and teaches modern European history at Northwestern College in Orange City, Iowa. Who says he doesn't carefully cultivate his students? He has the parts to prove it.

Greg Littmann is a head on a plate and is Associate Professor of Philosophy at SIUE. It publishes on the philosophy of logic and evolutionary epistemology and has written over twenty chapters for volumes relating philosophy to pop culture, including books on *The Big Bang Theory*, *Breaking Bad*, *Doctor Who*, *Planet of the Apes*, *Sherlock*

Holmes, and *The Walking Dead*. If it tells you that it wants to whisper something in your ear, don't fall for it, because it's just trying to bite you.

JONATHAN LOPEZ completed his undergraduate degree in Integrated Science with a minor in Philosophy at the University of British Columbia. During this endeavor he has built up a great deal of sympathy for the monster's feeling of forlornness.

MICHAEL MENDELSON is an Associate Professor of Philosophy at Lehigh University. He spends far too much time watching the Universal Studios *Frankenstein* films. He is also preoccupied with an approach he refers to as "Philosophical Gothic." Thus far, no one else has succumbed to this deluded project.

NICOLAS MICHAUD teaches as Florida State College, Jacksonville. He has dedicated his life to the work of Dr. Frankenstein and now believes he has discovered the secret to immortality, which he is willing to sell for a low, low price . . . really.

CAROLINE MOSSER is a PhD student in comparative literature at the University of South Carolina. She is an incorrigible hoarder of Frankenstein paraphernalia.

SPYROS PETROUNAKOS studied Philosophy at the University of London. He is a freelance editor, writer, and translator based in Athens, Greece. He thinks that Mary Shelley would have been delighted to know that Frankie went to Hollywood.

JANELLE PÖTZCH holds a degree in philosophy and English and works at the Institute of Philosophy I at Ruhr-Universität Bochum, Germany. She is close to completing her PhD thesis on applied ethics, and is just waiting for the powerful thunderstorm which will enable her to bring it to life.

TRIP MCCROSSIN teaches in the Philosophy Department at Rutgers University, where he works on, among other things, the nature, history, and legacy of the Enlightenment and of its version of the problem of evil. The present essay is part of a broader effort to view literary works and traditions such as Shelley's through the lens of Neiman's understanding of the same. He lived for much of his adolescence in Lutry, just a little ways down the coast of Lac Léman from the Frankenstein home in Geneva, though, as far as he knows, brought no monsters into being during that time.

William Rodriguez, worked on his PhD at the Florida State University in the areas of Religious and Philosophical Ethics. He teaches applied ethics at Bethune-Cookman University, specializing in bioethics, war and peace, economics, religion and violence, and science and religion. His fascination with the horror genre began as a child when he would watch *Creature Features*. It was here that he was exposed to the Universal monsters, Hammer Studios monsters, and countless other horrifying creatures of the night.

Joe Slater is a creature of the night who lurks in the alleys and taverns of St Andrews. When not scaring women and children, he likes to dabble in ethical theories.

Luca Tambolo completed his PhD at the University of Trieste in 2008. Among other things, he published a book on the philosophy of Paul Feyerabend. Just like the young Victor Frankenstein, he strives to become ridiculously famous one day.

Peter D. Zuk is a graduate student in philosophy at Rice University. His research interests include metaphysics, moral philosophy, philosophy of mind, early modern philosophy, and the weighty existential implications of bestowing the gift of life upon the dead.

Bits and Pieces